"This collection of chapters, written over a period of twenty years, provides a vivid depiction of the psychoanalytic experience as a laboratory, where all sorts of questions about human development, the therapeutic value of talking, and the nature of cure can be answered by the analyst who really listens."
Vicki Semel, Executive Director, Academy of
Clinical and Applied Psychoanalysis

"Lucy Holmes' papers on women pick up where Freud left off on femininity, throwing light on the 'dark continent' of the female mind."
Lucie D. Grosvenor, LCSW, Executive Director
Emerita, Psychoanalytic Psychotherapy Study Center

Women and Psychoanalysis

This remarkable collection charts the professional growth of one psychoanalyst from student to seasoned clinician to provide a guidebook for how psychoanalytic theory is conceptualized, created and tested in the analytic session. Specifically, the book traces the development of thinking on the place of women in psychoanalysis and how psychoanalysis has changed how it views and treats women.

Using the techniques of qualitative psychoanalytic research, Lucy Holmes presents new theories of female development grounded in drive theory and expands and enriches Freud's phallocentric ideas about women. Validated by over 30 years of clinical experience with female patients, her work demonstrates how these theories affect women in analysis, in group and in their personal lives. Later papers focus on the process of psychoanalysis itself, using the laboratory of the analytic session to study how talking changes the neurological structure of the brain; to reflect on the concept of "cure" in psychoanalysis; and finally to tackle the tenacity of the repetition compulsion.

Exploring topics across women's lives, such as childbirth, anger, identity, death, humor, leadership and madness, this unique collection of papers is ideal for practicing clinicians and theorists of psychoanalysis.

Lucy Holmes is a licensed psychoanalyst in private practice in New York City, where she is a faculty member and training analyst at the Center for Modern Psychoanalytic Studies, the New York Graduate School of Psychoanalysis and The Center for Group Studies. A former president of the Society for Modern Psychoanalysts, she lectures widely on female development and the technique of modern group analysis. Her previous book *Wrestling with Destiny* was published by Routledge in 2013.

Women and Psychoanalysis

The Collected Papers of Lucy Holmes

Lucy Holmes

LONDON AND NEW YORK

First published 2021
by Routledge
2 Park Square, Milton Park, Abingdon, Oxon OX14 4RN

and by Routledge
52 Vanderbilt Avenue, New York, NY 10017

Routledge is an imprint of the Taylor & Francis Group, an informa business

© 2021 Lucy Holmes

The right of Lucy Holmes to be identified as author of this work has been asserted by her in accordance with sections 77 and 78 of the Copyright, Designs and Patents Act 1988.

All rights reserved. No part of this book may be reprinted or reproduced or utilised in any form or by any electronic, mechanical, or other means, now known or hereafter invented, including photocopying and recording, or in any information storage or retrieval system, without permission in writing from the publishers.

Trademark notice: Product or corporate names may be trademarks or registered trademarks, and are used only for identification and explanation without intent to infringe.

British Library Cataloguing-in-Publication Data
A catalogue record for this book is available from the British Library

Library of Congress Cataloging-in-Publication Data
Names: Holmes, Lucy, 1945-author.
Title: Women and psychoanalysis: the collected papers of Lucy Holmes/ Lucy Holmes.
Description: Abingdon, Oxon; New York, NY: Routledge, 2021. | Includes bibliographical references and index. |
Identifiers: LCCN 2020029334 (print) | LCCN 2020029335 (ebook) | ISBN 9780367560867 (hardback) | ISBN 9780367560874 (paperback) | ISBN 9781003096375 (ebook)
Subjects: LCSH: Psychoanalysis. | Women and psychoanalysis. | Women–Psychology.
Classification: LCC RC451.4.W6 H65 2021 (print) | LCC RC451.4.W6 (ebook) | DDC 616.89/17–dc23
LC record available at https://lccn.loc.gov/2020029334
LC ebook record available at https://lccn.loc.gov/2020029335

ISBN: 978-0-367-56086-7 (hbk)
ISBN: 978-0-367-56087-4 (pbk)
ISBN: 978-1-003-09637-5 (ebk)

Typeset in Garamond
by Deanta Global Publishing Services, Chennai, India

For Robert J. Marshall

Contents

Preface   xi
Acknowledgments   xv

PART I
Women   1

Introduction   3

1 The object within: childbirth as a developmental milestone   8

2 The oppression of childbirth   31

3 The internal triangle: new theories of female development   45

4 Women in group and women's groups   62

5 Hell hath no fury: how women get even   75

6 Masculine and feminine: differentiation and integration   86

7 The technique of partial identification: waking up to the world   97

8 Gender dynamics in group therapy   107

PART II
Psychoanalysis   119

Introduction   121

9 A single case study of a fascination with death   127

10	Marking the anniversary: adolescents and the September 11 healing process	143
11	Humor and psychoanalysis	150
12	Leadership and psychoanalysis	154
13	Myth and psychoanalysis	157
14	Becoming an analyst: learning to live with madness, aggression and the unknown	166
15	Wrestling with destiny	171
16	Why talking cures	179
17	Beyond cure	186
18	Reaching the repetition compulsion	195
19	The analyst in winter	203
	Index	219

Preface

I started work on this project out of a simple desire, encouraged by my students and colleagues, to have all my papers in one place. When the task of assembling the papers was complete, I was able to look at the collection as a whole and realize it had something to say about the intellectual and emotional growth of one analyst. I also saw that the assembled papers had become a sort of instruction book, a manual of exactly how psychoanalytic theory is developed.

Freud was the first psychoanalytic researcher, and the theories he created have an objective reality because they are always grounded in the human body. Male human beings have penises, and women do not. Human beings come into the world totally dependent on an object for feeding and care. The universal vicissitudes of suckling, toilet training, and the growing, troubling awareness that we are not the center of the universe for that crucial object who keeps us alive create mind and develop character. All human beings have to deal with the two central problems of existence: that we are alone in our bodies, and that there are others that we must deal with unless we give in to psychosis.

There is also anecdotal evidence that many of Freud's theories reflect his own personal psychological challenges. His theory of the unconscious was developed in part by the analysis of his own dreams. His ideas about women and the feminine proclivity to hysteria reveal a lot about his relationship with his mother. The concept of the death instinct was created in a world that had become insane, with Hitler invading Austria, and Jews being killed in the streets of Europe.

After she read my first book, my sister commented that my theories about pregnancy and the importance of introjected objects for women were all about myself. I felt exposed and humiliated by this remark at the time, especially because I knew she had a point. But I have come to realize that the arduous task of developing theory, from the literature review to the gathering and analysis of clinical data, is a dreary and daunting task if it is not infused with a narcissistic passion to understand our own issues and character. Taking our research questions very personally infuses the whole process with relentless enthusiasm and creativity.

I encourage my students and supervisees who want to write to use their own struggles as a place to start. A male supervisee who has suffered with an oppressive sense of shame all his life is now carefully studying his patients who deal with the same issue. He has gone to the psychoanalytic library on the web and is happily devouring everything that has ever been written about shame. The paper and the book he is currently writing are projects he is devoted to, and I think his writings will make a real contribution to the literature. Another supervisee had a patient who was the victim of sexual misconduct at the hands of a professor at the institute where both she and her patient studied. My supervisee was outraged, not least because of the abuse she had endured in her own life, and she led a committee which ultimately expelled the offending professor from the institute. She is currently writing a paper, which she hopes will develop into a book, about the unconscious ways that academic institutions, including psychoanalytic institutes, ignore, deny, and therefore collude with sexual misconduct. Two female therapists I consult with are writing a book regarding women and power and healing themselves in the process. One is Asian and grew up in a family and a culture that devalued women; the other was told by her father that "you can't climb a tree in a skirt," a phrase which has become a metaphor in her life to suppress her ambition. The book they are writing together marks the end of their repetition compulsions to be "less than" men.

I was fortunate to experience certain serendipitous convergences in my own professional life, where personal challenges (namely pregnancy, divorce, and the bumpy journey of my own analysis) happened at a time when I was being educated at the Center for Modern Psychoanalytic Studies about qualitative psychoanalytic research. The rigor of really focusing on one control case, developing a " burning question" about something I did not understand but wanted to know about the patient, methodically writing down after every session what the patient actually said, and then analyzing the data collected, demanded a scientific discipline that broadened my ability to think and reason. Out of the stacks of process notes I carefully collected, I had to look for themes and relationships in the material to help me create hypotheses that answered my research question. These hypotheses had to do a good job of explaining the facts, and any hypothesis I generated from the patient's words had to be tested in future sessions. Did the patient say things in the next weeks and months that confirmed my hypothesis? Did the hypothesis allow me to generate new ideas about the patient as the treatment proceeded? If so, I could be assured that the hypothesis was a good one. While I was gathering data, I was also required to conduct an extensive literature review. What did other psychoanalytic writers have to say about the dynamics present in my control case? Did these writers help me have new ideas about my case and its dynamics?

The qualitative psychoanalytic research required of me at the institute was arguably the most important part of my training. It taught me how to listen objectively and to follow my intense desire to understand my patient relentlessly. Most importantly, it helped me develop passion about exploring things I didn't understand and gave me a road map that has guided me in all of the writing I have done since.

When I experienced pregnancy and childbirth, I knew on a visceral level that those experiences had rewired my mind. This was just a hazy intuition at the time. I didn't really understand what had happened to me, but I knew that I cared deeply about exploring what effect pregnancy has on the female psyche. And thanks to my psychoanalytic training, I had the tools to answer my burning questions about the female mind. The eight papers on women in this collection are products of the extensive research I did in the women's groups I led over a ten-year period. I was able to answer to my own satisfaction, the burning question about why pregnancy is such a developmental milestone in a woman's life and how it creates dynamics in the female mind that affect feminine functioning in groups and in life. My first book, *The Internal Triangle,* was a product of this research.

After I exhausted my exploration of women, I turned my scientific eye on the repetition compulsion. This curiosity was fueled by my own analysis, the patients I work with, and a personal crisis when I decided to end my marriage. Why, I wondered, did human beings recreate situations that had caused them so much suffering in childhood? Children of alcoholics became drunks. People who had suffered abuse early in their lives abused their children. Men with cold narcissistic mothers married cold narcissistic women. My clinical practice provided me a laboratory to conduct research on the repetition compulsion. My own analysis gave me some ideas about how the talking cure can rewire the brain in a way that allows us finally to outgrow our repetitions. My second book, *Wrestling with Destiny*, focused on these issues

When I was 15 years into my psychoanalytic practice, I developed new research questions about what I was observing with my patients. I saw that the people who were the best talkers, the ones who had the least ambivalence about happily "saying everything," were the ones who consistently got better, no matter their diagnosis. My curiosity about the therapeutic value of putting things into words occurred at the same time that I became aware of exciting developments in neuroscience which generated new ideas about how talking rewires the brain. The paper "Why Talking Cures" was the result of this second happy convergence.

Over the years, I had some satisfying outcomes in my private practice when patients who had barely been able to function when they started analysis were beginning to enjoy meaningful, satisfying lives. I was surprised to observe that many of the patients I considered "cured" kept coming back for more analysis, just as I had in my personal analysis. Listening to them helped me generate new ideas about why psychoanalysis can continue to be therapeutic even when pathological dynamics have been resolved. The paper "Beyond Cure" addressed these issues.

The final paper in this collection illustrates that I am continuing to research challenges that have a personal meaning for me. "The Analyst in Winter" discusses a daunting issue: growing old. Reading the literature, listening to my patients, and doing some self-analysis on my aging body and mind have broadened my perspective and provided some solace to the narcissistic injury of aging and human transience.

My hope is that this book as a whole charts the development of psychoanalytic theory from the catalyst of personal psychic and somatic conflicts, through a literature review enlivened by one's own unique journey and the questions it generates, to the long process of collecting clinical data and studying how it provides insight.

Acknowledgments

I want to acknowledge my appreciation to the following publications for graciously giving me permission to reprint the following articles:

Modern Psychoanalysis, the journal of the Center for Modern Psychoanalytic Studies, for:

"The Object Within: Childbirth as a Developmental Milestone," 25:1, 2000.
"The Internal Triangle: New Theories of Female Development," 25:2, 2000.
"A Single Case Study of a Fascination with Death," 27:1, 2002.
"Hell Hath No Fury: How Women Get Even," 29:1, 2004
"Becoming an Analyst: Learning How to Live with Madness, Aggression, and the Unknown," 31:1, 2006.
"Wrestling with Destiny: The Promise of Psychoanalysis," 32:1, 2007.
"Why Talking Cures," 33:2, 2008.
"Masculine and Feminine: Differentiation and Integration," 34:2, 2009.
"Beyond Cure," 37:1, 2012.
"Reaching the Repetition Compulsion," 39:1, 2014.
"The Analyst in Winter," *Modern Psychoanalysis*, 43:2, 2020.

International Journal of Group Psychotherapy for:

"Marking the Anniversary: Adolescents and the September 11 Healing Process," 55:3, 2005.
"The Technique of Partial Identification," 59:2, 2009.

Group, the journal of the Eastern Group Psychotherapy Society, for:

"Gender Dynamics in Group Psychotherapy," 35:3, Fall, 2011

Part I

Women

Introduction

As a young student of psychoanalysis, I learned that the theories of Sigmund Freud were deeply rooted in the body. In his "Three Essays on the Theory of Sexuality," Freud (1905) described the development of human beings from infancy to adulthood as a series of stages: the oral, anal, phallic, latency, and genital. In this model, physical experience creates mental representations. What the body is concerned with at any given time early in a human life creates excitements, frustrations, and gratifications that form lasting psychic structures and individual character.

Freud believed that human beings are innately bisexual, that is to say that infants are more interested in erotic gratification than they are in the sex of the object that provides it. Young children almost universally express the impulse to be both sexes, and the journey to adult sexuality is a challenging one. A crucial part of this journey for Freud was focused on the penis or the lack of one. The fear of losing the penis or the humiliation of never having one, thrust boys and girls into the rigors of the Oedipal complex, where the stormy seas of primitive longings for the mother and rages induced by her treacherous infidelities with the father buffet children around till they land, not always smoothly, on the shores of heterosexuality.

Freud has been criticized for his phallocentricity by many modern psychoanalysts. Feminists have gone even farther, relegating Freud to the quaint and irrelevant annals of history where we store religious orthodoxy and Victorian views on sexuality. I have always found the more strident denigration of Freud wildly ungrateful. Despite the fact that his theories are laced with the taint of the bourgeois, hysterical environment into which he was born, he managed to put conceptual tools in our hands that have revolutionized how human beings think about themselves. Among these are the theory of the primitive unconscious and its power, the deep humanity of bisexuality and homosexuality, the ability of the mind and the fantasies it creates to influence the body, and the "talking cure," which was the first concept to acknowledge that words can rewire the brain.

Studying Freud expanded my consciousness and engaged my intellect. He simultaneously enriched and enraged me. I wanted to think like he did. The physicality of his theories made them seem inevitable, grounded in reality in a way I admired. I was less enamored of his ideas about women as anatomically deficient human beings. His description of women as "little men" induced fury and contempt in me.

Still I was suspicious of my own negative feelings about Freud's theories of femininity and female development. Was I being defensive, I wondered? After all, I was just a student of psychoanalysis. Who was I to question the genius who created it? I tried to accept the sad fact of my symbolic castration. It wasn't until I became pregnant and gave birth to a child that I felt empowered enough to fantasize about expanding on Freud's ideas about women. Freud himself had given me permission to try to do this. In 1932, he acknowledged that his theories of femininity were "incomplete and fragmentary," and he advised his readers to "wait until science can give you deeper and more coherent information" (Freud, 1932, p. 135). After childbirth, I dared to think that it wasn't science that would expand theories of female development; it was a return to Freud's focus on the body, preferably piloted by a woman. I set out to create a theory of female development that paid as close attention to the pregnant female body as Freud did to the organed male.

When I was pregnant, gave birth, and nursed my infant, I did not feel castrated. On the contrary, the swelling belly of pregnancy, the orgasmic power of labor and delivery, and the animal pleasure of feeding the infant with my phallic, life-giving breasts left me feeling authentic and strong in a unique way that I had never before experienced. More importantly, I had the conviction, just a sort of unformed intuition at the time, that the experience of pregnancy and childbirth had changed my mind in a profound way. I decided to devote my doctoral work to the study of childbirth as a developmental milestone. I felt totally absorbed in my ambition to create a developmental theory for women that pays as close attention to the feminine body as Freud did to the penis. I wanted a theory that doesn't look at women as deficient men, but rather as anatomically correct human beings whose bodies can perform massive miracles.

As part of my research for my doctorate, I started my first group, composed of women for whom pregnancy and childbirth were burning issues. They were either pregnant and happy about it or unhappily pregnant and considering an abortion. There were also women in the group who were struggling with infertility, and several who were about to celebrate their 40th birthdays and coming to the realization that further delaying pregnancy was soon becoming a decision to remain childless. My second group was at an obstetrical clinic in the South Bronx. Most of the pregnant women in that group were in their teens, and unlike the group in my private practice, they were dealing with the challenges of poverty and racism. Nevertheless, themes in the two groups were remarkably consistent. As the women in both groups talked, I was constantly amazed by all the "ghosts" in the room. The women were there, of course, but so were their unborn babies, their mothers, and their fathers. I came to the conclusion that females internalize their mothers and fathers early in their lives in a very vivid way, and when they become pregnant, they project all their fantasies about those parental introjects onto the child growing in their womb. Even more interesting to me was that the process of childbirth seemed to provide an opportunity to eject all those fantasies into the real world, giving the mother a new power over her introjects and the fantasies about them. My groups provided me with clinical evidence of why childbirth is uniquely empowering and how it changes the female mind in a maturational way.

Out of all this passionate energy came my theories of the internal triangle and childbirth as a developmental milestone, as well as a revolutionary zeal about obstetrical practices in the United States, which produced the paper "The Oppression of Childbirth." This diatribe, written just after I received my doctorate, was so polemic that no one would accept it for publication. I include it here with affection for my youthful fervor and with a conviction that it provides an informative and telling history of Western childbirth practices. I also still believe that a lot of what I had to say was and is true.

In the ten years after I had completed my PhD, I was delighted to feel my theories were confirmed. Among the women in my private practice and groups, I discovered much clinical evidence supporting the importance of internalized parental introjects. The papers published about women from 2002 to 2011 were based on this clinical research. "Hell Hath No Fury" focused on the elegant ways that women get revenge without sacrificing their femininity. One of the most important and fascinating techniques they use is an unconscious identification with an internalized object to torture others the way they were tortured early in life.

The other five of these papers deal specifically with women in groups. Gender has enormous importance in group therapy, both in group members and in group leaders. Developing these papers gave me a heightened appreciation of how useful men and women can be to each other in group therapy, and brought me to a conviction I still hold: an important goal in any psychoanalytic treatment is to help women to think more like men, and men to think more like women. It enhances and expands the egos of both sexes to free themselves from the constraints of rigid masculinity or femininity.

It has been almost 20 years since I wrote my first article about female development, and in those years, gender theory has exploded and expanded. The binary of sexual difference has become a rainbow of possibilities with the gay and lesbian community continuing to add initials to its LGBTQ ranks. Older analysts like me have learned to be very cautious about pronouns with people who come to our offices for the first time. At best, this expansion of thinking about sexuality and gender has given voice to the myriad gendered fantasies, states, and embodiments that human beings are capable of, and that have often been unrecognized and debased by society, and unmet by justice (Corbett, 2011). It has also returned us to Freud's idea about the universal human tendency to bisexuality, with the new twist that *all* sexualities that limit object choice, including heterosexuality, involve the utilization of primitive defenses, such as denial and splitting. In this model, conventional masculinity and femininity, historically considered the gold standard of mental health by psychoanalysis, are essentially symptoms, defensive structures created to repress homoeroticism and other gender anxieties. Harris (2005) describes gender as being "softly assembled," with each person's idiosyncratic sexual identity being his or her unique creation. From this perspective, *all* sexual orientations and gender identities require explanation (Hansell, 2011). Certainly this is an idea that modern psychoanalysts should happily embrace, suggesting as it does, that it is therapeutic for any human being, no matter what her or his sexual orientation, to think and talk about how he or she developed and expresses a unique gender identity.

The danger in this perspective, of course, is that heterosexuality becomes "problematized" in the same way that bisexuality, homosexuality, and transsexuality have been in the past (Chodorow, 1992). The rage of human beings who have historically been labeled deviant by many pillars of the mental health field has sometimes led to a bellicose stridency that pits "us" against "them." Some vocal claims that sperm banks have rendered men obsolete or that a male homosexual couple doesn't need a woman to make a baby verge on psychotic thinking, denying the animal fact that it takes a sperm and an ovum to create a new human being. Less grounded in reality, but probably even more important, is the idea that human beings need exposure to both the masculine and the feminine to achieve their full potential.

As I worked with the patients in my two childbirth groups, I began to realize that one of the goals I had for the women in the groups was a mental freedom derived from liberating their fantasy life from the rigid ideas culture had imposed on them about gender. Though the women who seemed to derive the most satisfaction from life were able to feel grounded in their procreative, female bodies, they were also eventually able to explore gender in a liberating and enriching way that embraced both femininity and masculinity. In all the groups I have organized since, one of my main objectives has been to help women be as assertive and creatively aggressive as men, while encouraging men to risk experiencing feelings of empathy and comfort that have always been associated with women. Exploring a less rigid and more inclusive gender identity ironically seems to anchor my patients in the reality of their sexed male or female bodies. Opposite sex identifications can be mastered and creatively utilized rather than being repressed (Bassin, 1996).

When *The Internal Triangle* first came out, I was speaking at a conference about my ideas about childbirth and female development. A female colleague of mine, protesting what she experienced as the reductionism of my theories, reported that throughout my presentation she kept thinking, "Don't fence me in!"

Certainly, psychoanalysis has always walked a fine line between developing theory that illuminates in its explanatory, descriptive capacity and theory that puts people into boxes. No single theory should begin to presume that it is the final word on something as complex and variant as human sexuality. Taken as a whole, psychoanalytic theory is a progression of ideas in which each new theory addresses the blind spots of the ones that preceded it. If theory fails to function as an open and evolving system, we become guilty of listening *for* a particular theory rather than listening *to* the particular patient in our treatment room (Fiorini, 2017).

I advise my students to immerse themselves in as much psychoanalytic theory as possible, and then use the knowledge they have gained as a tool box, pulling a theory out of the box when something a patient has said in session brings it to mind. In that moment, if any given theory helps the analyst understand the patient on a deeper level, it is a successful theory.

References

Bassin, D. (1996). Beyond the he and she: Toward the reconciliation of masculinity and femininity in the postoedipal female mind. *Journal of the American Psychoanalytic Association*, *44S* (Suppl.), 157–190.

Chodorow, N. (1992). Heterosexuality as a compromise formation: Reflections on the psychoanalytic theory of sexual development. *Psychoanalytic Contemporary Thought*, *15*(3), 267–304.

Corbett, K. (2011). Gender regulation. *Psychoanalytic Quarterly*, *80*(2), 441–459.

Fiorini, Leticia Glocer (2017). *Sexual difference in debate*. New York: Karnac.

Freud, S. (1905). Three essays on the theory of sexuality. *Standard Edition*. London: Hogarth Press, 7, 125–245.

Freud, S. (1932). Femininity. Lecture XXXIII, New introductory lectures on psycho-analysis. *Standard Edition*. London: Hogarth Press, 22, 112–135.

Hansell, J. (2011). Where sex was, there gender shall be? The dialectics of psychoanalytic gender theory. *Psychoanalytic Quarterly*, *80*(1), 55–71.

Harris, A. (2005). Gender in linear and nonlinear history. *Journal of the American Psychoanalytic Association*, *53*(4), 1079–1095.

Chapter 1

The object within
Childbirth as a developmental milestone

Childbirth is a developmental milestone in feminine life, as psychically significant for women as the Oedipus complex and adolescence. It provides opportunities for maturation and psychic reconstruction and reconfiguration unique in the life cycle. My two-year work with two groups of pregnant women confirmed that female development is not something that ends when adolescence is over. Rather, feminine developmental issues continue to be reworked in conflict and resolution throughout a woman's life. Dynamics derived from the pre-Oedipal and Oedipal periods are not abolished or abandoned. They are built upon and integrated into the personality in compromises of ever-expanding complexity.

Bibring et al. (1961) defined a developmental phase as a turning point in the life cycle leading to intense disequilibrium which results, in favorable circumstances, in specific maturational steps toward new functions. Given this definition, pregnancy and childbirth qualify as a legitimate developmental phase. Like adolescence and menopause, pregnancy is a crisis which creates profound life changes with which women must deal. Pregnancy demands a reworking of the relationship to one's internalized parental objects, particularly the resolution of the infantile aspects of those relationships. Bibring et al. described the specific task of childbirth as the redistribution of the cathexis of self-representations and of object representations. A specific sequence and alteration of the woman's object libidinal and narcissistic positions occur in pregnancy. This article will detail exactly how these new psychic constructs occur. Deutsch (1945, p. 56) called pregnancy a "kind of late maturation." It is helpful to female growth and functioning because it tends to thrust a woman's inner world into the object field where it can be dealt with in terms of reality. Of course, this maturation can be achieved in other ways, but pregnancy and childbirth, because they are rooted in the body and often cause women to regress to their own pre-Oedipal, indeed their intrauterine life, provide powerful primitive fuel for unconscious change.

The groups

Several themes emerged about pregnancy and childbirth in my work with women. The first and most apparent is an idea that Freud (1931) first discussed: pregnancy forces women to confront their own mothers. In the unconscious, getting pregnant means "becoming my mother." The simple statement, "I'm afraid I'll turn into my mother," was virtually a universal idea in the minds of women contemplating childbirth, and I began to see that it reflected both a fear and a wish. Women who absolutely refused the notion of "becoming my mother" were the ones who decided not to have babies or were infertile, despite their conscious wishes to have children (Spotnitz and Freeman, 1969).

A childless woman who had been raised in an orphanage said, "I have no mother. I don't know how to mother." Another infertile woman, who had had no contact with her mother for two years, remarked, "My mother just has to realize that I am not her, and she is not me." Sometimes this rejection of maternal identification was instigated by the woman's mother. A 53-year-old childless woman told me,

> I think on some level, my mother didn't want me to be a mother. She was the only one who was allowed to be a mother, so I had to be something else. She told me once that she thought she had never really given birth to me, never really let me be born. She hadn't let me separate from her. When I look back on my life, I always said I wanted children, but I didn't act like I did. I think I made the decisions I made because I didn't want to turn into my mother, and the only way not to turn into my mother was not to be a mother.

Women who were able to forgive and accept their mothers seemed more readily to accept the mothering role themselves. Annette told us about her own mother who had not protected her against sexual abuse from her stepfather, "My mother did wrong to me, but I forgave her because I loved her. She should have protected me, but she was afraid. When she got cancer, I nursed her till she died. She was vomiting blood, but I rocked her like a baby." Annette, pregnant for the second time, wanted to study social work because, "I like to help people. I like to take care of them." She was fiercely protective of her own child: "My mother never protected me, but I carried my girl around on my back." She seemed to be saying, "I am a better mother than my mother was." She gained power over her maternal introject with her own motherly stance.

Pregnancy reactivates a longing to be mothered and the wish to be a baby. Regressing to orality, women in both groups talked endlessly about chocolate milk and fried foods. Dreams reported by the women were often set in their "mothers' houses," a symbol of the womb, expressing the wish to return to the pre-Oedipal, even prenatal symbiosis. One pregnant woman reported the following dream, "I dreamed I saw this big, beautiful house, and I thought, 'It's so nice. My mother and I can live there.' But then my mother fell down the stairs and got killed." The wish to be symbiotic and the idea that birth (falling down the stairs) ends that symbiosis and obliterates the union with the mother were apparent in the dream. One of the most frightening things about pregnancy for many women is the regression to prenatal and pre-Oedipal periods that it involves. Naomi said, "I feel like I'm losing myself to my body." Another patient complained, "I cry all the time, and when I look in the mirror, I look just like a weeping infant, a big baby." This regression often involves the danger that the woman will be engulfed by her pre-Oedipal mother, and fear of this danger plays a part in many cases of infertility (Davis, 1985).

The idea that pregnancy implies a return to issues of symbiosis, while childbirth seems to permit the termination of that symbiosis with the woman's own mother, is illustrative of a paradox in pregnancy: it requires an identification with mother for the unconscious to permit pregnancy, but by identifying with mother enough to get pregnant, a woman can finally in childbirth achieve true individuation and psychic separation from mother. More specifically, women can achieve pregnancy only by having a certain unconscious willingness to confront the maternal introject. The maternal introject in women is a synthesis of two imagoes: the pre-Oedipal mother and the passive, "feminine" mother who is the inheritor of the Oedipus complex. It is important to remember that, for both sexes, the pre-Oedipal mother is not "castrated." Rather she is a primal omnipotent figure. Her breasts, the part-objects which introduce the baby to the world, are protruding organs of activity and penetration, the source of life. Crowell (1981) discussed the toxic aspects of both the powerful mother introject and the depressed, passive, feminine image of mother. Fears of regressing and becoming the phallic pre-Oedipal mother's helpless infant, as well as anxieties about becoming the passive, masochistic mother of the Oedipus complex play a significant part in both infertility and early pregnancy. By identifying with the "feminine" mother and submitting passively and masochistically to pregnancy, women overcome those fears and truly identify, for the first time in the life cycle, with the powerful pre-Oedipal maternal imago, thus achieving individuation and autonomy while integrating a feminine identification. The process of gestating the fetus and pushing it out into the world permits the ego a new stance toward the maternal internalized object. Childbirth seems to facilitate true identification with the phallic mother of the pre-Oedipal period, so that the self is no longer controlled or dominated by its maternal imago. Pregnancy allows separation from the engulfing mother in a uniquely feminine way. In childbirth, the woman gains the power her mother had in the pre-Oedipal period, and by total identification with that power, women reconcile autonomy and femininity. They can at last identify with their mothers without submitting to engulfment. A patient who had recently had a baby and whose mother was staying with her to help her take care of the newborn, made the following observation:

I was changing the baby, and my mother was watching, and I said, "Here, Mom, take her while I throw this diaper away." And I gave the baby to my mother, and she took the baby, and she was very nervous, and I had a revelation while I watched my mother hold my daughter. My mother was *scared*, and she felt inadequate, and she was afraid she was going to hurt the baby. And then, I saw that she got angry at the baby for giving her all those awful feelings, and just then, the baby started to cry, and in that moment, I understood everything about my own character and how it was formed, all the sadness and guilt and shame that's a part of me. I've hated my mother, but in that little moment, I realized she couldn't help it. She did the best she could. I identified with both my mother and my daughter. I understood exactly how my daughter felt, and for the first time, I understood my mother too. I didn't know which one of them to hold. But I put my arms around my mother. I loved them both, and I loved me too. And for the first time, I felt in control of my life. Because I understood everything.

This patient played the role of phallic mother to both her own mother and her new baby. She got "control of my life" by simultaneously identifying with fetus/self and self/mother, and viewing the pre-Oedipal scene with a healthy observing ego which was powerful because it "understood everything." This opportunity to perceive the pre-Oedipal situation as an adult observer, while identifying with all the characters in that situation, is one of the beneficial aspects of childbearing. It allows for an unconscious integration of the complex endopsychic world.

The paternal image

This integration is characterized by a strengthening of ego in relation not only to the internalized mother, but also to the paternal introject. Another paradox of pregnancy concerns the internalized father. Pregnancy, or even the thought of pregnancy, tends to heighten aggression toward men in a woman's mind (Spotnitz and Freeman, 1969). This aggression directed toward males was particularly strong in the group I ran for disadvantaged women. Men were "mama's boys" who acted like "big babies." One woman said, "Sometimes I wonder who's pregnant, him or me? All he does is lie around, sleeping and eating and expecting to be waited on." Another told her boyfriend, "Any idiot can make a baby, but it takes a man to be a father." When he hit her in response, she said, "You're never going to see this baby. If something is trash, you put it in the garbage. I sent him back to his mother."

Annette reported, "Since I been pregnant, I been having the scariest dreams. They're all about killing. They're all about killing little boys. Once I dreamed I was killing a baby, and a little boy was helping me." Later, Annette had another dream about killing a male: "I dreamed I had an abortion, but the baby came out, and it was talking to me. It was a little boy baby, and it started talking to me. It was horrible." Almost every woman in the group said from time to time, "I don't need no man in my life. I got my baby, and that's all I need." A woman who arrived with her week-old infant said about the father of her child, "I don't want no part of him. I don't need him around. I'll be fine by myself. I can take care of my own." There was a sense that since the women had their fetus/baby, they didn't need a penis. But there was also a wish to be babied by their men and rage at them for their unwillingness to mother them. As one patient said,

> When a man gets a woman pregnant, it's his responsibility to provide for her. He has to make a home for her and take care of her and the baby. But these men are such children. They can make these babies all right, but then they go back to their mothers and act like big babies themselves.

Primitive competitive triangles between a pregnant woman, the father of her child, and his mother were commonly reported, and these conflicts always struck me as being more about who would be allowed to be babied than about Oedipal, sexual rivalry.

In my other group, there was talk of men abandoning women in pregnancy. The women were not sure their partners would protect and support them. A patient had the following dream:

> I was nine months pregnant, and I started to hemorrhage. There was all this blood, and I was so scared. I was in my mother's house, the house I grew up in, and she was screaming at me. Somehow it was my husband's fault that we were there. I don't know how it worked, but somehow, he was allowing it. He was there, and he wasn't protecting me against my mother. He was accommodating her. We were trying to go to the hospital, and my mother wanted to go with us, and I didn't want that, and my husband was siding with her.

This dream, both a fear and a wish, seems to say that the husband was putting her at risk by getting her pregnant, which meant abandoning her to the engulfing pre-Oedipal mother. Another woman resisted pregnancy because her husband would work 14-hour days and render her a victim of their baby: "I'll be alone and in a panic, just like my mother was." Many women reported anxieties about their husbands leaving them. I often felt that all the fear of being abandoned by men was actually an unconscious wish to get rid of them.

Several women were able to use their pregnancies to forge new relationships with their actual fathers and their paternal imagoes. Lily, who had always handled her father with a defensive and distant friendliness, reported "finally telling him off" after her baby was born. A woman in the group who had just given birth reported, "I finally let my father have it after all those years of being silently offended." Another patient spoke of "feeling more like my father's mother than his daughter" after she gave birth.

Many of the pregnant women in both groups verbalized the idea that when pregnant they were not going to be dominated by men anymore. Lily called it "training" her husband, while Martha called it "threatening." The women in the disadvantaged group said over and over that at about eight months into the pregnancy, their men, who had been acting like big babies and withdrawing from them throughout most of their pregnancies, wanted to be "under" them again. But the women held back: "Let him see how it feels."

After their babies were born, several of the group members related interesting stories about their new babies and their own fathers. I heard often of the importance of presenting the newborn to the father. One woman said:

> When I got home from the hospital, my mother and father came over, and I felt so glad to see them. I felt really close to my mother, but it's funny. When they came in, I right away gave the baby to my father. For some reason, it was very important for him to hold the baby. I just wanted to present him with his grandson.

Another patient with a male analyst told a remarkably similar story:

> I took the baby to my first analytic session after we came home from the hospital. I had had this fantasy for days that I wanted my analyst to hold the baby. Just hold it. I don't know why. When I arrived, I asked him if he would mind holding the baby just for a moment before I lay down on the couch. He was initially reluctant, and I could see he was uncomfortable. But I said, "Please, just for a moment. It's very important to me." He took the baby, and she looked up at him, and he was silent for a moment, and then he said, "Oh my, this is a very special baby." I felt euphoric.

Langer (1992) talked about the fetus as something "stolen" from the mother. These vignettes seem to confirm this idea. Women seemed to act out the idea that their babies were fathered, not by their husbands, but by their fathers or their father representatives. Childbirth had, on an unconscious level, finally made them Oedipal winners with the childish fantasy of obtaining a penis/child from their father at last fulfilled.

This data lent credence to the theory that pregnancy initially heightens aggression toward the internalized father, but finally achieves a restructuring of the relationship between the ego and the paternal imago, with the self acquiring a new authority in terms of the paternal introject. Childbirth seems to help a woman experience herself as what Benjamin (1988, p. 12) called a "sovereign equal" to a man, not by a defensive imitation of masculine power, but by an identification with a truly female power. The internal relationship shifts from one between a subject/father and an object/self and becomes a more integrated interplay between subject and subject. The new relationship between ego and paternal imago is what Benjamin called "a dance of mutual recognition" (p. 130). In some cases, women actually seemed to use their pregnancies to replace their mothers on the level of fantasy and shift the internal relationship from one between father/female child to father/mother.

One reason that pregnancy and childbirth can give a woman this new sense of power is that, in many ways, pregnancy functions for women as a penis does for men. Simone de Beauvoir wrote eloquently about how the penis operates for men. She felt that the major benefit of the penis, as an organ that can be seen and grasped, is that it allows a boy to partially identify himself with it. de Beauvoir (1952, p. 278) writes:

> He projects the mystery of his body, its threats, outside himself, which enables him to keep them at a distance. Because he has an alter ego, in whom he sees himself, the little boy can boldly assume an attitude of subjectivity; the very object on which he projects himself becomes a symbol of autonomy, of transcendence, of power.

de Beauvoir (1952, p. 278) talked about the double role the penis plays:

> It is for him at once a foreign object and himself. It becomes an alter ego, ordinarily more artful, more intelligent, and more clever than the individual. The penis is regarded by the subject as at once himself, and other than himself; its functions are midway between the voluntary and the involuntary, and because it is capricious and, as it were, a foreign source of pleasure that is felt subjectively. The individual's specific transcendence takes concrete form in the penis, and it is a source of pride. The phallus assumes such worth as it does because it symbolizes dominance that is exercised in other domains. If woman should succeed in establishing herself as a subject, she would invent equivalents of the phallus.

I suggest that pregnancy and childbirth function as equivalents of the phallus. Like the penis, the fetus is self and non-self, both subject and object, and this double role gives a woman the self-containment and self-reliance that the penis gives a man. Like the penis, pregnancy compensates for early narcissistic wounds, the old trauma of feeling "organless." Like the penis, the pregnancy and the fetus represent bodily symbols of independence from the engulfing pre-Oedipal mother. The newborn, like the phallus, can be seen and grasped and partially identified with. A new mother can see the self/object that is her child and know that the child can function. A woman's internal conflicts and anxieties can be projected onto the fetus and kept at a distance, providing the same function that de Beauvoir (1952) described in terms of the penis. The baby/fetus is its mother's phallic alter ego, an object over which the mother can assume an attitude of subjectivity, yet at the same time feel that object to be a part of the self. In giving birth, a woman achieves what little boys achieve with the castration complex: detachment and autonomy from the maternal imago. Just as the penis allows men to see themselves as totally separate and independent from women, so does the protruding belly of pregnancy give women that independence from the maternal imago.

If the fetus can be seen as equivalent to the penis as a dynamic in psychic functioning, it is significant that women give up the valued self-object in a way that men never have to. Castration fantasies are crucial to male development, but they remain fantasies; men are never required to relinquish their penises as women must lose the pregnancy and the fetus in childbirth. The loss of the phallus/fetus means that women must perceive the self/object as a separate object, and this is a process which is painful and by no means ever completely accomplished. Chodorow (1978) effectively described the boundary confusion and lack of individuation so common in women. But the projection of the self/object into the outer world, as traumatic as it is, can have positive psychic consequences. It can act as an impetus to individuation and a remedy against narcissism. In *Psychoanalysis and Feminism*, Mitchell (1974, p. 383) discussed the path out of primitive narcissism:

> The object is first realized as an object in its absence. Both the recognition of the separateness of the object and (it is the same thing) of the self can, then, only come through a knowledge of absence. For One to exist at all, two are needed, even if the second is in fact the reflection in the mirror. Because he stayed hooked on his own image and couldn't tolerate its absence, Narcissus never constituted himself as subject. The very self, the subject, is only created in difference. The illusion of primordial unity is Zero that misthinks itself as One.

The dual whole of man/penis or woman/fetus can be experienced as narcissistic bliss, but for women that bliss is shattered by labor and delivery. And though the termination of that bliss is painful, it also provides a pathway out of narcissism, the inability to recognize the other as a separate object. The ability to see another who, until moments ago, was a part of the self makes it impossible to narcissistically deny recognition of the object world of separately sentient others, and equally impossible not to identify with those others on some level. The loss of self/object then, with its demand that the object be realized as both like the self and different from it, becomes a maturational leap for a woman. Childbirth helps women achieve what Benjamin (1988) called "intersubjectivity," where sameness and difference between two subjects (not a subject and an object) exist in the healthy tension of mutual recognition. So, the loss of the child/penis can be a developmental milestone, albeit an agonizing one, which can be an experience as traumatic as death.

Childbirth is certainly linked with death in the unconscious. The loss of the self/object in childbirth is one reason for this link. Another is the primitive regression to a symbiotic union and the loss of that symbiosis which are associated with the death that childbirth symbolizes.

Over and over, my clients talked about childbirth in ways that brought death to mind. They were "losing control." They had "to go through this alone." They talked of "going someplace I've never gone before." Everything was going to change. There was a tremendous fear of the "unknown": "I just can't imagine how it will be." Lisa talked incessantly about her fear of the pain of birth, and she insisted that "I have to go through it alone. I don't want nobody to see me suffer or scream. I'm scared, I'm scared, but it's just something I have to get through." She could have been talking about birth or death, and her remarks demonstrated the link between them. When the first pregnant woman in my group actually gave birth, the group didn't meet for several weeks. Everyone called in sick or didn't show up. It was like, with the actual birth of a child, the group had become a place as frightening as death.

Because the baby is both self and object, childbirth is a loss of both, a kind of death. Postpartum grief and mourning that are experienced as depression are common in women. The loss of self/object that pushing a baby into the world implies was eloquently described by a patient who talked about the hours after the birth of her baby:

> I lay in bed weeping. I felt the loss of her so profoundly. I thought of all the people, long dead, who had helped me make her. My husband's father, I never knew him, but his blood is running though her veins. My grandmother, who died last year, and all the generations and generations of my family way back to Ireland, all dead, who helped me make her. I realized that now, just as the hour and day of her birth is determined, can be written down on a birth certificate, so the hour and day of her death will be written on a death certificate someday. As long as she was inside me, she was safe, immortal, a timeless fantasy. Now I have lost her to the world. She is flesh and blood, limited, manifest, and ultimately mortal.

It is the triumph of life over death that makes a successful childbirth experience empowering and ego-enhancing. Pregnancy is dangerous, but it is in confronting that danger that women overcome entropy and become truly alive. Experiencing childbirth means feeling in a primitive way what it is to be human, to be a part of an essentially uncontrollable process that started before we were born and will continue after we die. Pregnancy and childbirth, as powerful life forces that can confront and triumph over the death instinct, were ideas that were apparent in all the trauma, violence, and death that were part of the disadvantaged group. Despite all the abuse they endured, women said over and over, "I have to be strong for the baby." Everyone wanted to go back to school or give up drugs because "it's not just me now." Indeed, pregnancy seemed to offer some protection against violence. One father who had picked up a pipe had second thoughts, "You know I can't hit you when you're pregnant." For all the women in both groups, pregnancy motivated them to stay connected to significant others and to move closer to objects that had been defensively pushed away.

Shifting object representations

One of the most interesting aspects of my research was the observation of shifting object representations in pregnancy. The fetus within is the receptacle for all sorts of fantasies and projections. It can alternately be perceived as the self or one of the internalized parental objects, as part of her body or the parasite that feeds on it, as the possessed or the possessor. Rabuzzi (1994, p. 5) described the infant within as the "motherself," a binary–unity which is both two and one at the same time, its parts consisting of mother and child in varying degrees of relationship. Poet Adrienne Rich (1976, p. 63) put it this way:

> In pregnancy, I did not experience the embryo as decisively internal in Freud's terms, but rather as something inside and of me, yet becoming hourly and daily more separate on its way to becoming separate from me and of itself. In early pregnancy, the stirrings of the fetus felt like ghostly tremors of my own body, later like the movements of a being imprisoned in me; but both sensations were my sensations, contributing to my own sense of physical and psychic space. The child that I carry for nine months can be defined neither as me nor not-me. Far from existing in the mode of "inner space," women are powerfully and vulnerably attuned to both "inner" and "outer," because, for us, the two are continuous, not polar.

The ambivalence and vacillation in a pregnant woman's feelings and fantasies about her infant create all sorts of maternal attitude changes during the course of fetal development. The vomiting experienced during early pregnancy can indicate a certain refusal of the pregnancy. One patient called the fetus a "tumor" when she was in the throes of morning sickness. Midway through pregnancy, the nausea usually abates, and many of my patients experienced a sense of peace and well-being. Though they were aware that the baby was there, mother and fetus often seemed in perfect attunement. This is how one patient put it:

> I loved the middle three months. For the first time in my life, I wasn't alone in my own skin. I felt "two in one." The pain of existential loneliness was gone, and I had no anxiety. I just felt like, "What could go wrong? We're together." The baby's movements were coordinated with mine and yet distinct. It was great. But then when the baby started getting so big, and its kicking really started to hurt, and I got indigestion and couldn't breathe and felt a foot jammed against my ribs. I began to think, "Why don't you get the hell out of there, you little intruder? You're wearing out your welcome." And at the end, I was terribly anxious

and conflicted. I wanted it to be over and at the same time, I was terrified of the labor and delivery. No way out.

This attunement followed by conflict between fetus and child was very common. When women approach delivery, all their primitive terrors come to life, and they fear they will die in birth. The conflict between retaining the precious fetus that has been part of the ego and yet also a treasured object and expelling the expanding invader is acute. As the pregnancy unfolds, a woman must increasingly separate the baby from her own ego and experience it as an object toward whom she feels both libido and aggression.

Psychoanalyst Alessandra Piontelli (1992) has, in recent years, used ultrasound technology to observe fetuses in utero. Piontelli's beautiful pictures of fetuses floating in the amniotic fluid make it clear that they possess character in the womb. Particularly in her observation of twins, Piontelli was able to offer dramatic evidence that two fetuses growing in the same woman display totally different patterns of activity in contact and withdrawal and in quantities of libido and aggression. These same character patterns persist after birth. Piontelli's work seems to lend credence to the idea that many of a human being's most deeply seated characterological issues are representations of sensory perceptions experienced in utero and recorded in the primitive unconscious in a way that makes them a powerful dynamic in the formation of psyche. In pregnancy, a woman unconsciously projects some of these early pre-feelings experienced in her own prenatal life onto her fetus. This provides an opportunity in pregnancy to unconsciously work through deep-seated prenatal issues by utilizing the projections onto the child within. Furthermore, the physical act of pushing a baby into the world is a psychic as well as a physical projection of the inner world to the outer world, and this means that the pre-feeling conflicts invested in the fetus during pregnancy are pushed from fantasy to reality where they become available to be utilized and resolved by the mature observing ego of the new mother.

Baby as self can manifest itself in terms of viewing the fetus as an alien intruder, the woman's own voracious intrauterine and pre-Oedipal self who wishes to eat her mother up and destroy her. Alternately, baby/self can represent an ego ideal, and for the sake of the beloved baby as the idealized self, the pregnant woman takes better care of herself, is more responsible, and has greater social consciousness. A pregnant woman I interviewed said:

> I grew up fast. Pregnancy had an immediate maturational effect on me. I used to have trouble doing the responsible thing. Like the amnio. In the past I would have been afraid it would hurt, and I would have just forgotten to do it. But now I thought, "No way am I going to forget this. This is important." It's not just me anymore.

The protective feelings that women verbalized and the common desire to talk to the unborn baby were examples of the fetus representing the infant/self and of the pregnant woman's wish to baby herself by babying her fetus. Even after the child is born, women experience the infant as an extension of the self, and the gratification of the child serves the same psychological purpose as the gratification of the self. In nurturing their babies, women identified with their own mothers and at the same time with their infants; in providing care, they re-experienced themselves as cared-for babies, thus sharing with their babies the possession of a good mother. Baby as self can also be associated with the idea of a defective self. Dreams of giving birth to monsters and retarded infants were common in my groups and reflected the fantasy of the baby as an inadequate, pathological self.

The fetus can also be perceived as an object, and again these object representations can shift and reintegrate during pregnancy and birth. Baby as alien can also represent a toxic introject, either maternal or paternal. Aggression against these representations was rampant in all my work with women and manifested itself as compulsive worry about the baby and about harming the baby, which I interpreted as unconscious wishes to destroy the fetus. Dreams of killing babies were common. In both groups, women obsessed about hurting their infants by sleeping on their stomachs, drinking coffee, buying dangerous baby gear, and countless other creative ways of destroying the object within.

The process of analysis leads to the re-externalization of internalized or introjected objects, and their reworking through and re-internalization in such a way that there is a radical change in mental structure (Loewald, 1962). Pregnancy and childbirth, particularly when experienced in conjunction with psychoanalysis, seem to provide the same function. Just as psychoanalysis allows people to be "awake and aware" about their intrapsychic dynamics and to develop an observing ego that can modulate and regulate conflict, so too can an educated pregnancy and a drug-free childbirth allow women to be present at the restructuring of their inner world that marks childbirth as a significant developmental milestone.

The interplay between internalization and externalization of introjected objects, along with the vacillating cathexis of the representation of the fetus as self and object, make childbirth a time of heightened identifications for women. Masculine and feminine identifications that have been in conflict in the endopsychic world of the internal triangle of maternal and paternal introjects and self tend to become more integrated. Rather than a relationship of subject/object which has characterized the dynamic between the paternal imago and the maternal imago and between both the parental imagoes and the self, a restructuring occurs that allows for a triangle of equal subjects. Power, autonomy, and individuation – "masculine" qualities which heretofore have often been the sole property of the internalized father – become associated with the maternal imago and with the self, and not in a defensively "masculine" way, but in a manner endowed with a truly feminine strength, the strength of the pre-Oedipal mother. The integration of "masculine" and "feminine" that the following case of Naomi illustrates was by no means the exception. Many new mothers demonstrated this new complexity of identifications.

In addition, the demand that pregnancy and childbirth make, insisting that a woman perceive a part of her self as an object, often sets up a heightened capacity to identify with the world and everyone in it. A patient described this dynamic:

> Since I got pregnant, I feel I have more empathy for people. I see how vulnerable everyone is, how pulled along by life. Maybe that's because I feel vulnerable and out of control, pushed along by the life force. But I just feel everyone's feelings. I feel connected to every other human being on a really deep level. I sense people's struggles, and I identify with them.

Another woman put it this way:

> After Emily was born, I just felt connected to everybody. I used to watch the news at night and see people dying in wars or starving in Ethiopia and feel indifferent, removed. Now I weep. It's as if it's happening to me now, to Emily. I want to get involved in helping people in some way.

The dual identification with "masculine" power and "feminine" connection that childbirth seems to help instigate achieves new levels of complexity and integration in the female psyche.

In conclusion, I would like to address the question of whether there is a true maternal instinct, an instinct toward reproduction in women. Freud (1932) believed this powerful wish was really a wish for a penis. Homey (1967) and other psychoanalytic theorists disagreed with Freud, believing that there is a biological instinct in women which compels them to have babies. Feminist writers have insisted that mothering is by no means innate; they insist that it is learned, that culture "brainwashes" women into having babies.

In working with women, I have come to believe that there is a powerful maternal instinct which has its origins in the intrauterine life of girls. I believe the maternal instinct is a repetition compulsion, a desire to return to oneness with the mother. Chodorow (1978) pointed out that all people who have been mothered have a wish to return to the exclusive symbiosis of the mother–child dyad. Men attempt to return to this unity in sexual intercourse, but this pathway is not open to women. By having a child, women can resolve and recreate the mother–daughter bond. Only in pregnancy and childbirth can women re-experience the narcissistic oneness that preceded the first sensation. From this point of view, pregnancy and childbirth are a wish to return to a state of non-tension, a death instinct in the service of life. It is this primitive integration of life and death that makes childbirth so awesome and so terrifying to every human being. And it is the triumph of libido over aggression that makes pregnancy so empowering. One of my patients talked about the "special club" that having a baby admits you to. No longer estranged from their bodies, women saw them as "the seat of magical powers." A new mother said, "I've changed. Now I know how things work. And now I know what I know." When the child leaves the body, it leaves a residue behind, a sense that goodness and power are inside rather than outside the body, a talisman to carry for life.

The case of Naomi

Naomi was three months pregnant when she came into treatment for anxiety. She said,

> I'm afraid I'm going to turn into my mother and just give up my whole life to motherhood, like my mother did. One reason I think I got pregnant so easily is that I have a very good mother, but she totally sacrificed herself to motherhood. I don't want that.

She was vomiting constantly. Naomi admitted her pregnancy was unplanned, "It wasn't my choice. I think I got pregnant because my husband wanted a baby so badly."

Naomi told me she came from a very close and traditional family. She said:

> The women have the babies and raise them, and the men kill themselves with work. My father is so sexist. You can't believe how he talks to my mother, though she holds her own. He's very rigid too. He insisted I go to dancing lessons. I wanted to drive a truck, but he wouldn't let me. My mother is a wonderful mother, but she never worked. I'm a feminist, and my mother was a feminist too, but look at her now. I watched my mother have nothing to live for but the children. She was the nurturer. So that's how I learned to be a nurturer.

Naomi was a stockbroker, but her pregnancy disrupted her ambitions regarding her professional life. She said, "This baby has screwed up all my plans to develop my career. I worry about giving up my job, my whole life. I want to work." Her mother was going to take care of the baby after it was born. "I feel a little guilty about this," she said. "My mother has been taking care of kids all her life, and she loves to do it, but I think she deserves a rest at this point in her life. Also, I worry that if my mother takes care of the baby, I mean, she's great, but I worry that we're both going to forget who the mother is." Naomi was just beginning her career, and her husband, a health care consultant, made much more money than she did.

> I want my husband to cut his work week back from five days to three, so I can work too, but he says it's out of the question. But I'm so worried

about my career. I don't want to be dependent on someone to put food on the table." She said, "I'm not feeling at all feminine or successful. I feel like a fat cow.

Naomi wore her red hair cropped very short, and she favored pants. She said,

> I would never wear a frilly skirt. I associate it with no choices. I really had no choices as a girl. I remember once I had a boyfriend who was an electrician, and he was showing me how light switches work, and I thought, "No one ever showed me any of this." No one ever gave me the option to be an electrician. I wanted to be a fireman. I feel so out of control now, and I guess I am, but that's part of life, and at a certain point, you just have to let go. I've got to keep working. I'm so scared I'm going to end up like my mother, just staying at home and never working again. Sometimes I really wish I had one of those "career woman" type mothers who are very successful in business. Why did I even think I wanted to get pregnant? I think it's because of my upbringing. I watched my mother have nothing to live for but the children, so I didn't know what else to do with myself. But I always envied my father going out of the house to his job. He was the provider. I think I want to be a combination of my mother and my father.

Naomi's feminism seemed to be in constant conflict with her pregnancy. She said,

> I think men are afraid to show their feminine side. Sexism is like racism. People say they hate minorities, and then they leave their babies with black people to raise. My husband wants no part of this baby. He won't go to the doctor with me. I'm having to drag him to the classes. And he absolutely refuses to cut back to three days a week.

The tendency to worry became more pronounced as Naomi's pregnancy progressed. "I worry all the time about eating the wrong things. I drank two Diet Cokes, and I feel so guilty." She worried about caffeine and would reassure herself by saying, "My mother drank, and she smoked, and all ten of us are fine." She worried about sleeping in the wrong position and smothering the baby. She worried about gaining too much weight. She worried about Sudden Infant Death Syndrome. She worried because she did not feel maternal and was not sure she would. She worried about disciplining the baby. "My father used to hit me hard, and I worry if I get mad, I'll start hitting. I get so mad at my husband that I feel like hitting him, but I never have. My father used to fly into rages, and now I fly into rages." Above all, Naomi worried about being inadequate in terms of pregnancy and childbirth.

> Everybody talks about how horrible the pain is, and I'm afraid. And lately I've started worrying again that the baby is not all right. Early in the pregnancy, I used to feel it was so creepy to have something growing inside me. Did you ever see the movie *Alien*, where all those creepy things were growing inside her? I used to feel so horrible thinking there was a little alien growing inside me. But then it went away.

When I asked Naomi what made it go away, she said, "I had an amnio, and that helped a little. But the sonogram made it seem real to me. I saw his arms and legs moving around, and I thought, "What could go wrong? He's perfect. He's fine." I think that's when I settled down and stopped thinking of him as an alien. Now I'm worrying again."

Naomi had wanted a midwife and a birth center for her delivery, but her father had insisted that she go to the family doctor, even though he was known as "Mr C-Section." Naomi was very worried she would have a C-section too, but opposing her father seemed out of the question. She spent a lot of time in session reassuring herself that episiotomies and C-sections were sometimes the best way to go. "I just worry that I'm going to get in there in labor and not be able to stand up for myself, and things will start happening to me."

Naomi and her husband bought a house in the suburbs. She was unhappy about the decision and hated the new house. I asked her why she would buy a house she hated. She said, "Because it was so important to my husband." The only thing Naomi liked about the move is that she would be right down the street from her mother. "I need to be close to my mother. I need her, but I feel so guilty about using her. She gave up her life for us."

As Naomi's due date approached, her anxiety increased.

> I think when I start my contractions, I'll go right to my mother's house. I just want to go right up to my old room and lock the door. I don't want my mother with me. I'd just like to have my husband and me alone together in my old room when I have the baby. I can't believe my due date is so close. I guess it never seemed real to me. Now I realize, I'm really going to have a baby. I know he's real. I feel him move. He kicks me in the ribs, and it really hurts, so I've always been aware that inside me is another human being.

I asked her if she liked that feeling. She said:

> I didn't at first. The *Alien* fantasy, remember? But I like it now. I just worry about getting him out. I can't believe my body will be able to push him out. Oh well, I can't control these things, so I guess I'll just relax. I'm getting scared of the pain. I'm afraid I won't be able to do it. My whole life will be changing. But there's nothing I can do about it. I just can't imagine how it will be. You can't know how something you've never

experienced will be, and I guess that makes you nervous. And I'm getting so uncomfortable. I don't think I can stand it much longer.

Naomi seemed more at peace with her husband's choices as the delivery approached. She gave up on the three-day workweek idea.

> He says he wants to be with the baby. But not enough to go to a three-day week. I guess if he wants to get ahead, that's not practical. All I can think about now is the baby. I'm very self-involved. I don't care about anything else. My sexist father was talking about politics, and I wanted to yell at him, but I just couldn't be bothered.

The Friday after this session, I got a call from Naomi. She was crying.

> They're going to induce me tonight. At first, they said they would give me till Monday to go into labor, but then they said, why wait? So, they want to do it tonight. I really don't want to do this, but they say it's best.

I said, "Do you feel ready or do you feel rushed?" She said, "I feel rushed. I'm a basket case." I said, "Can you advocate for yourself? Can you tell the doctor you want to wait the weekend and see what happens?" She said, "I don't feel I know enough. Who am I to question the doctor?" I said, "Tell your baby it's time to go into labor."

When she called again, Naomi had had her baby.

> It was horrible and wonderful. When I got to the hospital, I refused to sign the consent forms because they waived my right to be consulted about anything. Finally, they wrote out a document I could sign. They were taking me to the delivery room at eight when I gave birth in the hall. There were no doctors. Next time I'm going with a midwife. It was so thrilling to see that little head sticking out of me. I was out on Sunday. I've been at my mother's ever since. Today on the way home, I started to cry. "Oh my God, I have this beautiful little son."

When she arrived at her next session, Naomi looked tired.

> I'm not doing so good. I just can't believe I'm a mother. I don't feel like a mother yet. Even though he's mine, I don't feel like he came from me. It was the most awesome thing I've ever experienced. I still can't believe I did it. They wanted me to lie down, but I insisted on standing up. And then as they were wheeling me into the delivery room, the baby's head crowned, and I was in a position so I could see it, and it was the most profound moment of my life. I put my hands down and felt the head, and I thought, "Oh my God, it's a baby!" I never really believed till that

moment. It was awesome. I'll never forget when I saw his head coming out of my body. We'll never be the same after that. It hurt, but it was the most beautiful moment of my life. I can't think about it now without crying. But it's not sadness. I don't know what the tears are about, but it's not sadness.

Naomi struggled in the weeks that followed with the masculine–feminine issues that had preoccupied her before the birth, but there were subtle changes. She was still the feminist complaining that:

Men are so rigid and self-involved. Women are taught to do what they have to do, whether it's enduring pain or being cut. We're trained to take care of and give pleasure. We give and give and never ask to get. Men just aren't trained to serve others. They have no idea how to mother. That's my responsibility, and I resent it. I'm the one who has to make sacrifices. Boys get trucks and blocks and camcorders for their birthdays. Look what we give girls – dolls and toy kitchens. What's the message? You're here to serve. I'm not going to give my best friend's baby girl a doll, even if I did see a beautiful one. Caretaking is held in contempt. You're only worthwhile if you have a career.

But then she added something new: "The truth is that I want to be the one to raise the baby. Why do I feel that I'm only worthwhile if I make a million dollars on Wall Street?" Naomi seemed to be experiencing the idea that she wanted the feminine role and could even find some dignity and authority in such a self-concept.

Part of this new thinking centered on her husband. She seemed to have given up on the idea of turning him into a co-mother and decided that women must assume responsibility in mothering. She said, "He wants to help, but how can he? He's willing, but I'm the one with the breasts." At times, Naomi expressed anger at her husband's inability to be a mother. "He will make no decisions about the baby. He treats me as the authority, and it's very annoying. He never takes care of the baby. He only plays with him." But she added something new: "I used to just passively accept all this stuff, but now I'm going to insist."

If Naomi's relationship with her husband had been altered, changes in her ideas about her mother were even more striking. She still was conflicted about her mother, saying through tears, "I feel so guilty because she is just exhausted taking care of all of us. I think she's a better mother than I am. She can calm the baby down in a way that I can't. My father would help, but he just doesn't know how." But then she expressed a new idea: "Now I can identify with my mother. I used to see her as self-sacrificing. But now I know. You do it for this strange kind of love. You just love that baby. It's like loving yourself."

In the next session, Naomi made her clearest statement about her conflicted identifications. She said:

> I think I modeled myself after my father. I didn't want to be so self-sacrificing. I got my MBA. But now that I'm a mother, I don't have any role model but my mother. My father didn't mother. He was a workaholic. So now that I'm a mother, I can't use my father as a role model. I always used to rail against staying home and being a mother, and now I think, "What's wrong with staying home and taking care of your kid?" We just feel we're not meaningful human beings if we don't have a meaningful career outside the home. But what could be more meaningful than raising a child? We play such roles. In my house growing up, the girls set the table and washed the dishes. The boys raked leaves and mowed the lawn. When we all went to work for my father, my brothers drove trucks, and my sisters and I filed like secretaries.

I asked why she thought her father was so sexist. Naomi said:

> My grandmother was very strong. She walked all over my grandfather. My husband comes from the same kind of family. His mother is very strong, and she dominates his father. I guess I'm pretty strong too. I really didn't want to become my mother, yet it's not so bad to become your mother. My mother is a good woman. She lived with this sexist man all her life, but she held her own.

In the weeks after the birth, Naomi spoke continuously about being out of control.

> I'm so tired. I've lost total control over my life. He doesn't sleep at all, and my career is a joke. I'm going to have to quit my job, I think. I was supposed to go in yesterday, and I just never made it. Here I am, sleepless, jobless, living with my mother, but it's great!

I asked her what was so great about it. She said, "To have someone you love that much. He's a person. He came out of me. I don't feel like I created him. I don't feel like this powerful creator. But it's just something so profound. Pregnancy is just a state of constant metamorphosis. Things are changing and growing all the time. How can you realize any of this before it happens?"

A few months later, Naomi decided to go back to work.

> I feel diminished that I'm not bringing money into the family. I'm not cut out to be a full-time mother. It's just not me. I feel like I'm a good mother. I was so worried that I had no maternal instincts, but it all just sort of kicks in naturally. I don't feel nervous now. I could be a full-time mother, but it's just too hard. I need time away or I'll go crazy.

Naomi's mother took care of the baby when she went back to work.

In the next session, Naomi said:

> You know, I've been thinking, womanhood is just a wonderful thing. I guess I feel a little sad. Have I ever allowed myself to feel like a woman? But on the other hand, if I had allowed myself to feel like a woman, would I have done anything different? I've been fighting it all my life, but really when I think of what I would have done differently…what? Wearing tops that are cut lower? I really wouldn't have done anything differently. And I've been thinking, maybe it isn't such a bad thing to let little girls have dolls. It teaches them one of the most important parts of life.

Discussion

Naomi's case certainly illustrates the struggle between masculine and feminine identification which is so common in pregnancy. Her ambivalence about pregnancy and the tremendous anxiety she was feeling when she came in for treatment were expressed in her simple statement: "I'm afraid I'm going to turn into my mother." The fact that Naomi was able get pregnant so easily was one of many factors which indicated to me that unconsciously there was a lot of libido directed toward her maternal imago. Naomi herself on several occasions verbalized the idea that she got pregnant because she had a "good" and "accepting" mother. It was clear that Naomi loved her mother and felt that she had protected her against her powerful, aggressive father. The mother Naomi was resisting identifying herself with was the masochistic, passive mother, the one who "totally sacrificed herself to motherhood." Naomi's vomiting early in pregnancy and her sense that the baby was an "alien" were indicative of her aggression toward this troublesome fetus who was going to turn her into her mother.

Though it was clear that Naomi had a persecuting father and a protecting mother, her identifications were quite complex. Her masculine appearance, her feminism, her wish to make her husband a co-mother, her desire to be a fireman, an electrician, and a stockbroker indicated that Naomi was identified with her phallic father. And yet, the paternal imago was not totally dominant or without conflict. Her inner world reflected the outer reality that a mother could hold her own against a powerful father. Though she valued masculine characteristics, she identified with her mother enough to get pregnant, and like her mother, she wanted to raise her baby herself. Her idea that she got pregnant and bought a house she hated to please her husband, reflected the fact that her masculine imago was so intrapsychically dominant that the self was compelled to take a submissive, "feminine" position to it. Her choice of her father's doctor and her "I don't know enough" attitude toward the doctor also illustrated this passive stance.

Though Naomi resisted her maternal identification, she also demonstrated a wish to regress to a symbiotic union with her mother. She often spoke about her desire to be close to her mother. She seemed to want to eat her mother up when she said, "I need to be close to my mother. I need her, but I feel so guilty about using her. She gave up her life for us." Her desire to "go right to my mother's house" and her "old room," but not to have her mother with her in the room indicated an impulse to return to the womb and be her mother's baby. But again, the maternal identification was not without conflict. Naomi devalued femininity. Dolls and toy kitchens were demeaning symbols of what it means to be female. Serving others and caretaking were perceived as contemptible.

In Naomi's inner world, the self seemed to take a subordinate position to both the maternal and paternal internalized objects. Despite her easy fertility, her feminism, and her wish to "put food on the table," Naomi could be quite passive. Her basic anxiety seemed to express itself when she worried that she was "going to get in there in labor and not be able to stand up for myself, and things will start happening to me." Caught in a triad where her mother "is a better mother than me" and her father could tell her how to run her life, Naomi was dominated by her internalized objects. Pregnancy and childbirth seemed to effect a positive change on that situation. She said toward the end of her pregnancy that she was "very self-involved." For the first time, she "just couldn't be bothered" with her father's political harangues. There were suggestions that the pregnancy provided her new insulation against the dominating paternal imago.

In the hospital, Naomi took an active stand in a setting that was inducing her to her old passivity. She refused to sign the consent form, refused to lie down, and later decided her next baby would be born with a midwife. She said, "I used to just passively accept all this stuff, but now I'm going to insist." After the baby was born, however, she complained that "I'm the one with the breasts." That complaint seemed to also contain a boast.

After birth, Naomi was able to identify with her mother in a much more conflict-free way. She said, "Now that I'm a mother, I don't have any role model but my mother. I can't use my father as a role model. Now I can identify with my mother. I used to see her as self-sacrificing. But now I know." Naomi was becoming aware that she and her mother were strong in a uniquely feminine way that enabled them to hold their own against the sexist masculine culture that attempted to denigrate and subjugate women.

How do we understand this positive change in Naomi? I suggest that several shifts in her psychic inner triangle occurred because of her pregnancy. The self became stronger in relation to parental introjects. The internalized father was no longer dominating the self and the internalized mother. Naomi was able to stop unconsciously competing with her father for power based on the masculine model. Her ability to give birth made her his equal in her unconscious, but on her own terms. She was also more in tune with the maternal introject, and this was due to a phenomenon that I saw over and over in my work with pregnant women. Childbirth seems to modify the nature of the "mother-in-me." A shift of identification occurs. The maternal representation moves from an identification with the passive, masochistic mother who is the heir of the Oedipal complex and returns to the relationship with the original phallic mother of the pre-Oedipal period. But additionally, the relationship with the maternal imago and self alters. The self gives up the submissive stance toward this phallic mother. No longer the baby to the engulfing mother, the woman incorporates the phallic mother within her own ego and experiences true identification with and individuation from the early maternal object. Thus, the original female problem of achieving autonomy while retaining female identification is resolved.

In many ways, Naomi's pregnancy helped her achieve the goal of being both her mother and her father. She did not become the mother who sacrificed her life. Using her more integrated identification with her father, she went back to work full-time. But she also embraced her femininity for the first time after "fighting it all my life." Childbirth helped Naomi get in touch with a uniquely female power and realize that "womanhood is a wonderful thing."

How does pregnancy achieve this new integration of the psychic triangle? An answer to this question lies in an examination of how Naomi experienced her pregnancy. She was full of fear and anxiety throughout most of it. She certainly equated pregnancy with death and danger. She talked about her condition in ways that we talk about death: "My whole life will be changing. There's nothing I can do about it. I just can't imagine how it will be. You can't know how something you've never experienced will be, and I guess that makes you nervous. It's so hard to imagine doing this, to think I'll be doing something I've never done before." I believe the unexplainable tears that are "not sadness" and that are experienced by so many women after birth are tears in response to the association of death and childbirth. We mourn the loss of infant/self, and we weep. Naomi, like many of the women I worked with who had babies, talked about "acceptance," and this is a word often associated with death, dying, and mourning. Childbirth is a triumph of life over death, and this enormous psychic feat empowers the ego to take charge of the internal triangle and integrate all its aspects into the personality in a constructive way.

Another explanation of this shift in the triangle can be gained by examining Naomi's vacillating cathexes of self and object representations in pregnancy. The early vomiting and the compulsive worry indicated aggression toward the pregnancy and the fetus. Naomi wanted to get rid of the intruder, smother it or poison it with Diet Coke. I believe the "something creepy" growing inside her was her own voracious wish to be totally dependent on her mother, to eat her up. Early in pregnancy, the fetus was the primitive self, threatening Naomi's life with the old fear of engulfing symbiosis. The sonogram made the baby seem "real" to Naomi. When she could perceive him as an object separate from herself, she resolved herself to the pregnancy. She liked to feel her son move and realize he was a real baby. Though it took her a while to "feel like a mother" and "realize he really came from me," Naomi was finally able to experience her female power. She said, "I don't feel like this powerful creator," but there were many indications that on some level, she did. She said, "To think my mother once held me like I hold him. That I was once that little. It touches something very deep." We see in the case of Naomi, a progression from the identification of the fetus with the helpless pre-Oedipal self, to the experience of the fetus as an object which enables the woman to identify with her own phallic mother, thereby triumphing over the powerless self-representation and achieving true individuation from the internalized maternal object.

References

Benjamin, J. (1988). *The Bonds of Love: Psychoanalysis, Feminism, and the Problem of Domination.* New York: Pantheon Books.

Bibring, G.L., Dwyer, T.F., Huntington, D.S., Valenstein, A.F. (1961). "A Study of Psychological Processes in Pregnancy and of the Earliest Mother–Child Relationship." *Psychoanalytic Study of the Child*, 16, 9–24.

Chodorow, N. (1978). *The Reproduction of Mothering: Psychoanalysis and the Sociology of Gender.* Berkeley: University of California Press.

Crowell, M. (1981). "A Response to Feminist Critics of Psychoanalysis." *Modern Psychoanalysis*, 6, 221–235.

Davis, E. (1985). *The Role of Aggression in the Psychobiology of Pregnancy and Infertility.* Cincinnati: Union Institute P.D.E.

de Beauvoir, S. (1952). *The Second Sex.* New York: Alfred A. Knopf.

Deutsch, H. (1945). *The Psychology of Women.* Vols. I and II. New York: Grune and Stratton.

Freud, S. (1931). "Female Sexuality." *Standard edition*, Volume 21. London: Hogarth Press, 225–243.

Freud, S. (1932). "New Introductory Lectures on Psychoanalysis: Femininity." *Standard Edition*, Volume 22. Volume, 22 Volume 22. London: Hogarth Press, 112–135.

Homey, K. (1967). *Feminine Psychology.* New York: W. W. Norton.

Langer, M. (1992). *Motherhood and Sexuality.* New York: The Guilford Press.

Loewald, H. (1962)."Internalization, separation, mourning, and the super ego." *Psychoanalytic Quarterly*, 31, 483–504.

Mitchell, J. (1974). *Psychoanalysis and Feminism: Freud, Reich, Laing, and Women.* New York: Vintage Books.

Piontelli, A. (1992). *From Fetus to Child: An Observational and Psychoanalytic Study.* London: Tavistock Publications/Routledge.

Rabuzzi, K.A. (1994). *Mother with Child: Transformations through Childbirth.* Bloomington: Indiana University Press.

Rich, A. (1976). *Of Woman Born: Motherhood as Experience and Institution.* New York: W.W. Norton.

Spotnitz, H., and Freeman, L. (1969). *How to be Happy though Pregnant.* New York: Berkley Publishing Corporation.

Chapter 2

The oppression of childbirth

Childbirth is women's talisman, manifest and indisputable evidence of the power and authority of "the second sex" (de Beauvoir, 1952). Female power, the ability to create new life, is the earliest and most profound source of power, and we all, men and women, fear it. The awesome, terrifying fecundity of women stands as a constant reminder that life and death are inextricably linked, and that both are ultimately out of our control. A birthing woman, both goddess and animal, inspires envy and fear, and on her body the entire history of patriarchal culture has been built.

Western culture is a masculine creation, both a response to and a recompense for the bodily supremacy of women. All the great institutions of patriarchy have been constructed to deny the primitive power of the female. Religion invented the concept of childbirth as God's punishment on women, disavowing the erotic, life-affirming aspect of birth and replacing it with the concept of childbirth as pain and suffering. Marriage and the family, patriarchy's most basic and effective institutions for the control of women, having successfully passed themselves off as nature (Millet, 1970), have asserted that the products of a woman's body belong to men and not women, and that those products can be judged legitimate or illegitimate in terms of their sanction by men. Technology, patriarchy's tool and favorite magic trick, has struggled to negate the simple truth that females, not males, grow new human beings; it can be argued that the whole history of obstetrics is an unconscious attempt to steal childbirth from the female sex. Education, industry, government, the arts, and all the other great cultural institutions which sublimate the feminine creative-generative impulse and which define man in his transcendence have been denied to women for most of recorded history out of deep unconscious envy of her reproductive power.

Psychoanalysis and radical feminist theory, philosophies which seem to be totally opposed, have ironically dealt with the frightening power of childbirth in the same way: they have devalued the experience. Psychoanalytic theory has, by and large, described women as a "series of lacks" (Chasseguet-Smirgel, 1970), and the feminine wish for a child as a displaced longing for a penis (Freud, 1924). Feminism presents childbirth as "that painful burden," (de

Beauvoir, 1952) an enslavement to the reproductive demands of the species which bears ultimate responsibility for the oppression of women by men. Childbirth is indeed responsible for all the patriarchal devices that relegate women to the role of the Other, but not because it is a burden, but because it is the supreme achievement of life and inspires primal envy and aggression in men which has historically been expressed in the cultural oppression of women.

Childbirth has traditionally been studied in a techno-rational way as a mechanical process which can be regulated and improved through the use of abstract science. There is no question that this is an important perspective from which to study the experience in our quest to make birth safe and comfortable. But birth, like death, is also a spiritual event. The emotional and psychological aspects of the experience profoundly effect its outcome and the lives of the people involved. Theory building based on science and abstract logic is a crucial area of study, but if we limit our thinking about childbirth to this essentially male way of perceiving the world, we masculinize the most feminine of activities and deny the deep psychological and spiritual complexity of the event. Perhaps because in our animal unconscious, we all know the power of reproduction dwarfs all other human endeavors, childbirth has virtually been ignored as a topic of psychological study. It is remarkable that in the hundred years since Freud began developing the body of theory which would come to be psychoanalysis, years that saw the concurrent development of a meaningful feminist theory, so little has been written by psychoanalysts or feminists about one of the most significant events of the female life cycle.

The history of culture's impact on childbirth is not only the honorable search for safety and health which organized medicine has sincerely tried to advocate and would like women to believe. A close investigation of childbirth practices in the last 250 years of cultural development reveals a rather sordid picture of submission and domination between women and their physicians not unlike the universal relationship between men and women painted by radical feminists. In the name of scientific objectivity, well-meaning doctors, historically male, have intruded upon the birth experience with tools and techniques, the vast majority of which have done more harm than good. Every meaningful advance in obstetrical procedure made since the invention of the first obstetrical tool, the forceps, has been made in response to the iatrogenic effects of the interventions of doctors in labor and delivery. It would be easy to explain the intricate dance between women and doctors in the childbirth experience as just one more instance of male aggression and female vulnerability, but the explanation would totally ignore women's role in their own submission. Psychoanalysis, particularly the recent work of feminist psychoanalyst Jessica Benjamin, has given us tools to look more deeply and meaningfully at why the culture of childbirth has evolved as it has.

Culture has always responded to the existential anxiety that birth engenders by producing the "expert." Whether that expert was priest or physician depended historically on the vicissitudes and alternating dominance of religion and science, but for most of recorded history all expertise has been in the hands of men. In the ancient world, learned men like Hippocrates and Soranus studied childbirth and organized a rudimentary science. The dawn of Christianity put an end to these scientific attempts and replaced them with the concept of childbirth as punishment for female original sin, the "curse of Eve." Any attempt to relieve a woman's suffering or even prevent her death in childbirth was considered heresy, an interference with the will of God. The intervention of a man of God, a priest, was required for purification and absolution of both mother and infant in Renaissance Europe. Early midwives, folk healers with knowledge of herbal remedies, were burned at the stake as witches because they attempted to challenge God's decree that women must suffer (Arms, 1986).

A physician named Peter Chamberlen invented the forceps in the early seventeenth century, revolutionizing childbirth practices, both physiologically and sociologically, and setting the stage for the slow but relentless masculinization of childbirth. The forceps, a set of two enlarged spoons cupped around the baby's head, could, for the first time, free an impacted fetus from the birth canal without killing it. Chamberlen kept the forceps a family secret for many years, operating the device under drapes. Forceps were perceived as almost magical, and armed with his wondrous "tool" a male midwife could, for the first time, penetrate the sanctity of the childbirth scene. After 1750, male physicians gained prominence in the courts of Europe and began to attend laboring aristocrats. In the French court, Louis XIV replaced the traditional birthing stool with a flat, horizontal table, arranging birth for the first time for the convenience of the physician rather than the mother (Arms, 1986). From this historic moment on, most women would give birth in the position usually assumed during heterosexual intercourse with a man's hand or "tool" in their vagina.

This conversion of labor into a symbolic act of sexual intercourse has historically been attributed to the allure of a new medical technology which could offer the safe birth of a living infant, and the forceps did indeed save lives, though they could and can cause more damage than they prevent. But if we look at the history of childbirth practices from a psychoanalytic perspective, deeper and more primitive reasons for the masculinization of childbirth emerge. Transforming birth into a symbolic coitus has unconscious psychological advantages for both sexes. Helene Deutsch (1945) discussed the unconscious bridge between childbirth and sexual intercourse. For both sexes, coitus unconsciously recreates union with the mother, a return to the womb, and this regression has advantages for both men and women in the childbirth experience. In symbolically engaging in sexual intercourse with his laboring patient, the male doctor assures himself that he is one with the source of all life, that indeed he is dominating it and controlling it. For woman, in the presence of the fear of death which childbirth represents, the symbolic coitus represented by her supine position and penetration by the man gives her the illusion that she is one with her mother, the original all-powerful protector.

The masculinization of childbirth came later to the United States than it did to Europe. The American way of birth was originally female-centered. Despite a Puritanical culture that told colonial women that the pain and suffering of labor or the birth of a defective child were evidence of God's contempt for the female sex, birth itself was a social affair, overseen but not controlled by the local female midwife. Female friends and relatives were invited to the home of a prospective mother to attend birth as experts, with expertise defined as having personal experience in giving birth. Colonial women moved about and labored in a variety of positions, and decisions were made in consultation. Birth was a joyous event, and there are few reports of women and babies dying as a result of this "social childbirth."

The idea of birth as an intolerable ordeal is a relatively recent one historically, a product of the Industrial Revolution and Victorian culture (Wertz and Wertz, 1989). The nineteenth century saw the rise of the medical profession, and a new childbirth expert, the obstetrician, almost obliterated the traditional female midwife of the colonial period in the United States. A change in women's attitudes toward birth went hand and hand with this revolution in maternity care: the hearty woman of colonial times was replaced by the limp and poetic Victorian invalid. Nineteenth-century medical propaganda designed to promote the new profession argued that women are fragile prisoners of a complex sexuality and must be "delivered" by male doctors from the ordeal of childbirth (Barker-Benfield, 1977). Women, whose historical areas of authority were quickly being replaced by the market and the factory of the Industrial Revolution, seemed to cooperate with this idea (Ehrenreich and English, 1979). Tied to a hearth and home which were no longer environments of meaningful, dignified, and necessary work, women embraced the idea of the erotic invalid as the best role open to them. Victorian standards of beauty in women leaned more toward romantic and perpetual fragility than vigorous health. It was almost considered ill-bred, particularly among upper class women, to be robust. These elegant invalids had relationships with their physicians which resembled nothing so much as illicit love affairs. Lying in darkened rooms, suffering from "nervous exhaustion," they waited in bed for the daily visits of their lover-doctors to examine their blighted female parts. Victorian culture demanded a nervous delicacy in well-bred women which gave rise to the notion that not only childbirth, but also sexual intercourse were painful but necessary wifely duties (Wertz and Wertz, 1989). By the end of the nineteenth century, Sigmund Freud equated hysteria and masochism with the "feminine" woman. For this delicate creature, pain had become pleasure.

In this cultural atmosphere of weak woman and physician savior, the idea of childbirth as too much to bear was born. The quasi-sexual attention women received from their husbands and doctors if they suffered and were in pain certainly fueled the search for drugs that would render childbirth an experience totally devoid of feeling. Providing pain relief during labor and delivery was probably one of the greatest contributions nineteenth-century obstetrics made to birthing women – but it was also its most powerful vehicle of control. Chloroform, introduced by James Young Simpson of Edinburgh and used in childbirth by Queen Victoria in 1853, was relatively easily administered at home; but the development of scopolamine or "twilight sleep" in the early twentieth century required elaborate facilities and careful supervision, and could only be accomplished in the hospital. Once a woman was under the influence of scopolamine, she had to be put into a specially designed crib bed which protected her from the violent thrashings that the drug induced. Since scopolamine was a dangerous drug, doctors insisted that all decisions about it be made by the physician, not the laboring woman. Though scopolamine quickly fell into disrepute after it caused the death of a feminist who had been its staunchest advocate, "twilight sleep" changed the cultural definition of childbirth from a natural, domestic event under the control of women to a dangerous illness which could only be managed in the hospital by medical professionals (Leavitt, 1986).

Pain relief, the issue that early twentieth-century feminists saw as liberation from the oppression of being female, ironically provided the impetus to move childbirth from the home, where the woman and her family were in control, to the hospital, where the physician and his increasingly complex tools possessed all authority. By the 1920s, the medicalization of childbirth was complete, with the overwhelming majority of women delivering in hospitals virtually unconscious. Dr Joseph DeLee, a prominent obstetrician and director of the Chicago Maternity Center, which ironically had a sterling record of safety and satisfaction with its home birth service, asserted that birth is a "pathological process." Dr DeLee recommended reducing birth to predictable patterns by using forceps and episiotomy routinely and prophylactically in normal delivery.

Despite the fact that neither of these interventions was subjected to scientific research to prove their benefit, they both became standard obstetrical practice. The drugs needed to mask the pain of these procedures and the requirement that women labor flat on their backs, slowed the process of birth and spurred the development of labor inducing medication. These new drugs speeded things up but made labor so painful that soon more anesthesia was administered. This "cascade of intervention" became the rule rather than the exception after birth moved to the hospital. And because of that intervention, birth had indeed become an intolerable and interminable ordeal. Labor and delivery became by definition high-risk crises, and the technology required to respond to those crises made the delivery room as alienating and dehumanizing as a modern intensive care unit. The spiritual, the emotional, and the intuitive, in short, everything feminine about birth, had been obliterated with the pain (Wertz and Wertz, 1989).

As medical research revealed the dangers of obstetrical drugs in the 1940s, a new movement towards natural childbirth emerged. It was led by British obstetrician Grantly Dick-Read, who delivered the babies of lower-class women in the 1920s and 1930s and believed that much of the pain of childbirth is connected to fear. Dick-Read first got this idea when a woman from a slum refused the chloroform that he offered her and gave birth without drugs. Later she said to him, "It didn't hurt. It wasn't supposed to, was it?" Dick-Read concluded that civilization and culture had brainwashed women into believing that childbirth is painful and dangerous. He wrote a book called *Childbirth Without Fear* which fostered the natural childbirth movement. In the book, the English doctor described childbirth as a spiritual event, a moment of woman's greatest triumph.

Later, childbirth activist Suzanne Arms went even farther than Dick-Read in questioning the whole idea of pain in childbirth. Pain is a symptom of disease and pathology, and Arms asserted that it is an inappropriate concept when applied to the discomfort caused by the hard work of the uterus during labor. Male obstetricians, who have never experienced birth, sell the idea of pain and treat their birthing patients as fragile, emotional creatures unable to endure the arduous ordeal of labor. An obstetrical nurse told Arms, "A doctor anesthetizes himself through anesthetizing a woman. He does it to avoid his own fears about pain." Like Dick-Read, Arms believed that most pain in childbirth is caused by fear, a fear induced by the stressful, alienating environment in hospitals and by the mindset sold by doctors that birth is dangerous and painful. This mindset is crucial for organized medicine to justify its place in the realm of normal birth. Arms accused doctors of paying lip service to the idea of natural childbirth, and then doing everything they could, through their dehumanizing stress and pain-inducing tactics, to ensure that women will "fail" (Arms, 1986).

Since the demise of scopolamine, obstetrical drugs have been improved and refined, but no relief from pain comes without a price: all anesthesia has negative effects on both mother and baby. The majority of births today include an epidural, a type of regional anesthesia injected into the lumbar region of a woman's back which holds the promise of allowing a laboring woman to be "awake and aware" during childbirth, while eliminating pain. Women today seem to equate pain-free childbirth with freedom from sexual oppression; modern obstetrical drugs have become a symbol of female liberation from the frumpy, bovine rigors of the child bed.

Epidurals are a vast improvement over earlier anesthesia, but the current rush to the hospital to mask the sensations of childbirth ignores some important evidence-based medical research. While skillfully administered epidurals can eliminate pain without reducing the urge or ability to push in the final stages of labor, epidurals often completely deaden all sensation, making pushing difficult and increasing the likelihood of forceps deliveries and C-sections. If an epidural is administered too soon, it can slow or stop labor, making the major abdominal surgery of C-section the only alternative. Indeed, spinal anesthesia is directly implicated in the dramatic increase in the C-section rate in the last 30 years. Epidurals are also associated with loss of consciousness, cardiac arrest, hypertension, headache, persistent backache, and numbness and weakness in the mother. In rare cases of an accidental lumbar puncture, lowering of the blood pressure and paralysis of the breathing muscles can occur. Dangers to the baby include oxygen deprivation, slowing of the heart rate, increase in the acidity of the blood, and loss of muscle tone, making it impossible to suck (Rooks, 1997).

Statistics about the dangers of obstetrical drugs are not the only evidence that a more natural childbirth might be better for mother and baby. There is also more and more evidence-based research that women who expect normal deliveries will have a safer and more satisfying experience in a free-standing birth center than in a hospital. A study of 15,000 birth center births, which appeared in the *New England Journal of Medicine*, revealed that birth centers are just as safe as hospitals for normal birth and safer if you factor in the very low C-section rate in birth centers. Women find the family-centered maternity care they receive in free-standing birth centers very satisfying, and their insurance companies like the cost savings, sometimes as much as 40 percent, that birth centers provide. A study of 12,000 women who used free-standing birth centers revealed that only 13 percent received any kind of sedative, tranquilizer, or anesthesia, and yet only 3 percent reported experiencing pain that was not adequately relieved. Nevertheless, when women are interviewed about why they consistently choose hospitals over birth centers, despite the research, one of the most common reasons cited is that birth centers don't offer epidurals (Rooks, 1997).

Most childbirth experts cite the dangers of obstetrical anesthesia when they encourage women to try natural childbirth, but this argument seems to fall on deaf ears. Certainly, epidurals have minor risks, but then so does natural childbirth – living is ultimately dangerous, and childbirth will always be a time of heightened danger, a confrontation with death. No relief from pain comes without a price. Most women who decide to take drugs trade pain for guilt, but even if they have to feel a little guilty or a little worried about the drugs, women don't want to be in *pain*, and that is that.

Does childbirth really "hurt?" The answer to that varies from individual to individual; what one woman considers painful, another might enjoy and even consider erotic. Birth narratives vary from reports of childbirth as the most painful experience life has to offer, to stories that describe pushing a baby into the world as a profoundly sexual pleasure, a transforming and spiritual moment in a woman's life. Even more important than individual differences in the perception of pain is the culture's collective agreement about how much childbirth hurts. Cultural norms define the appropriate stance toward and behavior in labor and delivery. In some cultures, women are expected to scream and shriek and suffer excruciating pain, in others, such behavior would be considered strange or even crazy.

Western culture, particularly American culture, insists that childbirth is almost unbearably painful. Literary heroines from Anna Karenina to Catherine in *A Farewell to Arms* and Melanie in *Gone with the Wind* have suffered and sometimes died bringing new life into the world. Modern culture expresses its attitude toward childbirth in hysterical, sweaty, excruciatingly painful but usually hilarious scenes in movies like *Look Who's Talking* and television situation comedies like *The Golden Girls*. Mothers who are otherwise loving and protective seem to be unable to resist regaling their daughters with lurid tales of the difficulties of getting children into the world, war stories from the trenches of the maternity ward.

But if birth is such torture, how do we explain reports from women such as this birth narrative cited in *Mother with Child* (1994, p. 101) by Kathryn Allen Rabuzzi?

> In the end, I had absolutely no pain, and I pushed very hard, and it was a very satisfying moment when I felt the baby moving through me. I did not even realize when the head had passed, but I think I shall remember all my life the sensations of sweetness and warmth which the baby's body gives as it comes out. The sensation lasts for only a second, but from that moment, I felt the child to be mine.

Or this:

> I felt myself expand infinitely outward. This did not exactly hurt; it was on "the other side" of pain, where *pain* is no longer an appropriate word. Possibly *ecstasy* will do. ... I was also "dying," "being born," giving birth ... [an] infinite outward and inward expansion.
>
> (1994, p. vii)

A patient of mine had this to say about her birth:

> After all the pain of labor, pushing felt fantastic. I've never felt so powerful, and yet it was as if I had nothing to do with it but get out of the way and let life renew itself. I could feel the baby being born. It was the most exhilarating moment I've ever known. The head was so big, and as it passed into the world, I let out a cry of joy and relief. Then I felt the limbs like slippery little fishes. It was the most erotic experience I've ever had.

Is this pain? Psychoanalysis has offered the idea that the feminine woman is masochistic, and for her, pain is pleasure. Can we explain the obvious pleasure these women felt by naming it masochism? Patriarchal culture would say this is so. It insists that birth is painful and dangerous, focusing on one aspect of labor while totally suppressing the magnitude of what is actually happening. But the reality of birth is very different. In one fleeting, irretrievable moment, a fully-formed new human being, which by its presence within the woman's body gives her the privilege of briefly defeating the existential loneliness that is the human condition, now enters the world through her genitals, the site of deepest physical pleasure. The vagina, though certainly challenged to the limits of its capacity, is doing what it was designed to do, and the sensuality of its fullness and the exhilaration of feeling the beloved infant being pushed into the world by her powerful, carnal, out-of-control body are profoundly satisfying. Analyst Georg Groddeck had a sense of this eroticism when he said, "The harrowing labor pains conceal quantities of pleasure that are denied to man" (Groddeck, 1976, p. 46). It is to console him for this painful denial that woman disavows what man cannot face: that in childbirth she doesn't need him. As she pushes her baby into the world, for one of the few times in her life, she is not a representative of "the second sex," the "Other." She is the completely alive, rapturously engrossed One, the source of life for another One with whom in this ephemeral moment she is merged in a struggle between life and death, poised on the boundary between the "me" and the "not-me." It is too much for both of them, man and woman, to bear. She must rename this "suffering" and allow him to "deliver" her.

The revealing statistics about the enormous number of modern women who choose drugs attests to the fact that today's woman, for all her so-called liberation, is just as afraid of her body as her nineteenth-century ancestors. Surely women have come a long way from the sexual hysteria of Victorian culture so aptly described by Isadora Duncan in *My Life* (1928, p. 61):

> crying out in pain, I was initiated into the act of love. I confess that my first impressions were a horrible fright and an atrocious pain, as if someone had torn out several of my teeth at once; but a great pity for what he seemed to be suffering prevented me from running away from what was at first sheer mutilation and torture.

Women at the dawn of the twenty-first century laugh at the idea of sex as a painful duty, but Duncan's description of the horrors of sexual intercourse could be used today to express most women's expectations about labor and delivery. Childbirth is the last frontier of female physical oppression, so polluted by the fear of pain that it is almost universally perceived as something to be dreaded rather than as the euphoric, erotic expression of raw female power that it can and should be.

Birth is the culmination of a complex and uniquely feminine sexual process begun with the intake and retention at the moment new life is conceived and terminated with the orgasmic giving and expelling of delivery. The passive yielding of sexual intercourse and the active mastering of childbirth are a continuity which are one of the deepest pleasures of female physical life. Yet most modern women are totally unaware of the intense sexuality of birth. Pain-killing drugs and highly technological hospital procedures are so effective at masking the erotic aspects of childbirth that birth's sexual nature has been virtually obliterated

In the techno-rational world of organized medicine, women don't give birth; they are the vessel from which the obstetrician and his tools bring the baby into the world. Indeed, it is the idea of pain and suffering itself that allows the reconstruction of childbirth as a scene where women are passive, and men are in control. If birth isn't pathological, if women aren't *suffering*, then technology and medicine, which are essentially masculine, become superfluous at the childbirth scene. I believe that this fact is ultimately the reason why American culture has painted birth as too much for women to bear. Childbirth as painful creates a pathway through which man can intervene in female creativity and claim it as his own, reinforcing the idea of man as active doer and woman as submissive object.

But if the masculinization and medicalization of childbirth have, on an unconscious level, been an attempt by men to dominate and control the very source of life, why have women cooperated in this patriarchal theft of their power? The reasons are complex. Historically, women have had good reasons to fear childbirth. Until recently, mutilation and death were not uncommon in labor and delivery, and we do have organized medicine and technology to thank for some of the real gains that have been made in childbirth safety. Indeed, it can be argued that since the discovery of antibiotics and the advent of AIDS, labor and delivery are safer than sexual intercourse. Yet despite the advances against the dangers of childbirth, there is no such thing as "risk-free" birth. Even in hospitals with the most up-to-date technology, bringing new life into the world can kill you, and that thought is scary. We all, men and women, fear the intense confrontation with carnality and mortality which childbirth represents. In the presence of this fear of death, it is understandably human to want to be "delivered" by an all-powerful protector. The masculine enterprise of obstetrical technology provides for all of us, male and female, the illusion of complete safety and control. Medicine has promised women salvation in the form of the "physician-savior," and women have sacrificed their own power to gain access to the fantasy of that omnipotent guardian. Through relinquishing control of the most creative moment of her life, a moment which more than any other represents the triumph of life over death, a birthing woman sacrifices her own profound power in order to create the physician's dominance and control in which she can then take refuge. She can remain childish and passive, exempt from the exertion and risk of being fully alive, while deluding herself with the idea that technology can guarantee that she will be saved from death.

Childbirth technology has always attempted to protect women from the pain and danger of labor, but it becomes cancerous when the compulsion with total control over the childbirth experience results in the worship of what is orderly, predictable, and controllable at the expense of what is alive. It is a denial of our vulnerability and mortality which ironically keeps women from living and feeling their innate carnal ability to triumph over death by creating life. Women offer themselves up as targets of often malignant technology because they can vicariously share with the physician the satisfaction of the illusion of being in control of the essentially and profoundly uncontrollable. Identification with the powerful authority of organized medicine allows women, through that identification, to take this power into themselves.

Margaret Mead addressed the unconscious collusion that goes on between men and women around the childbirth experience. Mead believed that woman consents to relinquish all cultural authority to man because his self-respect requires it to counterbalance her more impressive contribution as child bearer to the species' physical continuity. She also made the point that the male imagination about childbirth, undisciplined and unformed by immediate bodily clues or experience, has probably contributed disproportionately to our cultural belief that childbirth is torture (Mead, 1949). This is no doubt true, but our cultural acceptance of the idea of birth as unbearable has more insidious roots than the male imagination running amok. The unconscious envy and misogyny that men harbor against women for their reproductive power is so much a part of patriarchal culture that women internalize this masculine attitude and then use these feelings to go along with and even derive pleasure from their own domination. Tainted with this induced need for self-punishment and the very real terror of risking death, women take the vast range of sensations of labor and reduce them to "pain." They allow and even welcome the drugs that exclude them from the mystery and wonder of what is happening to them.

The problem with this unconscious collusion between men and women to deny the existential risk involved in childbirth is that when women dodge the challenges of freedom, they also sacrifice the euphoric physical and psychic transformation that a good birth experience represents. In removing all pain, indeed all sensation, from labor and delivery, birthing women obliterate one of the most profound experiences that life has to offer, an experience which can empower a woman in a uniquely feminine way.

When woman and physician collude to eliminate sensation from the ecstatic pleasure–pain experience of childbirth, they perpetuate the idea, so beloved by modern culture, that all feeling is dangerous and suspect, that intense feeling is too much for human beings to tolerate and must be muted with drugs, alcohol, and the diversion of the simulated stimulation of movies and television. They perpetuate the idea that we are not strong enough to face our existential vulnerability and must deny it by deadening and controlling our experience. But there is a price to be paid for this denial. When we eliminate the pain of childbirth, we also mask a euphoric, erotic, and empowering moment. A woman pushing her infant into the world without the death of drugs is at once deeply embedded in her flesh and transcending it in the ultimate act of creation. Integrating sensuality with mastery, she is intelligently and imaginatively enterprising and riding fully alive on a continuity of life that flowed long, long before she was born and that will continue long, long after she is dead.

This powerful, fleeting moment provides a path for a woman out of the submissive role which patriarchal culture would too often have her play. The carnal strength, the glimpse of immortality that a good childbirth experience provides for a woman gives her an authority which is unique and which no one can take away from her. In facing her extreme vulnerability, fear, discomfort, and existential loneliness in labor and delivery and conquering them to create a new human being, she learns a lesson that she can then teach the world in any arena that she chooses to enter; and that is the lesson that allows us to face the sad fact that we are not omnipotent, that most of the truly important features of existence are out of our control, and still experience the autonomous, honest pleasure of creating, of making dramatic things happen. Once a woman experiences her own strength and power, she will have a different attitude for the rest of her life about difficult situations and intimidating authority figures. Triumphing over the fear of birth gives her authority over all her fears. She becomes empowered in a uniquely feminine way.

Surely everyone could agree that childbirth is difficult, strenuous work, but then so is running a marathon, and no one is suggesting to women that the sensations of running 26 miles should be masked with drugs. To eliminate the pain would be to eliminate the glory of the experience, the whole point of which is to transcend and triumph over the daunting physical challenge. But women are so tainted with the patriarchal idea of birth as torture that they think of it in terms of pain, not challenge. Labor and delivery are perceived as malignant, polluted, and torturous. Rarely are they viewed by women as an opportunity to know and come to terms with our own complicated, pain-enduring, multi-pleasured female physicality, and to convert that physicality into both knowledge and power.

Birth is not an illness or an operation. It is a turning point for women of extraordinary physical and psychic significance, an opportunity to experience a deeply spiritual transition unlike any other moment life has to offer. I have written elsewhere of childbirth as a developmental milestone in a woman's life as psychically significant as the pre-Oedipal period, the Oedipus complex, and adolescence. Childbirth is a confrontation with and a triumph over primitive fears. It provides an opportunity to be in control of the experience of projecting the inner world to the outer world. This projection is a physical and psychological feat of astounding significance, and it means that women come out of childbirth with new psychic constructs, new relationships to their own introjects (Holmes, 2000).

Women are being oppressed in the most insidious way when childbirth becomes what one obstetrician called "birth to *The Price is Right*," (personal conversation, 1989) referring to the hospital wards where rows of laboring women, dead from the waist down, watch television while their babies are being born. These women are losing something they can never have back: the experience of feeling their bodies accomplish the creative, sexual, mysterious event which is the highlight of feminine life.

I am not suggesting that women should turn their backs on some of obstetrical technology's real gains. Of course, we should do all we can to ensure that childbirth will be safe, and certainly there are high-risk women who will require medical intervention and anesthesia during childbirth. Overwhelming pain during labor is inhumane, and it is the responsibility of anyone who provides care to birthing women to attend to their pain. But do we need to routinely offer women the riskiest method of pain relief before we try less dangerous methods, and to do so without informing them of the negative side effects of such methods?

Research now exists which shows that alternate forms of pain relief such as those offered by nurse-midwives are highly effective in reducing or eliminating the discomfort of labor. First, it is important to avoid painful technological intervention, such as IV, internal fetal monitoring, forceps, and episiotomy unless it is absolutely necessary. Moving around and changing positions during labor, applications of heat and cold, hydrotherapy, massage and other touch therapies, and breathing and relaxation techniques can all be helpful. Women are better equipped to deal with pain during labor if they are educated about pain before they give birth. Every pregnant woman should be interviewed about her expectations and fears about pain and her desire for specific methods of pain control. Women who are likely to require narcotics or an epidural belong in a hospital for birth, but that decision should be made only after a woman has been informed about the dangers of these interventions, and indeed the dangers of hospital birth, and also about the availability of alternate methods. Above all, women need to have continuous, focused support during labor and delivery. I am not talking about the idle chit-chat of nurses changing IV bottles or watching a fetal monitor, nor of the nervous and insincere reassurance of a frightened and woefully unprepared husband. Focused support is best given by an experienced caregiver and involves constant physical touch, maintaining eye contact during painful contractions, talking through everything that is happening, and advocacy for a woman's plans. Research studies have shown over and over again that women who receive this continuous support during labor need less anesthesia and are less likely to later describe their births as painful, exhausting, or terrifying (Rooks, 1997).

The modern American stance toward childbirth is a largely unexplored stronghold of misogyny. Pregnancy, probably more than any other milestone of female development, provides a symbol of power which corresponds to the power of the penis, the masculine phallic energy so beloved by American culture. The swelling, protruding belly of pregnancy speaks to the primitive unconscious with the primal power that the phallus has for both sexes in early childhood. Perhaps it is because pregnancy has this primitive power that it has been reframed as a painful burden by patriarchy and that the experience of childbirth has been virtually obliterated by technology. The liberation of labor and delivery from the abuses of the medical model is an appropriate place for feminism to set its next battle. The frontier for that battle will be within the minds of women, because it is female consciousness, hopelessly muddied by masculinized concepts about birth, which must be altered if we are ever to free pregnancy and childbirth from the sexist paradigms which corrupt them.

References

Arms, S. (1986). *Immaculate Deception: A Look at Women and Childbirth in America*. New York: Bantam Books.

Barker-Benfield, G.J. (1977). *The Horrors of the Half-known Life: Male Attitudes toward Women and Sexuality in Nineteenth Century America*. New York: Harper Row.

Chasseguet-Smirgel, J. (1970). *Female sexuality: New Psychoanalytic Views*. London: Karnac Books.

de Beauvoir, S. (1952). *The Second Sex*. New York: Alfred A. Knopf.

Deutsch, H. (1944, 1945). *The Psychology of Women, Volumes I and II*. New York: Grune and Stratton.

Duncan, I. (1928). *My Life*. New York: Boni and Liveright.

Ehrenreich, B., and English, D. (1979). *For Her Own Good: 150 Years of the Experts' Advice to Women*. New York: Anchor Books.

Freud, S. (1924)."The Dissolution of the Oedipus Complex." *Standard Edition*, Volume 21. London: Hogarth Press, 1931.

Groddeck, G. (1976). *The Book of the It*. New York: International Universities Press, Inc.

Holmes, L. (2000)."The Object Within: Childbirth as a Developmental Milestone." *Modern Psychoanalysis*, 25, 1.

Leavitt, J.W. (1986). *Brought to Bed: Childbearing in America, 1750–1950*. New York: Oxford University Press.

Mead, M. (1949). *Male and Female*. New York: HarperCollins.

Millet, K. (1970). *Sexual Politics*. New York: Doubleday and Company.

Rabuzzi, K.A. (1994). *Mother with Child: Transformations Through Childbirth*. Bloomington: Indiana University Press.

Rooks, J.P. (1997). *Midwifery and Childbirth in America*. Philadelphia: Temple University Press.

Wertz, R.W. and Wertz, D.C. (1989). *Lying-in: A History of Childbirth in America*. New Haven: Yale University Press.

Chapter 3

The internal triangle
New theories of female development

It is ironic that despite the fact that the majority of human beings involved in psychoanalysis today, both analysts and patients, are women, many aspects of feminine psychosexual development remain what Freud described as a "dark continent." The history of psychoanalytic theory has been dominated by a tendency to see human development as male development, with women viewed as "a catalogue of lacks" (Benjamin, 1988, p. 94). In the last 25 years, feminist psychoanalysts have attempted to address the integrity rather than the "difference" of female maturation and development, but many attempts at new theories have a basis more in sociology, anthropology, and politics than psychoanalysis. Much of the new literature borrows heavily from the school of object relations theory in addressing the feminine need for "connection" and the importance of issues of boundaries and merging for women. But almost 100 years after the creation of psychoanalysis, a coherent theory of female development based on the cornerstones of the unconscious and drive theory has yet to be formulated.

Early theories of female development

Freud (1932) was a male genius, and psychoanalysis has traditionally been a phallocentric theory. Freud himself acknowledged that his theories of femininity were "incomplete and fragmentary" (p. 135). Freud never answered his question to Marie Bonaparte, "What do women want?" (Gay, 1988, p. 501) to his own satisfaction, but the body of work he did leave on femininity provides a starting point for a discussion of the psychology of women.

Freud (1905) asserted that an important sexual theory of children is that there is only one genital: male. The penis and clitoris can be seen, while the ovaries and womb cannot, and small children react to this fact by assuming that the boy's penis is "bigger and better" than the girl's clitoris, and that she therefore functions as a "little man" (Freud, 1933, p. 118). At about the age of four, the boy realizes that girls are missing a penis, and at about the same time, the girl realizes she is missing one too.

This painful discovery that boys have something where she has "nothing" initiates the girl's Oedipal conflict. She develops penis envy and hates her formerly beloved mother for the fact of their mutual castration, and so she turns to her father with the incestuous wish that he give her a child. Freud (1924) saw this wish for a child as a displaced longing for a penis.

Because a girl's castration has already occurred and can no longer be feared, girls don't experience the dramatic destruction of the Oedipus complex typical of boys. This, according to Freud, has several consequences. One is that the Oedipus conflict in girls disappears or becomes repressed much more slowly, and in fact may persist throughout a woman's life. Another consequence is the relative weakness of the superego in women. Freud attributed a larger amount of narcissism to women, asserting that they need to be loved far more than they need to love.

In "Female Sexuality," Freud (1931) discussed the importance of the pre-Oedipal period for girls. The female reaches the Oedipus complex only after a long and intense attachment to her mother. Both boys and girls develop hatred for the pre-Oedipal mother for many reasons, but boys can displace their hatred onto their fathers as rival; girls are necessarily more ambivalent. When a girl turns away from her mother in favor of the father, there is a marked reduction of active sexual impulses in favor of passive ones. Freud equated activity with masculinity and passivity with femininity. But he went on to say that every individual is a mixture of masculine and feminine characteristics, and that often much activity is required to achieve passive aims. The suppression of women's aggression, which is prescribed for them constitutionally and imposed on them socially, favors the development of masochism, and therefore Freud (1932) saw masochism as truly feminine.

Helene Deutsch (1944; 1945) wrote about a "feminine core," the foundation of the feminine personality, which is characterized by three essential traits: narcissism, passivity, and masochism.

Female passivity, according to Deutsch, is activity turned inward. Girls, like boys, have active aggressive and sexual impulses, but because the clitoris is unable to gratify these impulses as effectively as the penis, the little girl inhibits her aggressive activity and turns toward a passive receptive style of functioning more suited to the vagina.

Like passivity, masochism is the outcome of a mechanism of instinctual reversal that turns energies directed toward the outer world inward. Passive drives of the ego are connected in both boys and girls to the mother, while activity and reality are centered on the figure of the father. But the father is more supportive of his son's drive toward activity and aggression than his daughter's, and so the girl encounters an inhibition of her ego development imposed by the outside world. The girl gives up her aggression and is offered a bribe for her sacrifice, the love and tenderness of the father. The renounced aggressive impulses are turned round to passivity, and they endow the passive state of being loved with a masochistic character. Feminine masochism, unlike moral masochism, which is characterized by guilt and self-punishment, is based upon the active impulse of a healthy ego to adjust to reality.

Narcissism serves as a counterweight to masochism in the feminine woman and guards the ego from a passive-masochistic decline. Healthy narcissism, the libido's taking of the ego for its object, protects the female personality from the dangers of the sometimes masochistic sexual goals of her reproductive functioning. The distribution of forces between the narcissistic ego and feminine masochism allows a sublimation of sexuality into eroticism that is uniquely feminine. The interplay of passivity, masochism, and narcissism is responsible for many positive feminine attributes: the enormous capacity for identification with objects, the rich inner life of fantasy and imagination, the ability to sacrifice self for a higher goal, and the tendency toward intuition (Deutsch, 1944).

Ernest Jones, Karen Horney, and Marie Bonaparte were other early theorists who devoted large parts of their careers to the study of female psychology. Bonaparte (1951), like Freud and Deutsch, was a drive theorist and believed that women are constitutionally and biologically bisexual. For Bonaparte, the central problem in feminine development was the masculinity complex. She saw the clitoris as an unsatisfactory little penis and insisted that women have less aggression and less libido than men.

Jones (1927; 1935) and Horney (1967) disagreed with Freud about several important aspects of female functioning. Jones asserted that femininity is innate, and that the masculinity little girls demonstrate is defensive. The vagina that Freud had asserted was "undiscovered" in childhood, Jones saw as "denied." Rather than emphasizing penis envy, he felt girls have an interest from a very early age in the inside rather than the outside of their bodies. Jones also differed with Freud in his views about the clitoris. He saw the clitoris as part of the female organ, not as a deficient substitute for the penis. He maintained that the wish for a child is not a displacement of the wish for a penis, but a true feminine wish.

Horney (1967), who agreed with most of Jones' ideas, was a great advocate of the influence of culture and society on feminine development. According to Horney, penis envy, the masculinity complex, and female masochism are not rooted in the anatomical-physiological-psychic characteristics of females but must be considered in the context of social organizations which oppress women. She argued that genital differences had been emphasized in analytic theory, while the great biological differences, namely the different parts played by men and women in the functions of reproduction, had been totally overlooked. Though Horney (1967, p. 42) agreed that penis envy is "an inevitable phenomenon in the life of female children," she asserted that women have in motherhood an indisputable and by no means negligible physiological superiority. Because girls have no external sex organ and don't come into their true sexual powers until adulthood, they are literally "in the dark" about their later superiority (Horney, 1967, p. 66).

The work of Jones, Horney, and Bonaparte left us with more questions than answers about several controversies in the theory of feminine development. The debates about whether femininity is innate or acquired, whether penis envy is anatomically or culturally grounded, whether the vagina is undiscovered or denied in early childhood, and whether men have inherently stronger drives than women are still raging. If we accept the most basic tenets of psychoanalysis, the first question seems to be the easiest on which to take a position. Freud rested his entire body of work on the concept that human beings are not born, they are made. The most fundamental idea of psychoanalysis is that it takes enormous effort to become logical, ethical, and civilized. Though most of us achieve an unstable victory over the primitive unconscious, it is with us all our lives. Acknowledging that the journey from animal to human being is a struggle, demands that we concede that femininity is no more innate than rationality or morality. Psychoanalysis insists that they must be explained to be understood.

Horney's cultural perspective on penis envy cannot be totally discounted, though it is perhaps fair to say that in any study of human development, drives are primary and precede culture. Ego is formed when sexual and aggressive instincts confront reality and adapt themselves to it, and sexist culture is certainly real. The passivity, masochism, and narcissism that Deutsch described can be seen as adaptations that female human beings have to make to live as women in the world. But there is an inherent danger in Horney's emphasis on culture to explain femininity. If sexist culture is given full responsibility for the difficulties of becoming female, it is easy to overlook the role that the primary thinking of the unconscious plays in making sexism seem like "second nature." Women's universal subordination can only be understood by an exploration of the early interplay of libido and aggression in very young girls which sets up a situation in which subordination is the best solution to a uniquely feminine problem. Passivity and masochism are sexual and aggressive instincts, originally directed at the outer world, turned inward; and this seems to be a classic example of a drive meeting the reality principle. In this case it is not only the demand of society that little girls be "feminine," but on an intrapsychic level, it is the demand that drives, originally directed toward objects, be turned back onto the self and internalized objects. Like the aggression and activity that are masculine drive derivatives, passivity and masochism are only "bad" if they function purely in the service of the death instinct unmitigated by Eros, the life instinct.

The question of awareness of the vagina is closely related to whether femininity is acquired or innate. Certainly, if girls are born feminine, then it is likely that consciousness of the vagina is there from the beginning. Clinically, this is a question which is almost impossible to answer with any certainty. Both boys and girls experience the pleasure of the fullness of a passive organ (the sphincter) in the anal period. Bonaparte (1951) contended that girls passively cathect the cloaca (the vagina and anus coenesthetically combined), and that this cathexis becomes the prototype for later vaginal functioning. Freud's idea that the erotogenicity of the clitoris is replaced by the vagina has been disputed by modern theorists. Women never relinquish the clitoris as an erotogenic zone; the vagina is an addition to their sexual pleasure, not a replacement, and this anatomical complexity reflects the psychic intricacy of women.

Just as difficult to prove is the idea that drives are stronger in men than in women. Given the immense diversity of human beings and a world that includes plenty of aggressive women and passive men, it is hard to accept Bonaparte's theory as inevitable. What is clearer is that the culture Horney felt was so important, as well as the modifications of the sexual and aggressive instincts in female development, dictate that male human beings have more permission to be aggressive and active, while women are expected to be loving and passive. This means that the vicissitudes of the drives are more complex in women than men, and they must erect more defenses against them. As Deutsch and Freud reminded us, it takes a tremendous amount of psychic activity to become passive in a way acceptable to both ego and id.

Gregory Zilboorg felt that the "woman envy on the part of man ... is psychogenetically older and therefore more fundamental than penis envy" (cited in Horney, 1967, p. 21). Given the developmental sequence which Horney herself confirms with her statement about little girls being in the dark about their sexual powers until the vagina and womb are discovered, this at first seems unlikely. The superiority of the phallus is a phenomenon of early childhood; the womb doesn't come into its own until much later. But Horney's theory of the primacy of woman envy becomes logical when we consider that for both boys and girls, woman is the original, omnipotent source of life. In the earliest stage of human existence, what Freud called the oral period, the organs of activity are the breasts. During this stage, all human beings, male and female, take the passive "feminine" position of receiving in relation to their mothers. It is in the first perception by the infant that the breast is not a part of itself, but a separate object attached to a powerful Other with her own subjectivity not under its control, that woman envy is born in every human being.

Melanie Klein and modern psychoanalytic theory on women

Modern analysis has emphasized the profound importance of the pre-Oedipal period for both boys and girls (Ernsberger, 1976). For both sexes, the infant's first symbiotic relationship is with a woman, and in that relationship, the woman is not castrated, but phallic and powerful. Her breasts, the part-objects which introduce the baby to the world, are protruding organs of activity and penetration, the source of life. To the suckling child, whether male or female, the woman is primally omnipotent, and the child is passive in relation to her.

Melanie Klein (Klein and Riviere, 1964) was one of the first theorists to address the significance of this universal situation. She emphasized the constant interaction between love and hate in this pre-relationship. The baby's mother is both desired and hated with all the strength and intensity that are characteristic of the primitive urges of the infant. The mother as the "good breast" satisfies all the baby's cravings and makes her feel secure, but she can also frustrate. These inevitable frustrations create destructive fantasies in the baby, and these fantasies feel like death wishes in that the baby may feel that she has really destroyed the mother with her hate and continues destroying her. This, according to Klein, has extremely important consequences for the mind. Feelings of guilt and distress now enter as a new element in the emotion of love. A pressing urge to make sacrifices develops in order to put things right and help loved people who have been harmed in fantasy. We acquire a capacity to identify with those we love, to put ourselves in their place.

The interplay between primitive love and hate during the oral stage that Klein described sets the stage for the child's first primitive identification with its mother. With the ingestion of milk, the infant, more or less on the level of fantasy, incorporates the powerful mother into herself and keeps her inside her body. This incorporation of the mother is driven by both libido and aggression and is both a wish to take the mother in and to destroy her. This "mother-in-me" is particularly strong in female infants, for reasons that Nancy Chodorow was to elaborate later, but it is important to consider that the first introjection is of an active phallic mother. When the primitive aggression, which Freud and Klein maintained is inevitable in the first relationship, asserts itself, boys, because they have a penis, are much better equipped to oppose the maternal object than girls. Later feminist psychoanalysts were to point out the importance for both sexes of the drive to separate from maternal engulfment and to frame penis envy in terms of the phallus as a symbol of separation from maternal omnipotence. This drive to oppose maternal omnipotence is fueled by the libido's love for the world and also by the inevitable aggression toward the mother. Klein provided an important contribution to the importance of early introjects and identifications in girls. The little girl's aggression toward her mother, first experienced in the oral stage as a wish to "eat her up" thereby replacing her, later develops into a deep resentment over the manifest evidence of their mutual anatomical deficiency. The girl feels guilty and conflicted about her wish to destroy her mother, and she develops a wish to make reparation, which is expressed as a capacity to identify with her mother. The early incorporation of the powerful maternal object redirects sexual and aggressive impulses, originally focused outward toward the mother, inward. It is because of the psychic space created by the incorporated mother, the "mother-in-me," that little girls become interested in the inside rather than the outside. Girls focus inward at a very early age, as Jones suggested, because of the specific challenges, unique to females, that they face in the pre-Oedipal and Oedipal periods. The tendency, more pronounced in girls than boys, to internalize objects sets up a rich, endopsychic world in females.

Crowell (1981) emphasized that girls and boys have very different experiences in the pre-Oedipal and Oedipal periods, because girls are mothered by an object of the same sex while boys are not. Nancy Chodorow (1978), another feminist psychoanalyst, theorized that sons are objects for their mothers, while daughters are more likely to be experienced in terms of narcissistic "oneness." Girls experience themselves as the self of the mother's fantasy, while boys become the Other. Because women are more likely to experience their daughters in this narcissistic oneness, the pre-Oedipal period is longer and more intense in girls than in boys, and women are more likely to experience boundary confusion and a lack of a sense of separateness from the world.

Girls enter the triangular Oedipal situation later, and they never completely renounce pre-Oedipal issues. The turn toward the father becomes a symbol of freedom from the dependence on and merging with the pre-Oedipal mother. The Oedipal girl's rejection of her mother is a defense against primary identification. It is, therefore, her own internal affair as much as a relational affair in the world.

The female Oedipal complex is triangular in a way boys' is not. Fathers do not become the sort of emotionally exclusive Oedipal object for girls that mothers do for boys. For girls, there is no absolute change of object, and this means that there is no single Oedipal mode or quick resolution of the conflict. Girls cannot and do not reject their mothers and women in favor of their fathers and men. They remain in a bisexual triangle throughout childhood and into puberty, and though they usually make a sexual resolution in favor of men, they retain an internal emotional triangle throughout life.

Chodorow (1978) described penis envy as the symbolic expression of the wish to detach from the mother and become autonomous rather than as a wish to be a man. A daughter does not have the different and desirable penis the son possesses to oppose maternal omnipotence, and she sees the father's penis as a symbol of independence and separateness from the mother. Chodorow saw Freud's notion that there is only one genital that people either have or are missing as a way the child defends himself psychologically against the overwhelming importance of its early mother image.

Girls do not define themselves in terms of the renunciation of pre-Oedipal relational modes to the extent that boys do, so regression to these modes feels less threatening to women than to men. From the retention of pre-Oedipal attachments to their mothers girls come to define and experience themselves as continuous with others. An ambivalent struggle for a sense of separateness and independence from the mother and emotional, if not erotic, bisexual oscillation between mother and father and between "mother–child" and "male–female" issues are themes throughout the female life cycle.

Chodorow is an object relations theorist, but her ideas reveal a basic problem for women concerning the drives: how does a human being direct the healthy aggression needed to separate from an object with whom they are originally merged in narcissistic oneness and with whom they must identify if they are to achieve maturation as a female? The solution to this problem requires an integration and fusion of the life and death instincts which is unique to females.

Jessica Benjamin (1988) addressed the paradoxical requirement that women must simultaneously separate from and identify with their mothers. Both boys and girls use the father to achieve separation from the mother, but the boy has a simpler path. His aggression toward his mother, which is experienced as so dangerous by both sexes, can be projected onto his father during his Oedipal complex. When that complex is shattered, the boy can deny and devalue his connection to his mother by achieving male identification with his father. The girl cannot disrupt her primitive symbiosis with the mother by using male identification to revolt against it. More importantly, the turning away of the girl from mother to father is problematic because, given the fact that most relationships between mothers and fathers are still permeated with inequality and subtle sexism, girls risk exchanging symbiosis for domination and control when they turn to their fathers. Fathers, because of the disidentification with women that their own Oedipal periods required, cannot see their daughters as they do their sons. They tend to unconsciously treat girls as nascent sex objects rather than subjects in their own right. Therefore, the use of the father to separate from the mother sets up the split, so common in women, between autonomy and sexuality. Little girls cannot use their connections to the Oedipal father either defensively to deny their dependence on the mother or constructively to forge a sense of separate selfhood. When her turn toward the father ends in frustration, the little girl redirects her desires, both sexual and aggressive, back toward herself, creating the passivity and masochism described by Deutsch and the muting of both libido and aggression delineated by Bonaparte.

Benjamin, like Chodorow, saw penis envy as a symbol of revolt and separation from omnipotent maternal power. She cites French analyst Janine Chasseguet-Smirgel (1970), who demonstrated that Freud's description of women as castrated and powerless is the exact opposite of a small child's unconscious image of the mother.

It becomes clear that penis envy itself goes through vicissitudes in the rocky road of feminine development. Beginning in the manifest, primitive awareness that boys have one more appendage than girls, which inspires a childish outrage not unlike the indignation when the cookie is unevenly divided around the nursery school table, it develops into a desire for the father's phallus which represents a fantasy of escape from engulfment by the omnipotent phallic mother. Finally, penis envy becomes entrenched in the humiliation of the Oedipal failure. The father's sexual rejection of his daughter is not as traumatic for female development as his refusal of her identification with his idealized autonomy and sexuality, represented by the penis. The defeated little girl's "lack," expressed symbolically in penis envy, is the gap left in her subjectivity by the rejecting father and the return to female identification (Benjamin, 1988).

New theories of female development

Chodorow and Benjamin both focused on the pre-Oedipal period in females, expanding on Freud's (1925) conviction that this period is crucial for girls. Infants of both sexes are originally merged in narcissistic oneness with the mother, but boys have a path out of this symbiosis that is not open to girls. The boy's penis is manifest anatomical evidence of his separateness from the mother. He clearly possesses something that the omnipotent mother does not, and he uses his gender identification with his father to devalue maternal power and deny his "mother-in-me." This defensive devaluation and denial are why his Oedipal conflict is "literally smashed to pieces" (Freud, 1925, p. 257). What is totally obliterated in the boy is the maternal introject, and in this act of psychic violence male chauvinism and domination is born anew in each male human being. The little girl, with no powerful breasts, no penis, and no child, finds herself "organless," and therefore much more vulnerable to engulfment by the mother. The only opposition open to her is her ability to fantasize the powerful mother inside herself. Therefore, she introjects her maternal imago and within the psychic space carved for this internal object, she masters the omnipotent mother by freely directing both her libido and her aggression toward the internalized object. This internalized relationship with the mother is an attempt to substitute activity for passivity. Unlike the boy who can psychically almost totally obliterate the maternal imago, the girl introjects the mother, thereby controlling her. The libido expresses itself in the idea that "I am just like my mother," while the aggression fuels the Oedipal idea, "I will replace my mother and have Father's penis for myself." Aggression toward this internalized mother drives a girl's Oedipal conflict as much as love for the world, self-assertion, or a sexual desire for the father does; and in her unconscious fantasies, the little girl wins the love of her father by attacking her maternal introject. Herein lies the seeds of masochism.

Though the little girl actively attacks the mother in her attempt to steal the father from her, she cannot approach the father actively. She has no penis and comes to the father with the wish to receive something from him. She is compelled to identify with the mother and take the passive position in terms of the father. This sets up a split in the introjected maternal imago. The original omnipotent phallic mother of the life-giving breasts is associated with the mother–child dyad, not the male–female relationship. The little girl, if she wants to win her father, must now modify the maternal imago and try to identify with the passive, submissive, "feminine" mother that is the father's sexual partner. It is here that the concept of "penis" and "child" get merged in the female unconscious. Having a child would give the girl the power of the phallic mother, while having the penis would gain her access to the power of the father. The father has both the penis and the power to give her a child, as he gave the mother, so the female child turns to him with the hope of receiving access to both masculine and feminine power.

Sad to say, for many reasons, the situation is doomed from the beginning. The little girl perceives that her genital is much too small for her father's penis, and she fears she may be destroyed by it (Horney, 1967). This creates anxiety not unlike the boy's fear of castration by his father if he has intercourse with his mother. The father for his part, if he is a good-enough father, is in no position to grant his daughter either his penis or a child. The cultural imposition of the incest barrier has hopefully restrained him in his impulse to have sex with and impregnate his daughter. But it is here that culture effects a more insidious prohibition. The father is a product of his own Oedipal travails, and very likely he has gained his masculine identity by devaluing and denying any dependence on females or any feminine identification within himself. He cannot perceive his daughter in the way he perceives his son, as an independent and autonomous subject. There can be no mutual recognition between father and daughter (Benjamin, 1988). He can only love her as an adored object. Whereas the father permits the son to identify with him, he unconsciously denies this tribute to his daughter. He rejects not only her desire for his manifest penis, but also her wish for the idealized phallus as a symbol of freedom from the engulfing mother. In so doing, he sets up a barrier to access to both the power of the female and the male. But his love for his daughter, so resonant of his love for her mother, tinged as it is with burgeoning sexuality, sends the unconscious message to her: "You will never possess a penis of your own, but you may someday receive a penis and a child, like your mother, provided you adopt the stance she has taken toward me."

Where does this leave the little girl? Her father's rejection of her certainly induces primitive aggression toward him, but if she expresses it directly, she risks losing the hope of ever obtaining either the promised penis or child. If she turns the aggression back on her mother, she threatens the basis of her feminine identity and her only hope for ever gaining the power of the penis and child. The aggression must be both muted and redirected toward the self, and her destiny becomes to wait and receive. She must learn to enjoy being passive; barred access to actively loving, she must eroticize being loved. It is not, as Freud contended, that women need to be loved more than they can love. They are given no choice. They can neither suckle their mothers nor penetrate their fathers; their active loving has no external port, and must, like their aggression, be turned back on the self. In this, they are aided by the love and tender feelings of mother and father, and by culture, which has trained both parents to be more overtly affectionate with little girls than little boys and to permit much less direct expression of sexuality and aggression in their daughters than in their sons. The redirection of libido frustrated in its active outer aim along with the internalization of tender parental feelings infuse the female ego with the healthy narcissism that Deutsch equated with femininity. Because she has no penis, breasts, or child in her womb to focus this self-love upon, the girl tends to cathect the self more globally. Not only her entire body, but the products of her mind, her thoughts and feelings, become eroticized, giving the feminine personality its sensuality and emotional richness.

The phallic pre-Oedipal mother has a short-lived existence as a construct in the psyche of both sexes. Boys, armed as they are with the penis that opposes maternal omnipotence, obliterate this primitive pre-identification with the mother of the good and bad breast very early. And though girls avoid this act of psychic matricide, they also lose their access to the powerful early mother for very different reasons, which have to do with the psychological wounds and stresses of the female Oedipal complex.

The infusion of secondary narcissism that Deutsch described in little girls is vital to female development because the reality of the female post-Oedipal position is harsh. The fact that female children adjust to that reality at all is a tribute to the enterprise of the feminine psyche. However, the adaptation the little girl makes at this period is a shaky compromise at best.

Left empty and depressed by her father's rejection of both her sexual and identificatory love at the end of the Oedipal period, the girl experiences a kind of mourning (Benjamin, 1988). Turning back onto the primitive mother imago within, the girl regresses to her earlier oral mode of identification and this time incorporates her idealized phallic father. This introjection of the powerful father achieves the same thing that the earlier maternal introjection accomplished: control over an essentially uncontrollable object, but it is not quite the same. When the female infant incorporated the phallic mother, it was a very primitive oral type of pre-identification, focused on bodily boundaries and the frontier between "inside" and "outside," a fantasy of ingesting the pre-Oedipal mother with her milk. The internalization of the Oedipal father is an introjection more than an incorporation. That is to say, it is a more highly evolved pre-identification because what is internalized is not only a mental representation of the object itself, but also the inherent qualities of and the conflictual relationship to that object. The more mature and reality-oriented female child of the post-Oedipal period internalizes not only the imago of the father, but also his feelings and behaviors. Since it is very likely that the father, because of the difficulties of becoming masculine in this world, has an unconscious or conscious tendency to defensively devalue women, this devaluation is internalized within the female psyche. So now the inner world consists not only of the residue, the mental image, of the phallic mother, but also of a real or fantasized relationship between maternal and paternal imagoes and between the self and those imagoes. Within the ever-expanding inner space of her complex endopsychic world, the girl is free to discharge love and hate toward her internalized objects.

The internal triangle of maternal imago, paternal imago, and self is unique to female development. Boys reject their maternal introject to identify with their fathers, and this sets up a dualism of male self as subject and female other as object in the masculine unconscious. In the female psyche, this clear opposition doesn't exist. To some extent, all three elements of the girl's inner world are subjects. The girl's internalization of both mother and father allows her access to both her powerful omnipotent mother and her powerful phallic father. This dual introjection is implicated in the bisexuality that Bonaparte and Chodorow asserted was characteristic of femininity. It is also responsible for women's unique way of looking at the world and framing morality. Freud's contention that the female superego is weaker than the male is perhaps too simplistic. The masculine superego is inexorable, impersonal, and independent of emotion because the boy has made a total identification with his powerful phallic father and obliterated his primitive identification with his mother. This enables him to think in dualistic terms about right and wrong, good and bad. What Freud described as a weak superego is actually a uniquely feminine morality based on the complexity of the inner world. Since females have a triadic unconscious cathexis, they don't see morality in terms of rules and logic. Any ethical issue must be weighed from a variety of perspectives, and thus, is never resolved easily.

Though the female triadic intrapsychic constellation provides women with an enormous capacity for identification, a rich inner life of imagination, fantasy, and intuition, and an ability to sacrifice self for others, these feminine virtues come at a high psychic price. Parental introjection presents a solution to the unique problems of the female Oedipal complex, but it also sets up new conflicts in the little girl's psyche. The shifting relationships and cathexes between the three points of the internal triangle have a profound effect on female psychic functioning, and the multitude of possibilities that exist between the three psychic structures allow for infinite individuality in female human beings. There are trends in the triangular relationship, however, which offer an explanation for several characteristics associated with femininity. For one thing, the triangle is not equilateral. Both the introjected mother, with the child that father gave her and the breasts to feed it, and the introjected father, with his powerful penis, have endowments that the little girl does not possess. The self is compelled to take a subordinate position in relation to these powerful introjects, and this intrapsychic process conditions females to submission, self-abnegation, and passivity, to what Dinnerstein (1976, p. 236) described as "the 'truly feminine' woman's monstrously overdeveloped talent for unreciprocated empathy." Even more damaging for feminine development than this subjugation of self to introjects, is the intrapsychic relation between the maternal and paternal internalized objects. The maternal imago, initially a primary identification with the omnipotent and phallic mother of the oral period, has her omnipotence challenged when primary penis envy is established, but it is the introduction of the paternal imago at the resolution of the Oedipal conflict that has the most detrimental influence on the "mother-in-me." When the girl introjects her Oedipal father, she identifies with his wish to dominate and attack the maternal imago. She derives pleasure from neutralizing the omnipotence of the internalized mother, but this assault on her primary female identification provides fertile ground for the masochism and submission associated with femininity. Her identification and cooperation with dominating man wins her vicarious power but at the price of devaluing her female identification. The muting of the drives which Bonaparte described is probably a defense against this toxic internal discord.

Latency brings about a repression of the conflict and initiates a period in which little girls pursue the acquisition of culture. The primary defenses of latency are projection and identification with the aggressor (Becker, 1974). These defenses enable the girl to project masochistic tendencies onto her mother and identify with her father. In this way, feminine eroticism and sensuality is temporarily abandoned for a more masculine focus on the outer world and school. Ironically, this active pursuit of what Edith Jacobson (1961, p. 174) called a *Weltanschauung* (view of the world) provides an initiation to patriarchal culture which can have a depressive effect on the preadolescent girl. Coming "up against the wall of Western culture," girls are in danger of losing their "voice" in their attempts to become feminine in a sexist society (Gilligan et al., 1989, p. 4). Gilligan's work seems to indicate that girls in early adolescence long to return to identification with a phallic mother. The conflict for Gilligan's research subjects is around finding a way to be both feminine and powerful. The problem for girls is that access to the primitive, powerful maternal introject of the first years of life is denied to them following the vicissitudes of the female Oedipal conflict. The intrapsychic conflict between the maternal and paternal internalized objects has demanded that female identification entail submission and passivity. The mother submits to the father, and the self submits to both in this internalized relationship. Vacillating between the maternal and paternal introjects, girls struggle to define and strengthen the self in the psychic triangle. Helene Deutsch (1944) discussed the bisexual nature of the prepubertal period in girls. The girl wavers between the internalized mother and father and wants to have them both.

With the strengthening of the sexual instincts at puberty, the libido toward internalized objects is intensified. But attachment to mother represents a greater danger than attachment to father. Libido directed toward the internalized maternal imago threatens a regression to the pre-Oedipal danger of engulfment by a phallic mother. Peter Blos (1958) writes about the decisive and forceful turn toward heterosexuality that girls make to defend themselves against the phallic pregenital mother. Identification with the father imago is heightened and revives the attack on the introjected mother. This two-sided discharge of aggression toward the mother creates a sense of guilt that is often expressed as attachments to same-sex friends and also provides impetus for the separation from primitive identifications which is adolescence's primary task. The girl's "best friend," whom she loves and with whom she shares everything, permits her to continue the experience of merging while denying feelings of narcissistic oneness with her mother (Chodorow, 1978).

Recent writers have disputed the classic analytic theory that the work of adolescence is to separate from mother and father and asserted that the task is to find a way to stay connected while differentiating from parental figures (Gilligan, 1982). This debate can be resolved, however, when we make a clear differentiation between internal imagoes and actual objects. It is not the mother and father that the female adolescent must relinquish, but her primitive introjects of them. In actuality, the psychic work of feminine adolescence finally allows the young woman to see her parents realistically with all the hope for true intimacy that that implies. Hyman Spotnitz discussed the adolescent's typical obsession with "memory romances," fantasies pertaining to the romances of the Oedipal period. In the "winter of childhood," the young girl turns inward to her childhood objects, an attempt to understand backward in response to the anxieties involved in living forward (Spotnitz, 1964, p. 223). Peter Blos (1958) challenged the analytic view that the Oedipal complex is completely resolved at the end of the Oedipal period. Like Chodorow, Blos asserted that the resolution is only a partial one, and that the Oedipal conflicts are not so much revived in adolescence as continued. The negative complex is particularly strong for adolescents and often manifests itself in intense hostility toward the parent of the same sex and a defensive clinging to the heterosexual component of the complex. Blos emphasized that the adolescent object disengagement through individuation proceeds in terms of internal, not external objects. Infantile parental imagoes perpetuate a belief in perfection, and separation implies a critical deidealization and humanization of the infantile inner world. The great maturational surge in cognitive functioning at puberty permits the formation of a girl's own view of the past, present, and future, with the past being subjected for the first time to a kind of reality testing. Residual historical traumas must be integrated into the personality where they provide organizers that promote the consolidation of the adult personality and account for its uniqueness. All elements of the internalized triangle must be deidealized and replaced by the mature ambivalence that permits a turn to the object world and a sexualized adult relationship.

In this difficult task of deidealization and reconfiguration of her inner world, the adolescent girl is aided by the infusion of narcissism that Deutsch felt was so helpful. In the psychic triadic constellation of the preadolescent girl, the self has been compelled to take a subordinate position to the parental imagoes. With the surge of narcissism typical of this period, the "I am I" is born (Deutsch, 1944, p. 95). This "I" is carved out of an intense internal struggle, characterized by what Deutsch (1944, p. 115) described as the "clash between progressive and regressive forces" in which the young woman vacillates between a wish to return to symbiotic oneness with a phallic mother and a desire to kill her off and identify with the phallic father.

The onset of the menses is a profound psychic event in the life of a young girl. Deutsch (1944, p. 149) said that menstruation "mobilizes psychic reactions so numerous and varied that we are justified in speaking of the 'psychology of menstruation.'" The first menstruation is usually experienced as a trauma. Deutsch related it to both the female castration complex and the reproductive function. The menses revives powerful feelings toward the mother, inspiring aggressive as well as sexual tendencies. Bleeding is associated in the unconscious with the old fantasy of castration, and the blame for that castration clearly falls on the mother's shoulders. The adolescent girl, like the mother, is unclean and shameful; they share "secrets." There is also intense erotic pleasure at the thought of these "secrets." At last, she is initiated into that society of females to which she was denied access so long ago. The onset of menstruation comes with the promise that one day she will share in the power of the phallic mother. Sexual instincts are reawakened from regression, and the girl takes her own body as an object of self-love and nurturance. Narcissistic vulnerability, particularly focused on the genitals, is expressed in the rejection of anything that might destroy their integrity. The vagina is alternately seen as something dirty and something very valuable (Deutsch, 1944). Unless penis envy, in any of its forms, is too intense, menstruation initiates a turn toward an identification with the mother, but again, this is not the phallic mother of the pre-Oedipal period. Now the identification is with a more passive, truly "feminine" mother, the "wounded" mother who bleeds. This shift in the maternal imago is fueled by aggression expressed in the idea that mother (and I) are dirty and debased, but it also has a libidinal component. Now the girl has a valuable "jewel," and like her mother, she can use her femininity to get the baby and the penis from her father. Because of this altered feminine identification, the sexual instinct becomes infused with feeling and spirituality, giving female sexuality its unique eroticism.

Menstruation can also alter the female self's attitude toward the paternal introject. Deutsch (1944, p. 121) reported that the unconscious idea of the young woman seems to be, "You didn't protect me from her." The menses is manifest evidence that identification with the phallic father is hopeless. The unconscious anger aroused by this final negation of identificatory love along with the surge of sexuality that menstruation initiates create a strong tendency in young women to turn away from their fathers toward heterosexuality in the object world. Originally, this love may be idealized and focused on an admired teacher or a famous film star, but eventually heterosexual object choices will be more realistic, with attraction containing unconscious residues of both maternal and paternal imagoes (Klein and Riviere, 1964).

The sexual impulses directed toward the internal father are redirected out into the object world, while sexual impulses toward the maternal imago express themselves in the wish for a child, which is the desire to return to narcissistic oneness with the primitive mother.

The adolescent girl must now deal with a conflict or a harmony of many contradictory elements. Questions of masculine versus feminine, active versus passive, and autonomy versus connection will challenge her sense of self. These questions become associated in her mind with the internalized parental objects along sexual lines. Much more than boys, girls incorporate traits associated with the opposite sex parent into their identities, though often after the trauma of the first menses and the identification with the wounded mother, these "masculine" qualities are experienced as unattainable ideals rather than integrated character traits. The internal maternal and paternal imagoes are seldom in harmony at this point in development; and though the phallic father rarely supersedes and deposes the passive mother, it is just as rare that the struggle between them ends in a tie. The intrapsychic problem for young women is that many of the qualities they most desire, active sexuality, autonomy, assertiveness, and power, are the provenance of the father within, and as such, threaten their female identification. The internal triangle lacks what Jessica Benjamin (1988) called "intersubjectivity," a situation where two subjects, different but equal, confront each other's differences in mutual recognition. The intrapsychic relationship between the father and the mother is one between the subject and the object; and though adolescence is characterized by the ascendance of the self in terms of introjected objects, the paternal imago can dominate the internal triangle in a way that makes the adjustment to femininity challenging. The healthy tension between self-assertion and recognition of and connection to the other is often not attained in adolescence. Young women often split their identifications along gender lines and become passive and depressed if they cathect the wounded mother, or ambitious and aggressive if identified with their phallic father imago. True integration of the complex female inner world is a task that continues for life.

References

Becker, T.E. (1974). "On Latency." *Psychoanalytic Study of the Child*, 29(1), 3–12.

Benjamin, J. (1988). *The Bonds of Love: Psychoanalysis, Feminism, and the Problem of Domination*. New York: Pantheon Books.

Blos, P. (1958). "Pre-adolescent Drive Organization." *Journal of the American Psychoanalytic Association*, 6(1), 47–56.

Bonaparte, M. (1951). *Female sexuality*. New York: International Universities Press.

Chasseguet-Smirgel, J. (1970). *Female Sexuality: New Psychoanalytic Views*. London: Karnac Books.

Chodorow, N. (1978). *The Reproduction of Mothering: Psychoanalysis and the Sociology of Gender*. Berkeley, CA: University of California Press.

Crowell, M. (1981). "A Response to Feminist Critics of Psychoanalysis." *Modern Psychoanalysis*, 6, 221–235.

Deutsch, H. (1944, 1945). *The Psychology of Women*. Vols. I and II. New York: Grune and Stratton.

Dinnerstein, D. (1976). *The Mermaid and the Minotaur: Sexual Arrangements and Human Malaise.* New York: Harper Collins.
Ernsberger, C. (1976). "Freud and the Modern School." *Modern Psychoanalysis*, 1, 17–32.
Freud, S. (1905). "Three Essays on the Theory of Sexuality." *Standard Edition*, Volume 7. London: Hogarth Press, 130–243.
Freud, S. (1924). "The Dissolution of the Oedipus Complex." *Standard Edition*. Volume 19. London: Hogarth Press, 173–179.
Freud, S. (1925). "Some Psychical Consequences of the Anatomical Distinction between the Sexes." *Standard Edition*, Volume 19. London: Hogarth Press, 248–258.
Freud, S. (1931). "Female Sexuality." *Standard Edition*, Volume 21. London: Hogarth Press, 225–243.
Freud, S. (1932). "New Introductory Lectures on Psychoanalysis: Femininity." *Standard Edition*, Volume 22. London: Hogarth Press, 112–135.
Freud, S. (1933). "New Introductory Lectures on Psychoanalysis." *Standard Edition*, Volume 22. London: Hogarth Press, 22, 7–182.
Gay, P. (1988). *Freud: A Life For Our Times.* New York, W.W. Nortonand Company.
Gilligan, C., Lyons, N.P., and Hanmer, T.J. (eds). (1989). *Making Connections: The Relational Worlds of Adolescent Girls at Emma Willard School.* Cambridge, MA: Harvard University Press.
Gilligan, C. (1982). *In a Different Voice: Psychological Theory and Women's Development.* Cambridge, MA: Harvard University Press.
Horney, K. (1967). *Feminine Psychology.* New York: W. W. Norton.
Jacobson, E. (1961). "Adolescent Moods and the Remodeling of Psychic Structures in Adolescence." *Psychoanalytic Study of the Child*, 16(1), 164–183.
Jones, E. (1927). "The Early Development of Female Sexuality." *International Journal of Psycho-Analysis*, 8, 459–472.
Jones, E. (1935). "Early Female Sexuality." *International Journal of Psycho-Analysis*, 16, 263–273.
Klein, M., and Riviere, J. (1964). *Love, Hate, and Reparation.* New York: W. W. Norton.
Spotnitz, H. (1964). "Adolescence and Schizophrenia: Problems in Differentiation." In S. Lorand and H.I. Scheer (eds), *Adolescents: Psychoanalytic Approach to Problems and Therapy.* New York: Harper and Row, pp. 217–237.

Chapter 4

Women in group and women's groups

Women in groups, like women in life, often tend to play the role of the "second sex" (de Beauvoir, 1952), that is, they subtly subvert themselves to the men around them. This dynamic is largely unconscious to both men and women, and both sexes play a part in creating it. It manifests itself in a multitude of complex patterns of man as subject and woman as object. It can be quite blatant, as when men do all the talking and talk only to other men, while the women sit silently; but often, it is expressed in a more elegantly intricate fashion. The clinician will find herself with a group where the men have "problems" and the women energetically attempt to "solve" them. In other groups, the men will talk about their lives, and the women will "identify" with them. In situations like these, women may be getting so much appreciation for their empathy and their insight, that it is almost impossible to spot the fact that the focus is firmly masculine.

The most skilled group leader, whether male or female, may overlook this tendency, since all men and women, because of the vicissitudes of becoming masculine and feminine, see this situation as "second nature." A female therapist with a feminist perspective may rush to see the men in her group as "oppressors" and the women as "victims," but if she does, she will be oversimplifying what is happening in a way that can be destructive to group members of both sexes. To resolve this sexist resistance and promote progressive communication between men and women, it is important for the clinician to consider how this dynamic develops in the unconscious of all people.

The internal triangle in female development

The domination of women is set up in the preverbal development of both sexes because of the almost universal fact that girls have a mother of the same sex while boys do not. While both males and females begin life in narcissistic oneness with a woman, boys must achieve their masculine identity through an almost violent disidentification with their mothers. The boy's penis, manifest anatomical evidence of his difference from his mother, gives him a path out of symbiosis that is not open to girls. He can identify with his father to deny the power of the mother and to obliterate the identification he has made with the female object in the pre-Oedipal period. What is "literally smashed to pieces" (Freud, 1925, p. 257) in boys at the end of the Oedipal period is the maternal introject, and in this act of psychic violence, male chauvinism and domination are reinvented in each male human being.

Little girls, with no penis to oppose the omnipotent mother, have a longer and more intense pre-Oedipal period. Mothers can more clearly see their sons as objects, while daughters are experienced as part of the self, and this sets up a tendency in women toward boundary confusion. Women struggle with issues of separation and individuation and feelings of primary identification and love unmitigated by the reality principle throughout life (Chodorow, 1978). I have written elsewhere about the complex ways women use identification to solve a uniquely female problem, which is the challenge of separating from the maternal object while still retaining a feminine identity. With no penis to oppose engulfment by the omnipotent pre-Oedipal mother, girls attempt to gain control by the introjection of the maternal imago. Girls incorporate the pre-Oedipal mother with the ingestion of her milk, and this "mother-in-me" is never destroyed as it is in boys. Instead, the feminine endopsychic world is rendered more complex at the end of the Oedipal period, when little girls resolve the conflicts of that difficult stage by introjecting the paternal imago as well. The internal triangle of maternal imago, paternal imago, and self is unique to female development; and girls utilize this triangle to provide some of the advantages of the penis: they gain control over essentially uncontrollable objects. Within the complex endopsychic feminine world, girls freely discharge both libido and aggression toward internalized objects.

Though the internal triangle provides women with an enormous capacity for identification with both men and women, rich imagination and intuition, and an ability to sacrifice self for others, it is important to remember that it sets up other challenges for women. The triangle is often not equilateral, and unconsciously, the self takes a subordinate position in relation to the powerful maternal and paternal imagoes. When the girl introjects her Oedipal father, it is not the primitive incorporation that was characteristic of the earliest maternal identification. This time, the girl introjects not only the imago of the object, but also the attitudes of that object and her relationship to it. Because of the challenges of his own development, the Oedipal father often has an unconscious wish to attack and dominate the powerful pre-Oedipal mother. This means that when the Oedipal girl introjects the father, she begins to identify with his wish to dominate and attack the maternal imago. This identification with the dominating man gives her the pleasure of vicarious power over the pre-Oedipal mother within, but at the expense of her primary feminine identification. This intrapsychic process conditions women to submission, passivity, and a compulsive, unreciprocated empathy that borders on the masochistic (Holmes, 2000).

Given the very real potential of this problem, it is easy to understand why many group leaders advocate women's groups. The argument goes that if men gain their identity by devaluing and denying any feminine identification within themselves, and if women compulsively lose themselves in identification and empathy, then it is particularly challenging in a heterosexual group for women to be perceived by either sex as independent and autonomous subjects. Only in a group where there are no anxious men to unconsciously subjugate and no opportunities for women to compulsively play handmaiden, can females be free to explore the integrity rather than the "otherness" of their issues.

Having run all-female groups for six years, I can attest to the fact that they can be highly effective, particularly for a certain type of "feminine" woman. These are women who, because of the difficulties of their own development, have become diffused in identifications. That is, the process of identification has become so compulsive that it is no longer in the service of the ego and deprives the woman of the full possession of her own personality. These women are often subjugated by their unconscious identification with an oppressive paternal imago, which expresses itself in a masochistic dependence or a compulsive, self-destructive identification with the men in their lives.

The "feminine" woman in group

Marilyn, a recently divorced woman, talked about a sense of emptiness. She said, "I don't know who I am if I'm not married. It's not that I enjoyed marriage that much. I just desperately need to know that I'm Eric's wife, because if I'm not, then who am I?" Marilyn was frantic to find a boyfriend, because "if I had a boyfriend, I could feel okay about myself." Marilyn was addicted to diet and sleeping pills, and she recognized this as a problem, but she idolized her male doctor, seeing him as the ultimate authority about her health and her savior in her attempts to deal with her feelings of emptiness and despair. It seemed that Marilyn's sense of self was so weak that she was compelled to look everywhere for an idealized father in whom she could take refuge, even if that refuge meant the erosion of her own ego.

Jane was very clear that she wanted to join a women's group. She said she had things to say that couldn't be said in the presence of men. When I explored what those things might be, she said, "I don't know. I just talk differently when men are present. I have to be the ingénue, the perpetual little sweetheart. Men take up so much space, and their needs come first." Jane described an incident when she had delivered her son to the apartment of his father and the father's new girlfriend. She said,

> My son started to cry. He didn't want to go in, so even though the girlfriend was there, I just took my son by the hand and marched in. I stayed

until he was comfortable – you know, like a dog pees on everything to mark his territory and then moves on?"

Jane blushed and giggled after she said this, and said, "Now that's something I never could have said if men were here!" When I asked why not, she said, "Men talk like that. Women are supposed to be lady-like." Despite his infidelity, Jane's husband moved back into her apartment every Christmas. Jane reported she put up with this because "it makes the children happy. And family means so much to him." Though Jane complained that she could "never do my own work or see my friends over the holidays. It's all about him," it never occurred to her that her needs had any priority over those of her husband and children. She said, "I don't know how it happens, but I lose myself. All my doors, my refrigerator, even my bathroom door are open to all of them twenty-four hours a day." Her total identification with her family's feelings defended her from any aggression she might have felt toward them.

Jane described her new boyfriend to the group as "very loving and attentive, just for me." But she also said, "being with him is like scuba diving, and I just have to come up for air every now and then. I totally immerse myself in his mind, his reality, and then I have to make myself some space so I can find myself again."

These feminine women were able to use an all-woman's group very effectively. With no masculine object present to compulsively play subject to, they seemed to carve out the time and the space they needed to begin to know themselves. Jane expressed the idea that "being in a group of women seems to slow me down, gives me the time to breathe so that I can find my own feelings." Marilyn compared the female group experience with going to the grocery store for the first time after Eric left her and their daughter went to college: "I stood in the aisle by the produce absolutely paralyzed because I knew what my daughter likes to eat, and I knew what Eric likes to eat, but I didn't have a clue what I like to eat. I was so busy taking care of their needs that I had never taken the time to find out who I am, even what I like to eat. So I had to figure it out."

Evelyn had been in a mixed-gender group with a male analyst with whom she had been in constant conflict, and finally, she left the group. Evelyn's individual analyst suggested that she might like to work with a female group analyst, and when I suggested a women's group, she liked the idea. In the first session with her new group, Evelyn described her difficult relationship with the leader and the other men in her last group. She reported a dream in which the male group leader was "raping me from behind, and I had to pretend to enjoy it." Evelyn was somewhat "shamed" by this dream, and was initially reluctant to talk about it. She said, "I'm a very sexual person," but she seemed to be embarrassed about it. A few weeks after joining the women's group, Evelyn reported another dream. She said, "It was sexual, like my dream of being raped, but this time I was riding a horse. I was in control, and it was very pleasurable." Evelyn told this dream with a sense of joy, and she made the association that this dream was about the new feelings of power she felt in the all-female group.

All these women had a rather impoverished sense of self, and in one form or another, they had all projected their oppressive internalized objects onto the people in their lives. In an all-women's group, each was able to begin to strengthen her own ego. Just as they did in life, all the women in the group compulsively gave themselves away in identification with the other, and so the group resistance became an obsessive "helpfulness." They all rushed to empathize, support, and rescue each other, and any aggression or frustration that arose was masked by the group myth: "We are just alike and feel exactly the same feelings, and we are here to bolster each other up against an externalized enemy." This group resistance actually had a positive effect on the individual members for many months. Most of the women achieved a new awareness, mainly by seeing themselves in the mirror held up to them by the support and encouragement of other members. It took many more months before these women could risk talking about any negative feelings toward each other, and when the aggression did finally appear, it often expressed itself in an unconscious identification with a parent, most often the mother.

For example, Teresa, who had initially been very quiet, began to monopolize the group about her difficulties with her teenage son, who was physically abusing her. At first, the group, true to form, listened attentively and sympathetically. Teresa's tirade about her victimization at her son's hands was quite consonant with the group resistance that aggression, if it existed at all, resided outside the group. Everyone offered Teresa helpful suggestions, all of which fell on deaf ears as Teresa, in her distress, became more and more repetitive and obsessive. As the weeks went by, the group deteriorated into a private session for Teresa while the others sat in silence.

Louis R. Ormont talks about the moment when a group congeals, that is, the time when the group has gone from being emotionally chromatic to monochromatic. This difficult state of affairs is usually brought on by a shared reaction to a particular member (Ormont, 1991). I could see that the other women were getting increasingly frustrated and angry with Teresa, but they seemed unable to put their thoughts into words. When I asked Teresa why she thought everyone was so quiet, she said, "I have no idea," and went back to her monologue. I tried bridging (Ormont, 1990), turning to Marilyn and asking her why she thought Susan was not saying anything. Marilyn said, "Well, I guess she doesn't know how to help." In desperation, I said, "Jane, what feeling does Teresa induce in you when she talks like this?" Jane looked flustered, paused, and said, "Well, of course, I understand how she feels, and I just feel so sorry."

I began to think that Teresa would destroy the group. After several months of this, Teresa phoned between sessions to tell me another horror story about her son. I said, "Bring it up in group." Teresa started the next group by saying, "I called Lucy about a problem I'm having with my son, and she suggested I bring it up here." This finally was too much. Jane said,

> I can't believe this. How could you do that, Lucy? We've sat here for week after week, imprisoned by Teresa, while she talks and talks. None of us can say anything or influence her in any way. We just have to sit silently and endure it while she tortures us. And you told her to bring it up in group? Why didn't you tell her to come in for an individual session and torture you for a while?

I said, "Why should I have to deal with this alone? What's your resistance to helping me out a little?" Jane said, "I don't know what to do. You're the professional." I said, "Well, as a professional, I'm trying to understand why this group sits silently week after week while Teresa talks." At this point Teresa exclaimed, "Wait a minute! Lucy, you told me to bring this up. I don't monopolize. I'm just doing what you told me to do." Susan said, "What do you mean you don't monopolize? We sit here in a box you've put us in week after week, and we can't speak because none of our problems are as important as yours, and none of our suggestions are helpful. I feel like you've tied us all up and are holding us hostage to your misery."

At this point, Teresa began to cry. She said, "I just had a memory." I asked her what it was. She said,

> When I was a little girl, my mother had a very unusual way of punishing me if I had done something bad. She would make me stand in the middle of the kitchen floor while she berated me. She could do this for an hour or more. I had to stand very still, and I wasn't allowed to say anything. I wasn't permitted to defend myself or apologize or disagree with her. I just had to stand there. Sometimes I had to go to the bathroom, but that didn't matter. I had to stand there until she was finished talking, till she was all worn out. And she could talk and talk and talk. I felt tied up and tortured.

Teresa's unconscious identification with her punishing mother allowed her to express anger in the group without ever being in touch with it. Until Jane's outburst, she had no idea that her monologue was enraging. She had used it to discharge aggression, while retaining her "feminine" identity as a gentle soul who was the victim of her male oppressor. Using her maternal imago to symbolically imprison, as her mother had imprisoned her, she was protected from her true feelings, which would have threatened her feminine identification.

Gradually, the group felt safer to express negative feelings not only toward me, but also toward other members. And as they were more frank with Teresa, she was able to give up her obsessive monopolizing and tell us the emotionally significant story of her life. Even later, she felt secure enough to express the feelings that her monopoly had masked: "This group doesn't understand the depth of my suffering and has no power to protect me from the abuse of my son."

Ormont (1991, p. 75) writes,

> An introject is a part object, a piece of some significant figure of the person's past, that remains incorporated in the psyche but has never been assimilated into the person's adult ego. It operates as a feeling, an attitude, a voice urging the person to act as the significant figure did. By implication, it urges others to act in the role of the patient himself.

Teresa, in an unconscious identification with her maternal introject, had tortured the group as her mother tortured her. Once the group resistance and the congealing it produced had been resolved, the other women were freed to give Teresa back to herself; that is, they verbalized the anger she was unable to experience.

Women in a well-functioning group are able to move through and play with the internal objects in the rooms of the other members' minds. They shape their relationships in the room according to what Bollas (1992 p. 50) calls "the idiom of the internal world." Each woman can bring along the personal spirits or ghosts of her internal triangle and, transfer them to a receptive place in another. When the group is functioning as a whole, and the leader is including all the members, the women are able to use both their compulsive need to identify and empathize and their aggression in highly effective ways. Identification provides a kaleidoscope of mirrors to each member, a multifaceted reflection of self that enriches each woman's understanding and acceptance of her own complexity. Aggression, used effectively, strengthens each member's sense of self against the oppressions of the endopsychic world of the feminine woman and frees her to use her empathy and identification, not in masochistic and compulsive ways, but in the service of her own ego.

Groups organized around female developmental milestones

Another situation in which women's groups are highly effective is when they are organized around the physical milestones of the female life cycle: the beginning of menstruation, pregnancy, and menopause. Though rooted in the body, these dramatic developmental events set up crises in psychic functioning, periods of intense disequilibrium that can lead, in favorable circumstances to maturation and the creation of new psychic structures. All these events create profound life changes with which women must cope: menstruation signals that you can never be a child again; pregnancy, that you will never be a single unit again; and menopause, that you will never bear children again, will grow old, and die. (Bibring et al., 1961)

During these traumas, a women's group can prove extremely helpful. It is often difficult, if not impossible, for women to speak about such quintessentially feminine events in the presence of men. The stresses on women during these life crises may make the identification with and empathy for men, which allow communication between the sexes to flow smoothly, almost impossible. As one pregnant woman put it, "I literally have nothing to give men right now. All I can think about is my own body." Men, for their part, because of the fear of their own maternal engulfment, usually find a focus on these feminine issues irrelevant at best, and deeply threatening at worst. Women sense this, and in unconscious compliance or conscious embarrassment, stifle the impulse to speak about the issues that are most pressing in their lives. I am reminded of a supervision group which contained five women and one man, all in their fifties. This group functioned very effectively and cooperatively in its presentation of patients until the day that the man was not able to attend the group. Spontaneously, the women began to talk about menopause, about everything from their anxieties about death to hot flashes and herbal remedies. At the end of the session, one of the female analysts said, "Well, I guess this was acting out in a major way, but I feel wonderful. I have absolutely nowhere to talk about any of this and I couldn't have talked about it here if Jeff had been here today!"

A pregnancy group

Lily, a woman who had recently discovered that she was pregnant with a much-wanted child, came into a group for pregnant women to discuss her mysterious "feelings of ambivalence." Her husband, Bob, was very excited about the impending birth, but Lily was filled with uncertainty, dread, and fear. She was afraid she would "turn into my mother" when the baby was born, and she was anxious about the discomfort of pregnancy and the pain of childbirth. She had miscarried in her first pregnancy, and I encouraged her to verbalize all her negative feelings in the group, because I believed this would help her achieve her goal of holding on to this pregnancy. She said,

> I can't talk to Bob about any of these fears. I get scared of making him resentful or angry. I think, in my gut, I'm scared to complain to a man. My father used to hit if we complained, and he wasn't interested in my feelings.

Oppressed by a harsh paternal introject which she had projected onto her husband, Lily had a lot of complaining to do, and she was able to use the pregnancy group very effectively to explore all the feelings her pregnancy induced. When she left the group after the birth of her son, she felt "much safer to be open with Bob about my feelings."

One of the most difficult feelings that pregnancy seems to induce in women is a primitive and seemingly unreasonable hatred and resentment

70 Women

toward their husbands and partners. Polly said, "I feel so alone in this pregnancy. He's not really with me, and he's not being supportive. I think deep down, I'm afraid he's going to abandon me and the baby." She reported the following dream:

> I dreamed I was nine months pregnant, and I started to hemorrhage. There was all this blood, and I was so scared. I was in my mother's house, my childhood home, and she was screaming at me. Somehow it was my husband's fault that we were there. I don't know how that worked, but somehow he was allowing it. He was there, and he wasn't protecting me against my mother. He was accommodating her. We were trying to go to the hospital, and my mother wanted to go with us, and I didn't want that, but my husband wasn't siding with me.

This dream expressed the idea that pregnancy forces a woman to return to her "mother's house," a frightening confrontation with the powerful pre-Oedipal mother of the internal triangle, and this confrontation is the fault of the man who impregnated her.

Not surprisingly then, dreams of killing men and boy babies are common in pregnancy and highlight the fact that pregnancy tends to heighten aggression toward men. A common thought verbalized among pregnant women is, "I don't need a man in my life now. I've got the baby, and that's all I need." The discharge of this aggression into language can have a very beneficial effect on the progression of pregnancy, but not to a marriage or to a woman's relationship to all the important men in her life. An all-women's group of pregnant women can provide a safe environment to discharge the anger (Holmes, 2000b).

A menopausal group

A group composed of women in their late forties and early fifties amazed me by never talking about menopause. For the first two years of the group's life, menopause seemed to be a taboo subject, and I wondered why it was never approached, since I was sure most of the women in the group were dealing with physical and emotional symptoms of the climacteric. Ruth was the first member to muster the courage to talk about this difficult subject. She had been on a trip to Alaska with her adolescent daughter, and they had fought bitterly. Ruth's daughter had constantly criticized Ruth on the vacation, and Ruth said, "I understand that she's an adolescent, and usually I can be understanding, but lately I feel like I'm going mad. I have hot flashes and insomnia, and when you are sleep-deprived, it's hard to feel motherly or understanding." Ruth expressed guilt about talking about her difficulties to the group. I said, "What do you mean? You're supposed to say everything here." Through her tears, Ruth said,

> It's so wonderful to hear that. I can't talk about these things to men, because it's not sexy to be menopausal, and I'm afraid they'll think of me as an old hag and turn their attention to all the beautiful younger women who seem to be everywhere these days. I can't talk about it with my children, because it will just bore them – or worse, scare them that their mother is going to get old and die. I feel like I remind everyone, including myself, of death. Even my best friend is no help. She won't even admit she's in menopause. She's just dealing with it with this rigid denial, and I feel so alone.

Ruth's honesty freed the rest of the group to begin speaking and suddenly, everyone was talking about the physical and emotional challenges they faced in this change of life. Alice, a very beautiful woman, talked about the narcissistic injury of watching your beauty fade, "I didn't realize what power there is in being beautiful until I began to lose that beauty." Edna, who had always considered herself "ugly," comforted Alice by saying,

> I've never been beautiful, so I never knew that power. That's probably why I went to medical school and cultivated my intellect. And you can do that too, Alice. The fading of your beauty may force you to find other sources of power – like brains and wisdom.

Several women expressed the idea that the grief and fear that menopause induces made them feel like a "burden" to everyone. But as they became freer to discuss their most painful thoughts, these feelings changed. Edna said to Ruth,

> You may feel like a burden to yourself, but you don't feel like a burden to me. In fact, listening to you makes me realize that maybe I'm not the burden I thought I was. Maybe I could risk talking to my husband about some of this. God knows I need his love and support right now. I've just been afraid I would be too much for him.

These middle-aged women were able to use their feminine tendency to identify to strengthen each other. They could say to each other, "Oh, I've felt just like that. I understand." Because of the female tendency to willingly take the object in, projective identifications between group members were very fluid and playful, and often, those projective identifications were articulated, transformed, and given back to the projector for recognition and reintegration into the self. "You don't have to defend and explain yourself to me," Alice said to Edna, "I'm not your critical mother, you know."

The women learned to separate and disidentify with some of the more painful feelings in a way that was even more helpful than their empathy for each other. Betty said, "I feel like a witch, I cry like a maniac, and I look like a cow. All I want to do is withdraw." Edna said,

I've felt like that too. But it's so interesting to me to be able to totally identify with what you're saying and also realize that you *don't* look like a witch, a maniac, *or* a cow to me. So maybe that means I can feel all those things about myself and still remember that I may not *be* all the things I feel. Maybe they're just feelings.

Because the women in this group could use each other in a variety of ways, both as an internal object and as an intersubjective other, their ego identities became strengthened and enriched.

Women in the pregnancy group described pregnancy as a "special club," and indeed there was a sense of exclusiveness and sanctity about the circle of women about to give birth, a conviction that no one but another pregnant woman could truly understand what they were experiencing. A member of the menopausal group laughingly called the group "a coven of witches huddled around the cauldron stirring our herbs and potions." Another member corrected her, "Not witches – wise women." An all-women's group during these challenging times in a woman's biological life can provide a safe space; indeed, these groups may be the only place that a woman can "say everything."

Women in mixed-gender groups

Critics of single-sex groups argue that the world is heterosexual and limiting group psychotherapy to one sex or the other is a resistance. The debate about single-sex versus mixed-gender groups is a lively one, with both sides energetically advocating for their position. This controversy mirrors a similar one in the field of education regarding girls schools versus coeducation. Recent researchers have described the impact of gender on educational experience and career aspirations. Gilligan et al. (1989, p. 4) discussed the drop in self-esteem that occurs in preadolescent girls when they come up against "the wall of Western culture." A 1991 nationwide poll of students (American Association of University Women, 1991) found that girls are systematically, if unconsciously, discouraged from a variety of pursuits, particularly math and science. However, a comprehensive survey of graduates of all-girls schools found that a girls school education gives young women a significant edge over their peers in all facets of life. Compared to women in the general population, a much higher percentage of these women go on to college and graduate school, and a striking percentage of women who have attained PhD degrees are graduates of single-sex schools. More importantly, the young women polled reported experiencing no drop in self-esteem at the time that Gilligan et al. described (Orenstein, 1994).

Though enrollment at all-girls schools is at an all-time high, mixed-gender schools still argue that sending a girl to a single-sex school is denying the fact that girls must learn to live and cope in the real, mixed-gender world. Many educators have taken steps to ensure that girls receive equitable treatment in mixed-gender schools, and they argue that this kind of educational reform will ultimately be in the best interests of women. Still many parents are not convinced. One staunch advocate of all-girls schools said to me,

> I am certain that my daughter is in a school in which, the president of the senior class, the winner of the science award, and the editor of the school newspaper will be girls. I don't think there are many coed schools that could say that.

The debates in education and group work will no doubt rage on, and probably choices of school or group will always best be made on an individual rather than an ideological basis. Though I have argued that for women with a certain type of character structure or a particular developmental challenge, a women's group can be meaningful and life-enhancing, women can also function very effectively in mixed-gender groups if group leaders are constantly vigilant in regarding important differences in male and female functioning. Traditionally, more masculine attributes such as self-actualization and autonomous functioning have been the most important qualities of mental health, and the ego or "I" so highly valued in psychoanalysis can sometimes dominate in a mixed-gender group. But female development occurs in the context of mutuality, and the ego or self strives to be enhanced in connection to others (Miller, 1976). The challenge in a group of both men and women is to help the men acknowledge and be comfortable with the essential need for human connection and relationship, while ensuring that women's need for connection is expressed in mutually enhancing relationship, not subservient affiliation. While men may fear entrapment and engulfment in facing mutuality, women fear aggression and the loss of relationship that may be its consequence: even success and achievement can make them feel dangerously isolated (Gilligan, 1982). One of the advantages of a mixed-gender group led by a leader sensitive to these sexual differences, is that both male and female fears can be acknowledged, discussed, and worked through.

The issue for women, whether in single-sex or mixed-gender groups, is the management of the complex world of introjected objects that is responsible for the feminine tendency toward empathy and intuition. This talent for identification, which can often become compulsive, is a woman's greatest strength and biggest problem. The challenge in any setting is to use her ability to connect with others in the service of her own ego and to develop the courage to verbalize her healthy aggression when identification and connection threaten to become oppressive. A useful technique in meeting this challenge is to encourage women to think about and express what they feel *toward* other group members, rather than what they feel *with* them. Often when encouraged in this way, women will discover that they have a negative feeling toward the person with whom they are in complete and compulsive identification. The expression of this negative feeling in words is the triumph of the self over the introjected object and can free a woman from the tyranny of her internal world. This triumph should be an important goal for both women's groups and women in groups.

References

American Association of University Women. (1991). *Shortchanging girls, shortchanging America*. Washington, DC: American Association of University Women.

Bibring, G.L., Dwyer, T.F., Huntington, D.S., and Valenstein, A.F. (1961). "A Study of Psychological Processes in Pregnancy and of the Earliest Mother–Child Relationship." *Psychoanalytic Study of the Child*, 16(1), 9–72.

Bollas, C. (1992). *Being a Character*. New York: Hill and Wang.

Chodorow, N. (1978). *The Reproduction of Mothering: Psychoanalysis and the Sociology of Gender*. Berkeley: University of California Press.

de Beauvoir, S. (1952). *The Second Sex*. New York: Alfred A. Knopf.

Freud, S. (1925). "Some Psychical Consequences of the Anatomical Distinction between the Sexes." *Standard Edition*, Volume 19. London: Hogarth Press, 243–260.

Gilligan, C. (1982). *In a Different Voice*. Cambridge: Harvard University Press.

Gilligan, C., Lyons, N.P., and Hanmer, T.J. (eds). (1989). *Making Connections: The Relational World of Adolescent Girls at Emma Willard School*. Cambridge: Harvard University Press.

Holmes, L. (2000a). "The Internal Triangle: New Theories of Female Development." *Modern Psychoanalysis*, 25, 207–226.

Holmes, L. (2000b)."The Object Within: Childbirth as a Developmental Milestone." *Modern Psychoanalysis*, 25, 109–134.

Miller, J.B. (1976). *Toward a New Psychology of Women*. Boston: Beacon Press.

Orenstein, P. (1994). *Schoolgirls: Young Women, Self-esteem, and the Confidence gap*. New York: Doubleday Publishing.

Ormont, L.R. (1990). "The Craft of Bridging." *International Journal of Group Psychotherapy*, 40(1), 5–30.

Ormont, L.R. (1991). *The Group Therapy Experience*. New York: St. Martin's Press.

Chapter 5

Hell hath no fury
How women get even

Getting even, if done correctly, is one of life's greatest pleasures. An important goal for any analysis is to help the patient get even in ways that give her satisfaction and don't land her in jail or in the back ward of a psychiatric hospital. Although all human beings savor revenge, most, unfortunately, seek it with unconscious and primitive methods that cause them as much suffering as the objects they are out to get. Beginning analysis can often be the first step toward constructive retribution, but as we know, it is an arduous, often painful process that requires courage and fortitude. The best revenge takes time and patience, but in psychoanalysis we begin the first time we come to the analyst's office to report the crime.

When thinking about getting even, my mind, of course, goes to women and the ways they choose to get even. I have a great interest in female development and psychology. This is my own revenge on my Texas family where women were supposed to be quiet and decorative and always select the wing when the chicken was passed. I have been getting even for almost 20 years by leading women's groups and encouraging women to *talk*.

Before I discuss my thoughts about female revenge, I want to emphasize that what I will describe to you are trends, not absolutes. Talking about masculinity and femininity in value-laden or absolute language is ubiquitous but overly simplistic. Much of what has been written about female psychology in the last 30 years has been burdened with that old adage of woman as victim and man as oppressor, and really this idea is insulting to both men and women because all of us are much more complex and creative than some radical feminists would like to paint us. Also, there are plenty of "masculine" women and "feminine" men in the world, so I hope you will take what I have to say as one analyst's report of some themes she hears over and over when her female patients are trying to get even.

When I think about the women I have listened to in the treatment room, three ways of seeking revenge emerge as favored female methods: women suffer, they seduce, and they repeat through identification. I have known several gifted women who have been able to do all three at once. Although there is enormous secondary gain in each of these methods, they all have major drawbacks to the patient, which I will discuss. I approach this topic with some humility since it requires revealing some of my less stellar moments as an analyst.

Suffering is probably the least satisfying and most self-destructive way a woman can get even, but it is very popular, and I think it is safe to say that it is more common among women than men, except perhaps in cases of schizophrenia. The degree of female suffering is widely variable. One of my female patients is married to a very wealthy and very controlling man who dotes on her by buying her beautiful clothes and jewelry, taking her on trips, and constantly redecorating their house in the Caribbean and their New York apartment. All of this makes his wife miserable. She is tired, bored, and listless. The husband, a retired businessman, has boundless energy. He wants to go to parties every night. He wants to go to China, India, and South America. My patient is tortured by this. Her favorite pastime is lying in bed reading women's magazines. She needs a lot of sleep. Her husband brings home Valentino suits. She weeps in response, worrying about money. He forces her to make dinner dates with other couples every night of the week, but she thwarts him by arguing with or insulting the women and coquettishly confessing to the men that her husband won't have sex with her. As you can imagine, their social dance card is getting shorter and shorter, which tortures the husband. In fact, these two have spent almost 40 years of their married life torturing each other. But here's the thing: my patient's suffering seems to be winning the battle over her husband's control because the husband is getting sicker and sicker, and now the wife is afraid he is going to die. Is this a wish, the final triumph of her revenge? Or is she genuinely afraid that he will die, and she will lose the object she has been enjoying getting even with all these years? I suspect that if she does manage to kill him with her suffering, she is going to get very depressed, despite her triumph.

This woman gets even with me by never making any progress. I find that, just like her controlling husband, I have plans for her. I want her to have a better marriage and get out of bed in the morning. Her refusal to go along with these plans tortures me. In the eighth year of treatment she told me, "The problem is my husband, and I am not going to get rid of him, so there's nothing you can do about any of this. You're stuck, and I'm stuck." I said, "Okay then – I guess all we're going to do is talk."

Of course, you're probably thinking, "We should all suffer like this woman," and if you are thinking that, you have a point. But on the other hand, I know she would get much more pleasure out of life if she gave up her aggressive suffering and followed my plans for her. I want her to torture her husband by going back to school and finding some friends where the relationship is not based on who has the largest diamond ring. I would like her to be an analyst like me. She's not going to do any of this because it is too much fun to torture me for wanting to control her, just like that lousy husband of hers.

Revengeful suffering can be pretty gruesome. Some women are willing to destroy their lives just to show the world what horrible mothers and analysts they have had to endure. I have worked for 20 years with a woman who arrives 20 minutes late for each session. She comes in and spends the next 20 minutes berating herself for never being able to get anywhere on time. In the first few years of treatment, she lost job after job because of this behavior, going from working as a copy editor at a newspaper to a job as a cleaning lady. She lost her apartment and had to move into a single-room occupancy hotel (SRO). All the while, she was spending her 30-minute session beating her breast about how defective she was. I told her the problem was not her. The problem was she had a defective analyst. When she tortured me by telling me what a failure she was, I told her we were a perfect match because I was a total failure as an analyst.

In the fifth year of treatment, the patient started talking about suicide. At this point, I was feeling pretty suicidal myself. I was fairly new at analyzing patients then, and I was ready to give it all up and jump out the window, so I went to supervision. My supervisor told me to tell this woman that she shouldn't kill herself. She should kill me because I was the problem. I followed my supervisor's advice, and I noticed that it worked pretty well. My patient reassured me that she could never contemplate murdering me, but she seemed rather pleased with the idea, and she began to get better. She got a job as a companion to a rich old man who fell in love with her and wanted to marry her. He moved her out of the dreary old SRO into a nice sunny studio and took her to Europe. She refused his offer of marriage, but she managed to keep this job for three years and get herself out of debt.

So, I decided to raise her fee by five dollars. When I told her, she said, "Well, I guess it's okay. Things have been going better for me, and you've never raised my fee before." But soon my patient was arguing with the old man. He was getting unbearably crabby because she was arriving two hours late to take him to the movies. After a few weeks of this, he threw her out, fired her as his companion, and stopped paying her rent. Back she went to the SRO, but worse than that, she stopped paying me. We talked at length about what was going on and when she was planning to bring me some money. But when her bill reached $1,000, I told her we were going to have to take a break until she could pay what she owed. I tortured myself for months about how I failed this woman. I thought about giving up the idea of being a psychoanalyst. I also contemplated downsizing my apartment since I couldn't even get people to pay me. My only consolation was that I fully believed that I would never see the patient, let alone her money, again.

Two years went by, and to my surprise I got a $1,000 check from my patient, followed by a phone call. She wanted to come back into analysis. With misgivings, I agreed. She came to my office and told me that since she left analysis, her life had been wonderful. She gave all the credit for this transformation to me. While she had been away, I had been constantly on her mind. Psychoanalysis was responsible for the fact that she now had a good job as a proofreader and could afford to pay her own rent on a sunny studio. She wanted to resume the analysis because she wanted a relationship with a man.

Since then, the patient has been getting even with me by engaging in anonymous and masochistic one-night stands. I have been tortured by this. Not only am I a terrible analyst, but I may be responsible for her death from AIDS. The only time she has managed to have a fairly constructive relationship with a man was the time we had to take another break in the treatment because of an unpaid bill. It seems this woman can only prosper when she is away from me. I have pointed this out to her and asked if perhaps I am the wrong analyst for her. She insists that I am the perfect analyst for her.

Lately, I have been asking my patient how she would like me to feel about her sexual activities. The thought that I would have feelings about her life is entirely novel to her. It will be interesting to see if she will have to leave me again to have a more productive sexual relationship. I suspect she will since it would give me too much pleasure to know she has stopped being promiscuous.

I think we've suffered enough with suffering. Let's look at seduction, another favorite female method of getting revenge. Seduction is much more fun than suffering, and it is highly effective as a form of revenge. The personal cost of seduction is not as high as suffering though there is still a cost. Women have been using seduction to destroy the object long before the Lorelei lured sailors to their death, but seduction as a dynamic in analysis has certain characteristics. The patient is usually, though not always, physically attractive. There is always an idealized transference to the analyst. The patient needs protection, she presents herself as extraordinarily vulnerable and delicate. She needs saving, and the analyst gets the idea that she can and should be a savior. My problem with patients like this has been that I love them too much, and when I love them too much, they always kill me off. In supervision when I talk about a countertransference of excessive worry, concern, or nameless longings, my supervisor always has to remind me that the sweet young thing on my couch is a potential murderer.

Let me tell you about Eve. Eve is a ballet dancer. When she came for a consultation, the first thing she said to me was, "Seven people are in love with me." I could see why. She was beautiful, delicate, and angelic looking. She was also full of feeling and very articulate. She cried easily. I wanted to take care of Eve, and she gave me the idea that I was perfect for the job. She called me a "wise woman" and a "goddess." She wrote a lovely poem about me and brought it to her session. She said that analysis was going to save her life.

Eve had a very sad history. Her father was an alcoholic and her mother was a heroin addict. She had been raped by a friend of her father's when she was 15 years old. I longed to be her good-enough mother. Eve dreamed and reported her dreams frequently. I always found them rather beautiful. She dreamed her father had taken her room from her. He took all her books and pictures from the shelves and filled them with bottles of alcohol. She looked for her diary and realized that her mother had stolen it. Her mother was there and said, "I didn't steal it. It's mine. Your thoughts and dreams belong to me." In another dream, Eve and her female roommate, to whom she said she felt sexually attracted, were swept away in a tidal wave. The wave threw Eve down and broke every bone in her body. A fireman, who was big and strong but like a robot, tied a rope around her ankles and rescued her by pulling her out. She wanted to have sex with him, but when she tried to embrace him, she couldn't move. Another man was there watching.

One day in the second year of her analysis, Eve came in and told me that she had gotten a job touring with a ballet company for the summer. She was going to take a three-month break from treatment. I suggested that we have phone sessions while she was away, but she refused. She couldn't even consider the idea; her mind was already on the road, and she had shed me and the analysis as easily as a butterfly sheds its cocoon. And so, she left. While she was away, I missed her terribly. I worried about her excessively. I received one letter, telling me how much she missed me and recounting what she was experiencing with the charm of Scheherazade and her Arabian tales.

One day after her return to analysis, Eve came in to tell me that she had had a very unsettling dream. She had dreamed that she and I had sex. She said, "I'm not a homosexual. How could I dream such a thing?" I said, "What's wrong with that dream?" Eve began to weep. She said, "I guess I'm so ashamed because the truth is I do love you and would like to have sex with you." What I said next was one of the big mistakes of my analytic career – a good intervention but about 30 years too soon. I said, "That's a nice fantasy."

There was a long silence. Then Eve sat up on the couch with a look on her face that truly frightened me. She appeared psychotic, sexual, and murderous. In that moment, I felt completely scared of her. She looked at me through lowered lids and said, "What are you trying to do to me?" I said, "What is it?" She said, "What are you trying to do to me? Do you want to sleep with me?" I said, "All we're going to do here is talk." She said, "What do you think I am, some kind of pervert?" I think I then said something intelligent like, "What do you mean?" Eve stood up and said, "I have to get out of here." I said, "The session is not over." She said, "I have to get out of here. You're trying to turn me into a lesbian." I said, "I think we need to talk about this. All we're going to do is talk, right?" She said, "I know what you're up to." I said, "What is it?" She said, "What they're all up to, that's what. I have to go." And she left.

I never saw Eve again. She never answered my calls. I was never able to get her on the phone. I wrote a letter telling her I thought the treatment had reached a crucial place and invited her in to talk. She never responded. For months, I tortured myself. I was a lousy analyst. Eve should sue me for malpractice. I was responsible for making her psychotic. My heart was broken.

Eve has gone on to become rather famous. I frequently read about her in the arts section of the *New York Times*. I'm sure she is still breaking hearts.

The problem with seduction as a way to get even is that it makes for a rather arid life. These sexy women are rarely sexual. All libido goes into being lovable to the object, and there is really no energy left to love. I once heard that babies need to be loved, but for adults a happy and meaningful life comes not from being loved, but from loving. The older I get, the more I realize this is true, though I might add that it helps to love people who aren't too invested in killing you off. Seductive people are in reality imprisoned by their own narcissism, and they get old very ungracefully, which I guess is our revenge on them.

Now I want to move to what I consider the most fascinating and creative way that women get even, and that is by identifying with the object. One of the things I have observed in my research with women is that because of the challenges of being female, women are inclined to internalize parental imagoes, both mother and father, very vividly. The internalization of the pre-Oedipal mother tends to be an oral pre-identification in which the mother is ingested with her milk, what Freud called a primary identification. The internalization of the father during the Oedipal period is more involved in that a relationship, as well as a mental representation of the object, is introjected (Holmes, 2000). Women use these parental imagoes in all sorts of interesting ways, but one of the most useful ones is to express aggression more or less unconsciously. Let me tell you about a woman who used her unconscious identification with her parental imagoes not only to get even with me, but also to try to destroy my group.

Heidi came to my office because she had heard that I ran women's groups. She had just left a group led by a man with whom she was very angry. She had decided that she needed to be in an all-female environment. Heidi had a rather lurid history. Her father, a prominent psychiatrist in Denmark, had had sex with each of Heidi's four sisters. Heidi was the only child who had been spared this treatment, and Heidi reported that this was because she was the youngest of the five daughters, and her mother had sent her father the unconscious message: "Don't you touch this one. She belongs to me."

Heidi idealized her mother. Despite the fact that Heidi's mother had never believed her when she tried to tell her about the incest that was going on right under her nose, Heidi described her as a "saint who bore everything with dignity." Heidi grew up in a house of secrets. Her sisters tearfully begged Heidi not to tell or talk. They were afraid their father would kill them all. When teenage Heidi tried to confront her father, he vehemently denied any wrongdoing and told her she was crazy. Heidi said, "I was the only one who knew everything. I held all the secrets."

At first, Heidi seemed to love the group. She talked about how liberating it was to know, for the first time, that she could really feel and say everything. Heidi had a very volatile temperament. She could easily fly into a rage if any other member of the group provoked her. Though she could be frightening, I felt Heidi needed protection when she was this angry, and I always tried to direct her anger at me. When I added a new member to the group, Heidi assaulted her. I said, "Listen, Heidi, you shouldn't be mad at Jennifer. You should be mad at me. I'm the one who added a new member." Heidi turned to me and said. "You! I'd like to cut out your uterus." Other members of the group expressed horror at this idea, but I said, "What do you mean? That's a very creative image. How should a child feel when a mother has a new baby?" This seemed to make Heidi feel very safe for a while. She told me how wonderful it was to finally have a therapist who wasn't afraid of her anger. She relished telling me she would like to "cut my tongue out" when I said something that annoyed her. She realized for the first time that she had other feelings toward the mother she had idealized and protected in her dangerous family.

At first, Heidi had no problem with me. Her problem was with the other women. Heidi managed to isolate herself from the group by frightening most of the other members with her rages. Until Heidi had arrived, this had been a group that had a fairly entrenched resistance that expressed itself in a compulsion to be "helpful" and in a denial that any aggression existed at all. Heidi, of course, flew in the face of this resistance, and suddenly I had a management problem on my hands. When Heidi expressed rage toward me, the other members rushed to protect me, and they worked hard to make Heidi feel guilty. They told her she was "too angry," that she was using anger to defend herself against other feelings. Though probably true, these interpretations induced even more rage in Heidi. She began to feel that, like her mother, I couldn't protect her. She saw herself as the "container for the truth" in the group. The other members and I were in a conspiracy against her.

Then I made another mistake that cost me dearly. I put a new member into this group without adequate preparation. A psychiatrist and friend of mine, a woman I trusted, sent me a referral, Angela, who she said would be wonderful for my group. Angela was articulate, a poet, and mother to a new baby girl. The psychiatrist had worked with her for several years. Angela had decided she wanted a group, and so she was sent to me. I interviewed Angela once, and she did seem perfect for my group. The group needed new members, so I put her right in.

Angela arrived for her first group. She told everyone about her poetry and her new baby girl, and then she said, "I'm planning to end my life this week." There was a long, astonished silence, which I broke by asking, "Do you have a plan for ending your life?" Angela said yes, indeed she did. She said, "I have a bottle of sleeping pills and a quart of vodka, and Friday night when my husband and daughter go to temple, I'm going to kill myself."

As you can imagine, most of the rest of the group was spent trying to save Angela from herself. I felt like a suicide bomber had come into my office and was threatening to blow us all up. I felt scared and very angry. I asked Angela if we could have a contract that she would hold off on her suicide and agree to come back to group next week. She said she couldn't be sure she could promise that.

And sure enough, on Saturday morning, I got a call from Angela. She said, "I won't be able to make group on Tuesday night. I'm in intensive care. I tried to kill myself on Friday night, but I didn't succeed. I'll be back to group a week from Tuesday. Tell everyone I said 'hi'!"

The next group was very lively indeed. When I announced that Angela had made an unsuccessful suicide attempt and would see us all next week, most of the group were furious. Happily, this event seemed to resolve the group resistance to aggression. All these lovely, polite women were furious with me. One said, "How dare you do this to us? How could you put someone in here who is suicidal? I feel like you tried to murder us all by putting Angela in this group."

Interestingly, Heidi, the usual container for the aggression, had another reaction. She burst into tears and said, "Oh, poor Angela! I loved her. She was wonderful. She's a person who's comfortable with primitive feelings. I felt we were soul mates. What hospital is she in? I want to call her and tell her to come back as soon as she can."

Janet, another member of the group, said, "What! No way is she coming back! I don't want her here. She's a killer." Beth said, "If she wants to kill herself, I wish she could at least be good at it." Beth was immediately chastised for this remark by some of the more upstanding members of the group, but Emily supported Beth. She said, "I'm furious at Angela, and there's a part of me that wishes she had succeeded." Heidi said, "How can you say that? Angela needs help, and we can help her. My sister tried to kill herself when my father raped her. Have a heart. Have some compassion!"

The rest of the group was devoted to the question: should I allow Angela to come back to the group? I was reluctant to agree to this. At one point, Heidi turned to me and said, "You seem so angry at Angela, Lucy." I said, "How should I feel about suicide? Should I be pleased?"

In the end, Heidi was so assertive in her insistence that the group could help Angela and that we couldn't abandon her, that it was agreed that Angela could come back. And she did. The next week she told the group that her suicide attempt had been an epiphany, a turning point in her life. She had acted out her mother's wish to destroy her, and now she realized she wanted to live. She wanted to make a commitment to the group.

Heidi was jubilant. She said, "I am so glad. I feel so close to you. I feel at last I have a companion who understands my primitive feelings. I know we can help each other, and you shouldn't worry about what Beth and Emily said about you." Angela said, "What did they say about me?" Heidi said, "Oh, nothing. It isn't important. What's important is that you're here."

But Angela was not to be deterred. She turned to Beth and Emily and asked, "What did you say about me?" Emily and Beth were both very flustered. They told Angela they couldn't remember what they had said, only that they had been very upset at her suicide attempt. Angela turned again to Heidi, "Tell me what they said." Heidi said, "They may not remember, but

I know the truth. I know what they said about you, but I can't tell. It's too painful. I'm afraid you'll use it to attack yourself."

So now we had an interesting dynamic. Heidi knew the "truth" about the other women, but it was too painful to reveal. This situation played itself out over several weeks. Angela wanted to know Heidi's secret. She put pressure on all of us to reveal the secret. Emily and Beth continued to assert that they couldn't even remember what they said and that it wasn't important. I tried to explore with Angela why it was so important that we reconstruct the session she had missed.

Angela said she couldn't stay in a group where people said bad things about her. I asked her if it would be all right if people didn't have good feelings about her suicide attempt. She said maybe so, but the feeling she wanted to induce in the group was concern. Heidi said, "Concern. Ha!"

And so, we arrived at the climax of this little drama. Angela came into group one night and confronted Heidi. She said, "I want you to tell me what was said about me in the week that I was away." I intervened and said, "Are we going to take Heidi's version of what was said or Emily and Beth's version of what was said as the truth?"

Heidi turned on me in a rage, "I know the truth. You may want to protect Emily and Beth and yourself, but I know the truth. Don't try to tell me I don't. Emily and Beth said they wished Angela had succeeded in killing herself, and Lucy agreed!" Emily said, "Oh, I don't think I said that. That doesn't sound like me. That's just not my style."

Heidi turned on Emily, "How dare you! My memory is excellent! I never forget anything that was said." I asked, "And what if others have a different memory?" Heidi said, "They may choose to forget, but I know I remember accurately. I can't help it if others can't face the truth." I turned to Angela and said, "Heidi's reality is the one true reality here." Heidi said, "I don't appreciate your sarcasm, Lucy. And that isn't all, Angela. Lucy said you are a big fat pig who monopolized the conversation." At this point, I lost it. "I absolutely refute that!" I yelled. Heidi stood up and said, "How dare you call me a liar." I invited her to sit down. Emily said, "There's something toxic in this room, and it's dangerous because it's indirect. You may be the container for the truth, Heidi, but I feel you want to sit back while we all murder each other."

Though I was shaking, I stood up to end the session and said, "This was a lively group. There were lots of angry feelings, and everyone did a great job of putting them into words."

Suicidal Angela went on to have many more productive sessions in the group. She became much less depressed and finally left the group after the birth of her second child. Heidi, however, did not fare so well. She came back to the group for a few more sessions but said, "I am exhausted by my own anger. I have turned this group into my original family, and I cannot stay."

Though I told her that the problem was mine, that I, like her mother, had not wanted to hear the truth and had not protected her from the other members of the family, Heidi seemed worn out and defeated. She left the group.

But the story is not over. A few months later, one of the members of this group came in and made a guilty confession. "I had dinner with Heidi last night. I know it's against the rules, but she's been calling me since she left, wanting to be my friend and go to the movies. Finally, I agreed to go out to dinner, and we had a wonderful time!"

Beth said, "That's funny. Heidi's been calling me too. I told her the group contract is no outside contact, but she said she's no longer a member of the group, so the rule doesn't apply to her. So far, I've resisted."

Another member said, "Well, I didn't. I did go to the movies with Heidi. I felt so guilty about it that I didn't dare bring it up, but since it's on the table…"

Emily said, "I can't believe this. Heidi's been calling me too. She said Lucy's rule is ridiculous, and anyway, a friendship is more meaningful than the group is."

A discussion followed about whether or not my rule was ridiculous. I said, "Should I modify the rule? Perhaps I should say it's okay to have dinner, but no sex. Or maybe sex is okay too. What do you think, Emily? Should we all have sex with Heidi? Or should everyone but me have sex with Heidi? I guess I won't be able to have sex with her since I'm the only one she hasn't contacted."

Angela said, "That's not true. She hasn't contacted me." Emily said, "Maybe that's because you're her soul mate." I said, "What do you say Beth? Should Heidi have sex with everyone but me and Angela? What do you think she's trying to communicate to us?"

The group was able to work this through, and it was finally agreed that the members would adhere to my rule and suggest to Heidi that if she wanted contact, she should come back to the group. Heidi never called to ask to return, but I did hear from her recently, right after this 12-year-old group ended. A few weeks after the group agreed to disband, Heidi called, saying, "I heard your group ended. You must be very sad." I said, "On the contrary. I feel very satisfied that the group was able to survive for 12 years, and that I learned so much from all of you." Heidi said, "Well, I just wanted you to know that I think it's too bad that it fell apart."

In the years I have practiced analysis, I have seen many women act out their rage in unconscious identification with one parent or the other, but I think it is safe to say that Heidi was the most dramatic example. Not only did she arrange to repeat her original family dynamic in the group with me cast as the consciously adored and unconsciously reviled mother, but she was also able to morph into her incestuous father and show me how it felt to be the only one who wasn't chosen.

In conclusion, I want to assure you that I have had some success in helping women seek revenge in more constructive ways. I think of the schizophrenic who is now a rather brilliant schoolteacher. Sorry to say, her mother is dead, but I'm sure she'd be disappointed. Then I worked with a woman who was jilted by her husband and suicidal when she came into treatment. She is now happily remarried to a much richer and much younger husband and has had the pleasure of watching her ex-husband go through three more marriages. A woman who spent most of her life acting like a Barbie doll in unconscious compliance with her father who thought of her as, and I quote, "a sexy little birdbrain" has recently finished her doctorate. I guess the difference with these cases was the evolution of the transference. These success stories were able to give up the pleasure of destroying the object. Self-enhancement as a form of revenge then became an enticing alternative. Cure, after all, is the ultimate revenge.

Reference

Holmes, L. (2000). "The Internal Triangle: New theories of female development." *Modern Psychoanalysis*, 25, 207–226.

Chapter 6

Masculine and feminine
Differentiation and integration

Freud (1912, p. 189) famously said that "anatomy is destiny," and according to the great man, if your destiny is not to have a penis, you are out of luck. Freud (1905) believed that little children of both sexes have the theory that there is one genital, and that genital is male. This is because they can see the penis and the clitoris, but the ovaries and womb are invisible. Children react to this fact by assuming that the boy's penis is bigger and better, and that the girl functions as a "little man." Freud (1932) thought that the little girl's symbolic castration had all sorts of unpleasant consequences: she was never really able to get over her Oedipal conflict; her superego was anemic; and most horrible of all, she had no real capacity to love since all her energy was focused on being loved. No wonder then that feminists in the 1970s took aim at Freud as a destructive and misguided male chauvinist pig. I can remember that as a young student at the Center for Modern Psychoanalytic Studies back in the 1980s, I balked at the concept of penis envy. Eventually, I had to reluctantly accept the idea. My change of heart came about through examining my own penis envy in my analysis and also in the observation of my daughter, who came home from nursery school one day dismal and outraged. "Mom," she said, "James can pee standing up." I said, "Yes, but you get to wear panties with ruffles on them." She thought about that and then shook her head sadly, "It's not enough," she said.

And indeed, it isn't. The penis gives the male sex all sorts of advantages. One of the most important of those advantages is that the penis helps little boys separate from the original pre-Oedipal mother – that engulfing and omnipotent figure that all human beings must free themselves from if they are to mature and become independent (Chodorow, 1978). The penis is manifest evidence that "I am not my mother," and is enormously useful in helping boys to escape from the merged symbiosis of the pre-Oedipal period. The boy clearly has something that the mother does not, and when his Oedipal conflict is resolved, he can use his identification with his father to devalue and deny any identification at all with his mother. Freud (1925, p. 257) stated that the Oedipal conflict in boys is "literally smashed to pieces." What is totally obliterated in boys is the maternal introject that was incorporated with the mother's milk in the pre-Oedipal period. At the end of the boy's Oedipal period, "I do not desire my mother" often becomes "I am nothing like my mother and cannot identify with her in any way." This idea promotes a dualistic way of thinking, with man as the subject and woman as the object. Now, for boys, there is an "I" and an "it" (Wilbur, 2000, pp. 110–111). This dynamic is responsible for ways of thinking that we associate with masculinity. It means that a tendency toward male chauvinism and the domination of women is born anew in each male human being. This is a dynamic that feminists need to understand in their attempts to liberate women. The oppression of women is cultural in many ways, but in a far deeper and more important way, it is set up in the human psyche very early in life. We all, men and women, have an unconscious impulse to control and subordinate the female sex because our first object in this world is a powerful woman who can feed us or let us die. We all have to find our own ways to subdue and control this loved and hated figure, and boys and girls find different solutions to this universal problem. I will discuss the female solution later, but first I want to emphasize that the male solution has some positive as well as negative aspects. The dualism set up by forever seeing self as subject and woman as object gives men a strong sense of right and wrong, a clearheaded, logical way of thinking that is less tainted with the primitive emotions associated with the pre-Oedipal period and a strong investment in the healthy phallic energy that built the Taj Mahal and invented the airplane.

Freud (1924) thought that girls never really get over their penis deficiency and that their symbolic castration is the focal point of female development and female pathology. He even thought that the feminine desire for a baby was only a disguised wish for a penis.

When I went through pregnancy and childbirth, particularly when the birth experience wasn't obliterated by becoming a medical rather than a spiritual event, I felt in some ways that I had grown my own penis. I felt very empowered. And I had the idea, just a murky intuition at first, that childbirth had changed my mind. By that I mean that I came out of the experience with a different psyche from the one I had coming into it. I began to believe that, like adolescence, childbirth is a developmental milestone for women. As a result, I decided to study pregnancy and childbirth in my doctoral work. For two years, I ran two psychotherapy groups for women. These groups consisted of pregnant women or women for whom pregnancy was a burning issue; that is, they desperately wanted a baby and were having trouble conceiving, or they were approaching their fortieth birthday and realizing that delaying having a child would soon mean they would never have one. For two years, I studied these women. One of the most striking things I observed was the number of ghosts in the room. When you sit with a pregnant woman, she is there, but so is her mother, father, and fetus. Women consistently experienced pregnancy as "becoming my mother," and if this idea was too repellent, they were often infertile. If a woman had made a stronger identification with her father than with her mother, she often verbalized ambivalence about pregnancy, or sometimes expressed a conscious refusal to consider bearing a child. If a woman was already pregnant, her fetus was definitely there in the room too, usually as an object of projection. The unborn baby was alternately experienced as like another object in a woman's life – mother, father, or perhaps partner – or it was experienced as an aspect of the self. If a parent had been perceived as ruthless or parasitic, the fetus was often experienced as feeding on its mother in a way that would destroy her. If a woman suffered from a lack of self-esteem, she frequently was convinced that her baby was defective or deformed, like the devalued self. When the unborn baby was the object of love from the mother, it was seen as the mother's own best self, her ego-ideal.

Bollas (1992, p. 56) wrote about "the ghosts within us," the internal objects that influence us. He described these internal objects as *"highly condensed psychic textures*, the trace of our encounters with the object world" (1992, p. 59). Listening to the themes played out in different ways in the minds of the women I worked with, I began to speculate that there is a strong tendency in women to internalize their parents. All these women in their own unique way seemed to be dealing on a fantasy level with an internal triangle of mother, father, and self. I also noticed that often the self, the woman's own ego, seemed to be oppressed by the fantasies surrounding the internal mother and father. I listened over and over as a drama involving these three intrapsychic characters unfolded within each woman according to her own unique script. I observed, as well, that the object within, the unborn baby, became the receptacle for all the projected fantasies involved in this script. A woman who described her dominating father as "a male chauvinist pig" was told by the doctors that her baby was a boy. She became obsessed with the idea that this baby was going to control and dominate her life, destroy her career, and turn her into a housewife. She had projected her father's attributes onto her unborn baby. Another woman, whose mother had gotten her addicted to crack cocaine when she was 13, was pregnant with her seventh child. She was able to stay away from drugs only when she was pregnant and nursing, and she was terrified because she had been diagnosed with lupus, and her obstetrician had told her that this must be her last pregnancy. "My babies protect me. I can be good when I'm pregnant," she explained. She had projected a good and protecting mother onto each unborn baby, and that fantasy had enabled her to be drug-free.

These projected fantasies were consistently present in the pregnant women I worked with. Even more fascinating to me was the fact that as the women began to give birth, there was a significant shift in the internal triangle. Before giving birth, the women seemed subordinated to the internalized mother and father, but the female self gained significant ego strength in the process of birth, especially if the experience was not masked by drugs and technology. I saw again and again that enormous psychic development occurred when the fetus, so often the focus of the internal drama, was pushed out into the world.

This transition from inner fantasy to outer reality consistently gave women a sense of empowerment. The infant, the repository of so many primitive fantasies and projections, could now be seen, held, controlled, and nurtured. In this triumphant transition, the mother's ego was greatly strengthened. The new mother was able to identify with her own mother in a new way, not as the oppressed, humiliated mother who was the heir of the Oedipal conflict, but as the life-giving, omnipotent mother of the pre-Oedipal period. This, I decided, is why childbirth is truly a developmental milestone (Holmes, 2008).

It was at this point that I began to wonder why all the women I worked with demonstrated over and over the lively triangularity that inhabited their psyches. How did the internal triangle get set up? What purpose did it serve? I decided to study various authors, beginning with Freud and Klein, to see what they had to say about early female development. I was struck by the Kleinian idea that in the pre-Oedipal and Oedipal periods children, on a fantasy level, introject early objects. According to Klein (1946), this internalization serves both the life and death instincts. It is both an act of love, a wish to retain and identify with the object, and an act of hate, a wish to eat the object and destroy it. Most importantly, it is an attempt to gain control and mastery over an essentially uncontrollable object. It suddenly occurred to me that since a little girl lacks a penis that would prove she is not her mother, she can introject the mother. If she fantasizes that mommy is in her, she has both eaten her up and gained mastery over her frightening power. That is an elegant solution to a uniquely feminine problem. Boys separate by disidentifying with mother, but girls don't have that option. To separate from an object with whom she identifies, the girl incorporates the power of the mother with her milk. Mommy is now inside rather than outside, and the girl has gained enormous control. Three-year-old girls demonstrate this fantasy of "mommy in me" with their dolls and their little baby carriages, while adult women in analysis verbalize the internalized mother.

Almost all of the female patients I have worked with also demonstrate a strong identification with their fathers. This identification may be healthy or pathological, but it is undisputedly present. As I studied the writings of authors like Benjamin (1988) and Chodorow (1978) about women and their fathers, I began to think about the difficulty of the Oedipal period for the female sex. The humiliations of the Oedipal defeat are especially challenging for little girls. Both boys and girls must relinquish the desire to have sex with the parent of the opposite sex during the Oedipal period. But boys are offered a reward for the sacrifice of their incestuous wishes, an identification with phallic power where, "I, like father, have a penis, and I can control and subordinate mother." Little girls have no such bonus. Not only are they denied their father's penis and with it any hope of receiving a baby from him, they are also denied access to any identification with the penis itself, that symbol of power and autonomy. Girls find themselves truly "organless" at the end of the Oedipal period. They have no breasts, no womb with a baby in it, and no penis. In the face of this multifaceted mortification, it makes sense that the female child would again use introjection to internalize the father. She does this for the same reason that she internalized the mother: if the object is inside rather than outside, she can freely discharge libido and aggression toward it. In short, she gains control.

Though the introjection of the powerful father achieves the same thing that the earlier maternal introjection accomplished, it is not quite the same. When the female infant incorporated the mother, it was a very primitive pre-identification, a fantasy of ingesting the mother with her milk. The imago introjected was a powerful woman with protruding, life-giving breasts, not the castrated, humiliated woman of the post-Oedipal period. The introjection of the father is a more sophisticated operation, more of a true identification. The more mature and reality-oriented little girl of the post-Oedipal period internalizes not only the imago of the father, but also his feelings and behaviors. Since it is very likely that the father, because of his own difficulties becoming masculine, has an unconscious or conscious tendency to devalue women, this devaluation is internalized within the female psyche. The introjection of the father makes the internal triangle complete, but it also totally alters the fantasized imago of the mother. When the mother was originally introjected, she was a powerful object with phallic breasts. When the father arrives on the intrapsychic scene, the introjected mother is subordinated and subdued, becoming the deficient, castrated figure that Freud associated with femininity. Within the complex endopsychic world of the female mind, the father attacks the mother, and both parents unconsciously subordinate and denigrate the self. Herein lie the seeds of female masochism (Holmes, 2008).

I am convinced that my theory of the internal triangle is a good one because it explains the facts well and helps us understand all those attributes, both positive and negative, that we attribute to femininity. A triadic unconscious gives women an enormous capacity for identification, a rich inner life of imagination and intuition, and a capacity to sacrifice self for the other that ensures that many marriages work and most newborns don't starve or die. That's the good news. The bad news is that the internal triangle is also implicated in some of the less admirable qualities of the truly feminine woman. Deutsch (1944; 1945), in her comprehensive work on female psychology, declared that women are passive, masochistic, and narcissistic. I believe the tendency to masochism results from the fact that the fantasized internal triangle is never equilateral. The mother with her protruding belly and life-giving breasts and the father with his penis possess powers that the little girl, who feels "organless" until her own puberty, doesn't have. This internal subordination sets women up to masochistically attack the self. Female passivity, as described by Deutsch, is aggression turned upon the self. I believe this passivity is facilitated by the tendency of the female ego to feel attacked by the internalized mother and father. Female narcissism is actually a triumph of self-love against the powerful internalized parents, and it is of tremendous help to women in their difficult journey toward healthy femininity.

Freud (1932) asserted that women have weak superegos. The more recent work of Gilligan (1982) has, however, reframed that concept. It is not that women have less morality than men, they just think of it in a different way. Whereas men tend to define right and wrong in terms of logic and rules, women tend to see morality in the context of relationships. Men tend to be dualistic – either you're right or you're wrong; women tend to look at things from several points of view. A masculine morality says if you rob a bank, you go to jail. A feminine observer would want to know if the bank robber was desperate to feed his family. This ability to see things from several different points of view is also a derivative of the triangularity of the female unconscious.

Freud (1932) also felt that women lack the capacity to love, but let's look at the little girl's situation at the end of the Oedipal period. The little girl has good reason to be furious with her father for denying her a child and with her mother for denying her a penis. But if she expresses her aggression directly or even experiences it consciously, she risks the loss of her feminine identity with her mother and her hope of ever receiving a penis and a baby. Her destiny is to become passive, to mute the aggression and turn it toward the self. Her best choice is to await the time when she will receive a penis and a baby from someone like her father. It is not, as Freud contended, that women can't love, they are given no choice. They can neither suckle their mothers nor penetrate their fathers. Their active loving has no external port and must, like their aggression, be turned back on the self. This redirection of libido and aggression infuses the female ego with the healthy narcissism that Deutsch (1944; 1945) described. Because she has no penis, breasts, or child in her womb on which to focus her narcissism, she tends to love herself more globally. Her entire body, as well as the products of her mind, her thoughts and feelings, become eroticized, giving the female personality its sensuality and emotional richness.

Clinical examples

The internal triangle is a useful theory not only because it explains many facts, but also because it has been of tremendous help to me in understanding my female patients. I developed the theory ten years ago as a working hypothesis, but it continues to be confirmed in what women say to me today. If the internal triangle is too oppressive, the clinical picture is a masochistic woman so imprisoned in her identifications that she is clueless about her own thoughts and feelings. Often, she is unconsciously angry at the person with whom she is totally identified. For example, my patient Elise, an anorexic who was a compulsive caretaker and helper in my women's group, was so committed to being understanding and self-sacrificing that she neglected herself. She obsessively mothered the other group members, even when they were angry and attacking her. Elise described her own mother as a very sad and unhappy person. Her mother was so immersed in her own misery that she badly neglected Elise. In unconscious identification with her mother, Elise neglected herself in my group, even seeming to enjoy being abused by the other members. Her obsessive helpfulness and empathy defended her against a powerful longing to be taken care of. Elise talked about her mother as a gentle victim. But after hearing about the tyranny of this victim for many weeks, the other women in Elise's group began to feel angry at her mother, and they invited Elise to be angry too. Elise said:

> Angry? I can't be angry at my mother. It's like attacking myself. It's like we're one person. I don't know where I end, and she begins. She's inside me. I was always the one who took care of my mother. She used to wash dishes without gloves, and her hands were blistered and cracked, and she loved it. She loved pain. She was always cutting her fingers and burning herself in the kitchen. It was a form of self-mutilation. Eating was torture. Every bite she put in her mouth, she talked about how fattening it was. And I'm like her. Even the things I enjoy, my ballet dancing, I do it till I'm abusing myself, like my mother.

Elise was so identified with her difficult mother that she couldn't even entertain the idea that she might be angry about her mother's neglect and masochistic suffering. In the here and now of the group, Elise compulsively identified with and took care of the other members so that she would never experience her own aggression.

Another of my patients, Gretchen, is oppressed by her father introject. Gretchen would be horrified to hear this analysis of her unconscious because she hates her father, who abused her and her mother for many years, not only verbally but physically. Gretchen's father had the macho idea that wives and daughters must submit and obey, and constantly told Gretchen's mother how stupid she was. He became enraged if his wife or his children dared to disagree with him. "His truth was the only truth," Gretchen said. Gretchen managed to escape her childhood environment and to get a law degree and a doctorate in mathematics. When she came into treatment, she was 37 years old. She had never had a good relationship with a man, but very much wanted to have a baby. She said, "I've spent my whole life proving I'm smart, but now I want to be a mother." Gretchen was skeptical about treatment. She wondered if I was smart enough to help her. She wanted answers from me, but when I told her the answer was for her to say everything, she told me that it was a ridiculous idea. She demeaned every word that came out of my mouth, but when I was silent, she told me that I bored her. She talked about the men who asked her out on dates in terms of their parts: his ears were too big; his penis was too small. If a man she was dating said one thing that she didn't agree with, she decided that he was not smart enough for her. She was mystified because every man she got involved with managed to escape. Gretchen has been in treatment now for five years, and she is involved with a man who says he would like to get married and have a family. The sex is great, but they fight constantly. They are sarcastic and attack each other. Gretchen has told me that she wants to keep this man, "Somehow he makes me feel safe and loved, and he wants to marry me. I want to be married once before I get old." I asked her if it would be possible to give herself an order to say positive and loving things to him whenever she has a positive feeling toward him. She was astonished at this idea and replied, "It's very hard for me to say loving things toward men. It's much easier to be belittling and sarcastic." Gretchen is getting close to a conscious awareness that she operates in a world under the control of that difficult father who demeaned and abused everyone. Though she consciously hates her father, her unconscious has identified with his power, domination, and monopoly on intellect.

The internal triangle manifests itself in the treatment room in myriad ways. Many women perceive reality as if they were in the mind of their own mother. This idea came to me in working with a patient who suffers from terrible anxiety attacks. When she is in the throes of an attack, she weeps and threatens to commit suicide. She tells me she is going to end up poor and alone on the street. She will be manipulated by her ex-husband until the day she dies, and there is nothing she can do about it. Though she presents herself as a helpless victim during these attacks, her eyes look narrow and angry, and I feel assaulted by her hysterical, inarticulate crying. Once, she sat up on the couch and said to me in a rage, "Do I have a sign on me that says, 'Abuse me!'?" When she did this, I felt that I was her abuser, that she was trying to kill me, and that I wanted to kill her in return. A few months later when we were enduring one of these storms of rage and grief, she put her hands to her face and said in despair, "I am in the mind of my mother!" When I asked her what she meant by that, she said, "All this is not me. I feel like I'm trapped inside my mother's mind and can't get out." This woman professes hate for her mother, who has been dead for many years. Her first memory is of her mother telling her she deserves nothing. From the age of five, her mother made her clean bathrooms and scrub floors and beat her when she didn't do a good job. Consciously, my patient expresses nothing but aggression toward this hateful mother, but she seems to be telling me that she can only perceive reality from her mother's point of view. Though she sees herself as a helpless victim, when she is in the middle of one of her anxiety attacks, she assaults herself and me in the same way her mother tortured her. Her fears of being evicted and out in the snow confirm her mother's idea that she deserves nothing. Once I said to this patient, "Your mother may be dead, but she has a three-room apartment in your unconscious." She laughed at that, and it seemed to help her realize that she can be as sadistic to herself and to me as her mother was to her.

Since my patient described her reality as the mind of her mother, I have listened for this dynamic in other women. A beautiful and privileged woman that I work with was an unwanted baby and an unloved child. Her mother loved to tell her three daughters that she never should have had children and that her happiness ended when they were born. My patient has a rich husband who loves her, beautiful children, and great talent as a singer. She is constantly going out to lunch, making tennis dates, and throwing parties. Yet she describes herself as friendless and as "a piece of shit" and her life as a sewer. Reality for her is the mind of her mother: she should never have been born. Another patient, whose mother was an obsessive perfectionist, lives her life in a state of perpetual anxiety. She fears that the plane is going to crash or that the food she prepares for a dinner party will be less than perfect. This patient said to me, "I can attach my anxiety to anything. It's not connected to reality." I asked what would happen if she just put it down for a while. She said, "Oh, no! I need it. If I put it down, even for a minute, I would leave here, go out on the street, and bam! I'd be run over by a taxi!" Again, the mind of the mother, a maternal introject that unconsciously attacks the self.

In addition to being oppressed by an internalized father or mother, many women struggle with a conflict between masculine and feminine identifications. Naomi was a pregnant woman who tortured herself throughout her pregnancy about becoming her mother, who never had a career and devoted her entire life to her children. Naomi loved this mother dearly, even idealized her. She said she became pregnant so easily because she admired and identified with her mother. But she saw her mother as oppressed. She served the father and her children in a totally self-sacrificing way. As a child, Naomi wanted to be like her father who had a successful business and all the authority at home. Naomi had earned an MBA. She wore her hair very short and refused to wear skirts because they made her feel powerless. She told me that if the baby was a girl, she would never let it play with a doll. "I'll give her fire trucks and scooters," she said. Throughout her pregnancy, Naomi struggled with her masculine and feminine identifications. But after her son was born, she said, "You know, I've been thinking. Womanhood is a wonderful thing. Have I ever really allowed myself to feel like a woman? Maybe it isn't such a horrible thing to let little girls play with dolls. It doesn't mean she can't drive a truck or have a career too."

After giving birth, Naomi was able to embrace and integrate both her masculine and feminine identifications. She identified with her mother in a new way, not as an oppressed victim, but as a powerful creator and nurturer of life. She enjoyed nursing her baby. But when he was a year old, she was able to call upon her father introject and go back to work on Wall Street and get a promotion.

Conclusion

This integration of the masculine and feminine is an important goal in psychoanalysis, whether the patient is male or female. I think male development and female development are very different, but I also want to emphasize that these differences are tendencies, not absolutes. There are plenty of masculine women and men who have feminine skills – quite a few in the profession of psychoanalysis. Male psychoanalysts are almost always very talented at identifying and empathizing. Lots of female analysts write books, found institutes and organizations, and are happy to consider themselves ambitious and competitive. We can explore male and female differences without denigrating either sex. Indeed, we need to value both the masculine and the feminine if we are to evolve and grow as a species. We can say that men tend, because of the challenges they face in the pre-Oedipal and Oedipal periods, to stress individuality, rights, and justice. Phallic energy ensures that we continue to have sex and that the enemy and game are killed when we need to survive. This phallic energy explored the earth and the heavens, developed culture, ethics, law, and launched rockets. The masculine tendency toward duality, toward seeing oneself as a subject and the rest of the world as an object invented science and medicine. An "I" looking at an "it" through a microscope discovered bacteria and DNA. This is a positive energy, and human beings, whether male or female, need to find that energy within themselves to have meaningful lives. Women, for reasons I have tried to enumerate, tend to emphasize relationships, complexity, and nurturance. I believe it is this feminine tendency that will ultimately save our environment and bring peace to the Middle East. Freud described women as deficient men, but lately there has been a tendency to define men as deficient women. This is just an unfortunate reversal of the sexism that feminists have been railing against for over 200 years. We need both perspectives to face the challenges of the modern world. It is good to explore difference and then to find ways to integrate what is best in order to move forward. This integration is vital if we are to help our patients develop and grow. Whatever has been repressed, whether masculinity or femininity, needs to be made conscious and integrated into the personality.

This integration is also essential to the profession of psychoanalysis itself. When we think in a dualistic, masculine way, we study our patients objectively and create drive theory and new ideas about human development. When we utilize the feminine perspective, we realize that although theory is useful, every human being who comes for treatment is a complex and unique person, not just an "it" to whom we apply our science. Through the feminine tendencies of identification, intuition, and nurturance, we meet each new patient with a mind that does not impose any theory on that patient, but opens itself up to what is before us in the here and now of the session. We need both the masculine and the feminine to be successful analysts.

While we were discussing penis envy in a class I taught at the Center for Modern Psychoanalytic Studies, a young woman said, "It's not so much that I would rather have a penis than a vagina; I want them both." Well, I say, why not? Exploring and enjoying the integration of the masculine and the feminine in our patients, ourselves, and the profession of psychoanalysis can be a unifying and life-enhancing experience.

References

Benjamin, J. (1988). *The Bonds of Love: Psychoanalysis, Feminism, and the Problem of Domination.* New York: Pantheon Books.
Bollas, C. (1992). *Being a Character: Psychoanalysis and Self-Experience.* New York: Hill and Wang.
Chodorow, N. (1978). *The Reproduction of Mothering: Psychoanalysis and the Sociology of Gender.* Berkeley: University of California Press.
Deutsch, H. (1944). *The Psychology of Women: A Psychoanalytic Interpretation.* Vol. I. New York: Grune and Stratton.
Deutsch, H. (1945). *The Psychology of Women: A Psychoanalytic Interpretation*, Vol. II. New York: Grune and Stratton.
Freud, S. (1905). "Three Essays on the Theory of Sexuality." *Standard Edition*, Volume 7. London: Hogarth Press, 125–245.
Freud, S. (1912). "On the Universal Tendency to Debasement in the Sphere of Love." *Standard Edition*, Volume 11. London: Hogarth Press, 177–190.
Freud, S. (1924). "The Dissolution of the Oedipus Complex." *Standard Edition*, Volume 19. London: Hogarth Press, 171–180.
Freud, S. (1925). "Some Psychical Consequences of the Anatomical Distinction between the Sexes." *Standard Edition*, Volume 19. London: Hogarth Press, 241–258.
Freud, S. (1932). "Femininity. Lecture XXXIII, New Introductory Lectures on Psychoanalysis."*Standard Edition*, Volume 22. London: Hogarth Press, 112–135.
Gilligan, C. (1982). *In a Different Voice: Psychological Theory and Women's Development.* Cambridge: Harvard University Press.
Holmes, L. (2008). *The Internal Triangle: New Theories of Female Development.* New York: Jason Aronson.
Klein, M. (1946). "Notes on some Schizoid Mechanisms." *International Journal of Psycho-Analysis*, 27(3–4), 99–110.
Wilbur, K. (2000). *A Brief History of Everything.* Boston: Shambhala Press.

Chapter 7

The technique of partial identification

Waking up to the world

All of us want our groups to be lively environments where members live in the moment, communicate emotionally and meaningfully with each other, and focus on building bridges to other people in the room which will facilitate mutual growth. That's the goal. But it's not always easy to achieve.

More often, especially with new groups or new group members, we see something different. We find ourselves dealing with people who are isolated in their narcissism. Like very young children, they want to play alone. Toddlers in a playgroup play like this. They sit, side by side, but the play is individual, with each child manipulating a toy or object that is individually pleasing, with very little awareness that there are other potential playmates sitting right beside them. If they become aware of the fact that there are other children around, they usually treat them as a toy that can be used, mistreated, and then pushed away. It isn't until the end of the second year of life that children are capable of seeing others as playmates who can be helpful in achieving a common wish of building or destroying something together. When these older toddlers recognize the usefulness of the children around them, then we can be pleased to observe that the child has moved from inner reality to shared reality, from egocentricity to companionship (Freud, 1960; 1965).

As a group therapist, particularly with a new group, I have often felt I am dealing with a bunch of very young children. Every member is playing with her own toy. The toy is more often than not a "story" the member is eager to relate, usually focusing on the way the world and the people in it have been a source of disappointment or pain. Each member wants to play with her story/toy by talking about it with very little awareness that there are other potential playmates in the room. If there is any object awareness at all, it is usually of me as the leader. But commonly I am experienced not as a real and separate object but as a toy to be used to focus on their sad story and then pushed away. Of course, to play well, a patient needs to develop a capacity to recognize and use objects (Holmes, 2008, p. 107). How do we help our groups make the transition from the primary process of narcissism to a healthy identification with others? In other words, how do we help people wake up to the world around them?

The whole history of group therapy has been a gradual progression out of narcissism and into progressive communication with others. When group therapy was first tried, it was based on a model of the leader doing individual therapy with each member while the rest of the group watched. Louis (Lou) Ormont has been a pioneer in giving us a new model of group therapy. Lou doesn't think of himself as a leader, as the sole therapeutic force in the room, and the person who has the responsibility to facilitate change for his patients. Rather, Lou sees the group as the agent of change. He is a master at harnessing the power of the collective genius of the group, an entity that is smarter than any of the individual people in the room. Lou works with bridging, helping members talk to and identify with each other. With these bridges, he fosters progressive emotional communication and immediacy. He creates an environment where people are no longer playing alone with their sad histories. They are talking to each other, sharing their thoughts and feelings towards each other, in the moment. And when that happens, a very exciting thing occurs. Rather than describing their unhappy pasts, people turn to their relationships in the room and begin to demonstrate the resistances and defenses which prevent them from living satisfying and meaningful lives. Their problems aren't described; they are lived in the here and now of the group, relating to the other members. And this immediacy makes the group an exciting laboratory where resistances and pathological patterns are available in the moment to be explored and resolved (Ormont, 1991b; 2001).

In building his bridges between people in the room, Lou searches the group for a member who might be a good playmate for the person who is talking. It might be a person who has a feeling, whether love or hate, that would prove of use in resolving a resistance of the person talking. Using his own feelings and intuition, Lou contacts the person who he thinks has the right feeling, saying something like, "Mary, what's your reaction to what John has to say?" Very often in bridging, Lou looks for a person who is able to identify with the person speaking. Indeed, Lou sees the ability to make a transient identification as the catalyst for all group exchanges. Lou defines transient identification as a brief inhabitation of another's identity, followed by a return to ourselves. These fleeting identifications open up avenues of constructive interchange (Ormont, 1991a).

The two main components of transient identification are empathy and intuition. Empathy is the ability to temporarily experience the world as the other person does. Empathy expresses itself in feelings and impulses. Intuition is using intellect and perception to understand what those empathetic feelings and impulses mean. Empathy brings us closer to people, while intuition brings us closer to meanings. Lou sees empathy and intuition as innate capacities of human beings. People who lack empathy and intuition have inhibited their innate capacity to identify with others, often because of narcissistic injury in their past.

As group leaders, we can help people unlock their inherent ability to make transient identifications using several different techniques. These include, modeling, educating, and resolving resistances. We model and educate when we trust and use our own feelings to understand others, and when we encourage other group members to do the same. We work on resolving resistances to transient identification by enlisting every member to help us (Ormont, 1991a). When a particular member is demonstrating a pathological pattern, we don't start analyzing him as if he were in individual therapy with us. We try to get the whole group involved. And everyone will have different reactions to the pathological problem. Some members will feel angry or impatient, some will identify with the resistance and feel empathy, and others may have new ways of looking at the problem or playing with ideas about it. But the point is that the resistance, the pathology, is confronted and understood from a myriad of different angles by group members. Transient identifications, coming from different members with different perspectives, reflect the complexities of our inner emotional life. We are all usually ambivalent about any important issue in our lives; that is, we have lots of often conflicting feelings about it. So the group, with its varied ways of looking at the same issue, can hold up a mirror to our complicated thoughts and feelings. We can hear painful truths from angry people when there is another person in the room who is sympathetic and working to support us when we're under scrutiny. In this rich environment of different perspectives, resistances can be worked through in the continuous flow of progressive communication between members.

Transient identification is a twofold process. In order to experience each other's feelings, there is a momentary letting go of who we are, followed by a return to ourselves. It is a complex process that requires knowledge and resonance, not only of what the other person feels, but also of what we feel toward them (Ormont, 1991a). The identification is partial because we don't get lost or overwhelmed in the other's reality. We can empathize and understand without blurring the psychic boundaries between self and other. In other words, the identification is an excursion, not a permanent relocation in another person's reality.

Much attention has been given to the first part of this process: the ability to know what others feel. Many people can't do this at all – they are too focused on themselves to know or care what other people feel. We call this problem narcissism, and it is everywhere. There is an enormous amount of literature about narcissism and the compulsive focus on the impoverished self to the detriment of object relations. We all are familiar with the self-preoccupied, attention-craving patient who has no capacity to care about what others feel and who isolates herself in a lonely world where her inner reality is the only reality.

But I want to focus on the second part of the process of transient identification: the ability to return to our own psychic reality after putting ourselves in another's shoes. This is a part of the technique of partial or transient identification which is too often taken for granted, but it can be quite challenging for many patients, particularly female patients.

Women have a tendency, more so than men, to get overwhelmed by their own identifications. That is, they often lose themselves in empathizing with others. This, of course, is not true of all women, and it also true of many men, but I think it is safe to say that oppressive and compulsive identification is more common among women than men. I have studied women in groups and written extensively about female psychology, but let me summarize briefly here and tell you that women tend to have a vivid psychic world of internalized objects that makes it very easy for them to be empathetic and sometimes means that they can get overwhelmed by their own identifications. I believe this is so because of a uniquely feminine solution to the problem of separating from early parental objects. All children, girls and boys, have a need to break away from the powerful pre-Oedipal mother, but boys have a simpler path toward that separation than girls. Their penis is manifest evidence that they are "not my mother." Like many other feminist psychoanalysts, I believe this is why girls envy the penis – it helps little boys gain their independence from the engulfing mother. Girls, with no penis to oppose the symbiosis with the mother, have to find another way to individuate. My theory, developed from ten years of work with women in groups, is that little girls tend, on a fantasy level, to introject the maternal object. What is the purpose of this fantasy of a "mother-in-me," to oppose the mother of reality? Internalizing the mother on a fantasy level gives the little girl a sense of mastery over her powerful original object. If the mother is inside, she can be controlled and manipulated.

Girls introject the father during the rigors of the Oedipus complex for the same reason: an internalized paternal object provides a comforting fantasy of control over the painful Oedipal situation. The internal intrapsychic triangle of mother, father, and self is a unique outcome of female development, and it has lots of advantages, including all the good things we associate with femininity. It provides women with an enormous capacity for identification with both men and women, rich imagination and intuition, and an ability to sacrifice self for others. But it is important to remember that it sets up other challenges for women. The triangle is often not equilateral, and unconsciously, the female self takes a subordinate position in relation to the powerful maternal and paternal introjects. This intrapsychic submission conditions women to develop some of the negative qualities associated with being feminine: passivity, masochism, and a narcissistic need to be loved which diminishes active loving (Holmes, 2008).

It also makes transient and partial identification difficult for women. Women who have a particularly oppressive internal triangle are often so suffused with identifications to past figures that they have trouble maintaining a sense of self. Often, they have no conscious awareness that they are obsessively controlled by other people's feelings. They don't even know that they are not the captains of their own ships. Many women project their inner dramas concerning the internal triangle onto people in the room. I want to give you some clinical examples of what all this looks like.

One day, a woman named Jessica came to the group, feeling guilty because she had had a fight with her boyfriend, which she herself didn't understand. She said:

> My boyfriend's father and mother came into town from California and wanted to take him to the Four Seasons. He asked me if I wanted to go, but I knew he was nervous about seeing them and wasn't really up to introducing me to them yet, so I told him I had to work. But the next day he called me and was going on and on about what a great restaurant the Four Seasons is, and I just blew up and told him he never thinks about my feelings. I've never even been to the Four Seasons. He said to me, "But I asked you to go!" And I said, "But I know you didn't really want me." And he said, "I don't understand women," and I didn't know what to say, because he did ask me after all.

What happened next was a nice little example of the differences between men and women regarding identification. Jack, a man in the group, said sarcastically, "I agree with your boyfriend. I don't understand women." Jessica looked even more crestfallen than ever at this remark, so I turned to a woman I knew was often able to identify with Jessica and said, "Liz, Jack doesn't understand Jessica. Do you?" Liz said, "Of course I do. Jessica can't be comfortable unless her boyfriend is comfortable. She feels his feelings more strongly than she does her own." At this, Jessica perked up, nodded, and said, "That's right, Liz. I knew he didn't really want me to go." Jack said impatiently, "But what about what you want Jessica? Why are his feelings more important than yours?" Another man, Tom, said, "He did ask you to go. You say he didn't want you to go, but he must have had other feelings too. He was just a little ambivalent." Jack asked Jessica what prevented her from accepting her boyfriend's initial invitation. She said, "I just wanted him to want me." Tom spoke up again and said, "I feel so annoyed at you, Jessica. Why can't your boyfriend be a little ambivalent and nervous without you getting all embroiled in his feelings?" I asked Tom, "Does that happen here? Does Jessica get all embroiled here in this room?" He said, "Absolutely. You do it with me too, Jessica. You do it with all the men. You're always so understanding of my problems, but I never feel you assert yourself much to help me or have a different idea. It makes me feel kind of lonely – like there's no one here but me." Liz jumped in and said, "You men just don't understand. Jessica experiences her boyfriend's feelings as her own. She's so identified with him, she doesn't even know what she's feeling. You guys don't appreciate how sensitive Jessica is." Jack said, "I appreciate how sensitive you are, Jessica. But I want you to start trusting your own feelings. How do you know it wouldn't have turned out great with his parents? They might have loved you, and you would have had a five star dinner to boot." Tom said, "I really don't care about your boyfriend or the Four Seasons. I just want you to be more direct with me, Jessica. I don't need a mommy to understand me. I need someone to be honest about their own feelings with me!" "Well," said Jessica, "Right now I feel a little pissed at the men in the room. And come to think of it, I guess I was angry at my boyfriend too for his ambivalence!"

This little vignette demonstrates to us how the two parts of the transient identification equation tend to split along gender lines. Women are very good at empathy, so good, in fact, that they can lose themselves in another's feelings. Men often do better knowing and asserting their own feelings. If the group leader understands and exploits this, she focuses on building bridges between the group members, particularly between the men and the women. Women can model empathy for men in a very helpful way, and men can deliver women back to themselves by focusing on awareness of self.

Jessica's situation also shows us how resistance has a better chance of being resolved when it is being worked on by several different members with different perspectives. All of the masculine criticism might have overwhelmed Jessica if Liz hadn't been able to make a partial identification with Jessica and explain her thought process to the men. With Liz's support, Jessica began to be able to take in what the men in the group were saying to her. At first, she felt angry, but her anger seemed to help her free herself from the compulsive identification that so often paralyzed her. As the group members worked with her on her resistance, Jessica was gradually more comfortable with verbalizing all kinds of feelings to the men in the room. She could empathize with their feelings, but she also became increasingly aware of her feelings toward them.

Here's another example of identification gone wrong. Betty, a beautiful, dynamic, and articulate woman, was very talented at making identifications with other group members, and I would often contact her when the group was struggling to understand someone. I would say something like, "Betty, what do you think is going on? Why is it so hard for Ralph to talk to Susan?" I did this for several reasons. I hoped that Betty's excellent intuition could shed light on the thorny resistances that were presenting themselves, and I also wanted to educate the rest of the group by using Betty as an example of making good transient identifications. Usually, Betty could intuit another person's inner process in a very helpful way. She would say something like, "Ralph is afraid of his feelings toward Susan. That's why he can't talk to her. He is very attracted to Susan, and he's afraid he's going to be rejected." This would get all the members of the group focused in a new way on the difficulties between Susan and Ralph, and soon this pair, who had been frozen, were talking in a progressive and emotional way. I was very pleased that Betty could be so helpful to the group with her ability to put herself in another's shoes, and many of the other group members expressed admiration and affection toward Betty for her ability to make these transient identifications. But a problem arose when I contacted Betty too often to ask her what was going on in the room. Some of the other members began to feel competitive with Betty and resentful of her – and angry at me for acting as if Betty was my favorite child. It would have been fine if these more silent members had been able to express their aggression toward Betty directly – and toward me for giving her too much attention. But often something more insidious would happen. Frequently, a person who had trouble talking and identifying would approach Betty and tell her she was frightening. "I wish I could talk to you," this seemingly shy person would say, "But I'm afraid of you. You're very strong, and I'm scared of being overwhelmed if I try to have a relationship with you. You might get angry with me, and I couldn't take that." Now I, as the leader, saw the projected aggression in this communication, and I immediately guessed that perhaps I should stifle my impulse to use Betty as a model. But what is interesting is what happened to Betty when people talked to her in this way. This intuitive woman completely lost herself in the face of the accusation that she was scary. When she heard this, Betty would immediately begin to attack herself, compulsively accepting the projection of the accusing member that she was a dangerous person. She would tearfully reassure the frightened person that she was harmless, and often after she had been accused of being scary, she would be silent for weeks. She was so focused on identifying with the other's feeling that she was dangerous, that she had no ability to consider her own feelings toward the accuser. Betty's guilty silences would induce other members to contact her, "What's wrong, Betty? It's not like you to not talk." They would tell her they missed her intuition. Betty would just shake her head and say something like, "I think it's time I let others talk for a while." Finally, I decided to intervene. When Robert, a group member who had originally accused Betty of being frightening, approached her and said, "I wish you would talk, Betty. I miss you when you're silent." I said, "What are you talking about, Robert? Betty is doing the right thing to keep quiet! If she spoke up, someone might get killed! Betty is a dangerous person! Better she shut up for the sake of the safety of this group!" This attempt to join Betty's resistance had the right effect. Betty turned on me and said, "How dare you say that, Lucy! After all the times I've tried to be helpful to this damn group, and you talk about me like I'm some kind of witch! It makes me furious!" I said, "I see that you're furious, and I'm very pleased that you're furious. You've got the right feeling to be furious when I call you a witch. What's less clear to me is why you have to put a bucket over your head when someone says you're scary." Robert said, "Lucy's right, Betty. The whole group suffers when you don't talk." Betty turned on him and said, "You! You have a fine nerve even talking to me. You're the one who makes me feel like I have to retreat. I'm so dangerous I might annihilate you. Isn't that what you think?" Leslie, another member who had an intuitive understanding of Robert said, "I don't think Robert really thinks you're going to annihilate him, Betty. I think Robert envies your ability to relate to others in here. It's just easier for Robert to tell you you're scary than to say that he feels competitive with you and wishes he could be as charismatic as you are." When Betty realized that she was angry at being called a witch, she began to be able to hold onto herself in the face of being attacked. She had new memories of a mother who always told her she was too big, too dramatic, too angry. Gradually, she started reacting in a totally new way in the moment. She would smile at the frightened person and say cheerfully, "That's right. You're right to be scared of me. I'm pretty scary, so watch out. I just may eat you up!" What usually happened when Betty said this, is that the scared person would get outraged and tell Betty how angry they were at her. "I thought so," Betty would say, "and really I prefer you to be angry rather than scared." Betty had made the leap from obsessive identification to a healthy partial identification. And how had she done it? By focusing on what she felt toward, not with, the other person. By recognizing her own feeling of anger, she was able to pick up the unconscious aggression of the scared person. She had made a partial identification, but had been able to come back to herself. Her new way of reacting was also helpful to our supposedly frightened person, as it helped him see that behind his fear were feelings of competition, envy and anger.

A very popular way that women express their aggression in unconscious identification with an early object is by suffering (Holmes, 2004). I'm sure you've all heard of patients like this. Often these women have had a mother who lived her life as a suffering victim, and these patients are quite talented in making even a very lucky life of privilege and talent into a sewer. They may have loving partners, beautiful healthy children, and creative abilities, but they are determined to see the world as bleak and unfriendly. I call this being in the "mind of the mother." They are unaware that the misery they perceive as objective reality is really the reality of an intrapsychic object who controls their perception and experience. They are usually very lonely, even in a room where many others have positive feelings toward them and helpful ideas about them. It can be quite a challenge to encourage them to give up their thunder cloud to make a transient identification with anyone, but this is the path out of their unhappiness. By modeling and education, we try to teach them to get interested in and experience new sensations. We work with other members to give these unhappy women new feelings to identify with, and we encourage them to have feelings toward others in the room. These women usually are able to begin to wake up by experiencing rage toward others for disrupting their story/toy. Their anger may be difficult for the group, but we should be encouraged when we see it because it is the first awareness that there are other people in the world, other realities to be considered. Love and pleasure come much later, and are only achieved when our suffering woman realizes that good feelings as well as misery exist in the world, and relief from suffering can be attained by an outward focus on objects. As Ormont likes to say, "Loving is infinitely more satisfying than being loved!" (personal conversation, 2007)

The talent for identification is a woman's greatest strength and biggest problem. It should be a tool, not a prison. Women in groups need help in managing the complex world of introjected objects which is the heir of the rigors of growing up female. The challenge is to help women use their ability to connect with others in the service of their own egos and to develop the courage to verbalize healthy aggression when identification and connection threaten to become oppressive. A useful technique in meeting this challenge is to encourage women to think about and express what they feel *toward* other group members, rather than what they feel *with* them. Often when encouraged in this way, women will discover that they have a negative feeling toward the person with whom they are in complete and compulsive identification. The expression of this negative feeling in words is the triumph of the self over the introjected object and can free a woman from the tyranny of her internal world (Holmes, 2002).

In mixed gender groups, we often observe that men are better at knowing and articulating their own feelings, while women are more skilled at identification. This difference, if understood and used by the leader, can be helpful to both sexes in developing the technique of partial identification. Women can help men develop empathy for others in the room, and men can help women understand and articulate their own feelings.

Encouraging our patients to make transient and partial identifications in the here and now of the group is the key to maturation and satisfaction for the people we treat. Skills learned and practiced in group will eventually be practiced in real life, and when that happens, life gets better. People become more successful in love, work, and play in the world. Waking up to others, being able to put ourselves in another's shoes, is one of the secrets of happiness in life, a comforting diversion from the suffering inherent in being existentially alone in our own skin. The dual skill of identifying with others while holding onto our own feelings is the pathway out of the isolation and loneliness of narcissism. When we can experience both self and other, life becomes complex, colorful, and meaningful; we can inhabit many worlds (Ormont, 1991a). But we have to be able to return from those other worlds to our own.

References

Freud, A. (1960). Entrance into Nursery School: The Psychosocial Prerequisites. *The Writings of Anna Freud, Volume Five*, 315–355. New York: International Universities Press.

Freud, A. (1965). *Normality and Pathology in Childhood*. New York: International Universities Press.

Holmes, L. (2002)."Women in Group and Women's Groups." *International Journal of Group Psychotherapy*, 52(2), 171–188.

Holmes, L. (2004). "Hell Hath no Fury: How Women Seek Revenge." *Modern Psychoanalysis*, 29(1), 49–61.

Holmes, L. (2008). *The internal triangle: New theories of human development*. New York: Jason Aronson.

Ormont, L. (1991a). "Establishing transient identification in the group setting." *Modern Psychoanalysis*, 24(2), 143–156.

Ormont, L. (1991b). *The Group Therapy Experience*. New York: St. Martin's Press.

Ormont, L. (2001). *The Technique of Group Treatment* (ed. Lena Blanco Furgeri). Madison, CT: Psychosocial Press.

Chapter 8

Gender dynamics in group therapy

In this post-feminist era, it is sometimes considered politically incorrect to generalize about the differences between the sexes. And indeed, a liberal and inclusive point of view about sexuality has great merit. Human beings are incredibly complex and diverse. We all know men who display qualities associated with femininity like empathy and intuition, and women who are as ambitious, competitive, and assertive as the most masculine of men. But to insist that there are no generalizable differences between the sexes is just as dogmatic a position as insisting that anatomy is, inevitably and irrefutably, destiny.

Having devoted a great deal of my professional life to the clinical study of the female mind, I can say with a certainty that grows with each year and new female patient, that women have unique psychic structures that are the catalyst for all the qualities that we associate with femininity: empathy, intuition, a talent for identification, passivity, masochism, and a narcissistic need to be loved. Women consistently display, on a fantasy level, an internalized triangle of introjected mother, introjected father, and self, and this triangle is hardly ever equilateral. In the unconscious, the female ego often subverts itself to the parental objects within. I have theorized that this often oppressive intrapsychic triangle is set up in early childhood when little girls use the fantasy of introjecting objects in much the same way that little boys use the penis: to separate from and gain mastery over the powerful and engulfing pre-Oedipal mother.

The little boy's penis is manifest evidence that he is not his mother, and during the Oedipal period, he makes a rather violent dis-identification with his mother to identify with his father and the power of the penis. Freud said that the boy's Oedipal complex is "literally smashed to pieces" (Freud, 1925, p. 257). What is destroyed is any identification with the mother, and henceforth, any tendency to empathize or identify with a feminine point of view will likely be laced with anxiety about a regression to primitive symbiosis (Holmes, 2002).

Girls, who experience themselves as "organless" in childhood, must find another way to break the early symbiosis with the mother while still retaining their identification with her. I believe they do this by incorporating the early mother with her milk. If "mommy is in me" on a fantasy level in the little girl's mind, then she has not only absorbed maternal power, but she has also gained enormous control over the mother. Father is introjected at the end of the humiliations of the Oedipal period and for the same reason: internalizing the father gives the little girl significant fantasied mastery and control over an uncontrollable object (Holmes, 2008).

Gender dynamics in group members

These differences in the way boys and girls solve the universal problem of separating themselves from the pre-Oedipal mother, play themselves out in groups in a variety of ways. Male group members often focus on self-actualization and autonomy, and this focus can help strengthen, not only male egos, but by example, female egos as well. Male energy can offer models for the creative use of aggression laced with humor and healthy self-assertion. Most women, on the other hand, have an enormous talent for identification and empathy because they are literally able to see things from three points of view. The triadic perspective of the feminine woman can be quite beneficial in group. The ability to use empathy and intuition to make a transient identification with another person facilitates immediacy and progressive emotional communication (Ormont, 1991, 2001a and b).

But gender dynamics can also cause problems in group. The challenges of growing up male have demanded that little boys make a dramatic dis-identification with their mothers. This means that any empathy or identification with the female can feel like a frightening regression to men. Women, because of the rigors of female development, often become overwhelmed and oppressed by their own identifications. Their tendency to empathize and identify with other group members can become compulsive, and they become so obsessed with being "helpful" that they lose all ability to know what they themselves are feeling.

When gender dynamics become malignant, the leader may find herself with a group where men do all the talking and women sit in silence. More often though, sexual tendencies are expressed more subtly. Men will talk about their lives, and women will empathize and identify with the male members. In this situation, women may be getting lots of gratifying appreciation for their sympathetic attention, and so it becomes difficult to spot the fact that the focus in the group is decidedly masculine. Though both men and women are doing what comes naturally, the group is stuck in a sexist resistance, with man as the subject and woman as the object (Holmes, 2002).

Group leaders who are sensitive to gender dynamics can do a better job of resolving this resistance and facilitating progressive emotional communication in their mixed-gender groups. Dr Louis Ormont (1991) talked about the importance of being able to make transient or partial identification in group. This ability requires a capacity for empathy and intuition, and it is a two-part process. First, we let go of who we are to experience the feelings of another. Second, we return to ourselves to experience what we feel toward the other. It is a complex process that requires knowledge and resonance, not only of what the other person feels, but also of what we feel toward them. The identification is partial because we don't get lost or overwhelmed in the other's reality. We can empathize and understand without blurring the psychic boundaries between self and other. In other words, the identification is an excursion, not a permanent relocation in another person's reality (Holmes, 2009).

Many men (though certainly not all) have a tendency to have trouble with the first part of this process. Letting go of their own sense of self to briefly inhabit the world of another can be a challenge because their masculinity demands a sense of autonomy, which is sometimes defensive and rigid. Many women (though not all), on the other hand, are challenged by the second part of the process of transient identification. That is to say, they tend to lose themselves in an oppressive identification and become so compulsively empathetic that they have no energy left to consider their own feelings.

These gender dynamics can be harnessed by a sensitive leader to mobilize men and women to be extraordinarily helpful to each other. Men must be encouraged to verbalize their fears about entrapment and engulfment before they can begin to risk identification with the other and experience the pleasure of human connection. All their anxieties about regression to symbiosis with the pre-Oedipal mother must be articulated and worked through. Women usually have resistances to aggression and autonomy which involve anxiety about the loss of relationship. The expression of anger risks abandonment. Even success and achievement can feel dangerous to them (Gilligan et al., 1989). These feminine fears must be acknowledged, discussed and worked through. Happily, men are perfectly equipped to help women resolve their resistance to having strong, autonomous egos; while women naturally possess the skills to help men discover the pleasures of connection to the other.

When sexist resistances are resolved, exciting progressive emotional communication begins to occur. When women are encouraged to think about what they feel *toward*, not *with* a male group member, they may be surprised to find that they are angry at the very person with whom they have been in compulsive and oppressive identification. The creative expression of female anger at a man for being self-involved or dominating the group can be an exciting wake-up call for both men and women. The anger paradoxically invites the man to stop contemplating the autonomous self and focus outward on the irritated woman who is confronting him. He is being offered, not a subjective handmaiden who understands him, but a true object whose difference from himself can enrich his world and promote his growth. Suddenly, there are two people relating to each other, where there had been only one, with the other acting as a subservient accessory to the male ego. Female anger also strengthens the woman's sense of self, fostering a new autonomy and opening up opportunities to perceive the world with a refreshingly masculine perspective.

Likewise, when men are encouraged by the leader to identify with the women in the room, to speculate what they may be feeling, exciting new dynamics develop. A man who has temporarily left himself to focus intensely on a female group member is a compelling figure. The rigidity required to maintain his defensive independence softens, and he can become remarkably articulate and reassuring. He is able to deliver his clear, logical thinking and comfort with assertive aggression to the woman with whom he is trying to identify. Empathizing with her feelings while offering his masculine perspective, he presents her with a new and exciting way of looking at things. In this encounter, both man and woman are enriched. When men are thinking like women, and women are behaving like men, a new kind of object love develops, characterized by an integration of the masculine and the feminine. Group members become skilled in both knowing their own feelings and empathizing with the feelings of others. They can hold and appreciate both a strong, autonomous ego and a desire to connect to others. Observing the differences in male and female functioning in a mixed-gender group has helped me understand that this integration of the masculine and the feminine is an important goal for the group leader.

Gender dynamics in group leaders

Gender dynamics are as important for the leader as they are for the group members. My personal and professional experience has given me ideas about this issue. I had the personal experience of being in a group led by a male therapist for thirty-five years and the professional experience of being the female leader of my own groups for almost twenty years. My first supervision group was led by a female analyst, and I am currently a member of a supervision group whose leader is male. These rich experiences have given me an opportunity to observe firsthand, dynamics that are characteristic of male and female leaders. Again, I want to emphasize that these dynamics are trends; they are not written in stone. Every leader brings his or her own unique combination of male and female attributes to work with groups, and each group has its own distinctive personality. That being said, the sex of a leader does color the environment of a group, the transference and countertransference of members and leaders, in ways about which I feel confident enough to risk some generalizations in the hope that they will help clinicians be mindful of gender and use it creatively.

The most basic generalization about a difference in the gender of leaders is that groups run by men have a father, while female-led groups have a mother. Though there are, of course, a myriad of possibilities within this matrix, there are also inevitable consequences of this simple fact. Yalom (1995) described the group as a family. Leaders are parental authority figures while members are perceived as peers or siblings. Like a family, the group is characterized by strong, sometimes primitive emotions and moments of intimacy. Inevitably, members will relate to the leader in ways that are reminiscent of the ways they interacted with a parent. Hopefully, familial conflicts can be relived correctively. Yalom's model of group as family gives credence to my idea that group members will unconsciously relate differently to a mother than to a father.

Mother is the infant's first object or rather pre-object. The infant behaves and functions as though he and his mother were a dual unity with one boundary. This closed monadic system is self-sufficient in its hallucinatory wish fulfillment. When the breast appears, the infant experiences it as part of himself, a satisfaction for his hunger which he, in his omnipotence, has conjured up. Mother's holding behavior, her primary maternal preoccupation with her infant is a symbiotic organizer for the baby (Mahler, 1968). At about three months, the newborn becomes dimly aware of a need-satisfying object, but the child's love for mother knows no bounds. It demands exclusive possession and is satisfied with nothing less than all. It is incapable of complete satisfaction, so it is doomed to end in disappointment and to give place to a hostile attitude. Mother love is characterized by oral and cannibalistic impulses. The infant expects the mother to love him without any need of giving anything in return (Balint, 1949). Deeply buried within us all is a longing to return to the illusory fusion with the early mother universe. The dream of potential access to the original mother/child unity claims a powerful place in the unconscious of every human being (McDougall, 1989).

The father plays a very different role with the growing child. Lacan (1977) talked about the function of the father in the development of the mind. The father (or the paternal function, since it is not always the biological father who intrudes himself into the mother/infant dyad) creates what Lacan called the paternal signifier, a "no" in the mind of the young child. (In French, "no" and "nom" have the same sound, indicating that the name of the father sparks a prohibition in the child's mind.) The paternal signifier opens up a space between mother and child, a space occupied by the name of the father and by the phallus, a symbol of complete union with the mother which preceded the child. When the paternal signifier is established, the child is able to give up his symbiosis with the mother and enter what Lacan (1977) called the symbolic space. A fundamental shift in the child's relation to language occurs. Absence of the mother can be tolerated, because the use of language symbolizes her continuing presence. When the child moves into the symbolic order and begins to use language, he gives up the idea that he is the sole object of his mother's desire (Hurst, 2000).

Blos (1984) discussed a patient who had an over idealization of him which reflected the father's role in the child's life in the first two years. The father is uncontaminated because he has never been a full-fledged symbiotic partner,

Lacan's restraining and punishing father is also, in some sense the child's rescuer, who saves him from his infantile delusions and the danger of engulfment by the mother. Father is the early personification of the reality principle.

Though these paternal dynamics can be very helpful for male leaders, there are other pitfalls for men running groups. Any therapist worth his salt is probably familiar with the concept of the primal horde (Freud, 1939). According to Freud, the first communities were organized around a powerful father who was worshipped and feared by his sons. The father alone had sexual access to the women in the group, and though the sons venerated the father, eventually they killed him and ate him, thereby incorporating his power for themselves. To atone for this patricide, the sons set up totems to worship and began to sacrifice animals in religious services to reenact their original crime. They also set up laws against incest and murder to protect themselves from their father's fate.

Freud's story indicates that behind all idealization of a powerful male figure lies primitive rage. We love our fathers, but we also envy their power and want to devour them and get power for ourselves. Men who run groups would do well to remember Freud's cautionary tale and be constantly vigilant about the cannibalistic and patricidal tendencies that idealization of the leader can mask.

These differences in dynamics of mother and father simmer just under the surface of any group. On an unconscious level, a male group leader represents the paternal signifier in a very helpful way. His phallic power inhibits regression in group and provides the "no" to any tendency to primitive, preverbal functioning. Rather than yearning for the original dyad, the members of a group run by a man enter the symbolic space and use language to express that yearning. It is easier in such a group to focus on one's peers and to talk rather than regress to the mother/child dyad where one has no language and can only scream to be fed. Because a male leader represents the "no," it is less threatening to the group for an individual member to get the attention of a male leader. The father/leader by his very nature prohibits the primitive dyad, so his focus on any individual member is less unsettling to the other people in the room.

A female leader is more likely to stir up pre-Oedipal longings and hungers, In a woman-led group, the desire for pleasure in primitive union with the mother is easily activated. Language is not a part of the early mother environment, and often members whose leader is female expect the leader to understand them without the need for explanation; indeed, they expect the leader to read their minds. An implicit demand to be understood without resorting to speech is always in the air. When this doesn't happen, and the female leader encourages words, fits of rage about the betrayal of the mother can erupt. Female leaders stir up preverbal hungers, which inevitably are frustrated, and this can mean that women who lead groups often have to deal with a specific type of primitive aggression. Contempt and devaluation of the female leader are often defenses against anxiety about the original mother's terrifying power. This dynamic can be particularly dramatic in the male members of a female-led group, and I believe this is because of the terror men feel when their autonomy is threatened. Adding new members to female-led groups is often experienced unconsciously as the birth of a new baby, the ultimate treachery of the pre-Oedipal mother. A female group leader can feel like a mother with too many children and not enough milk. It is important for women to remember that they may have to work harder than a male leader to get their groups to use language and focus on each other rather than their hunger for and anger at the pre-Oedipal mother.

A group

Several years ago, I added a new man I'll call James to this long-running group. James had been an individual patient of mine for many years. He had become articulate and confident, and I was sure he would be a good addition to the group. Michael, a long term member of the group, immediately formed a close and intense relationship with James. They had similar histories, and Michael told James he felt like he had a new brother. Though these two men were very close, they also would frequently get into arguments which would degenerate into loud, attacking screaming matches. They would curse and call each other names, and I was hard pressed to stop this antler rattling. Sometimes the other men would join in the fight, and chaos would ensue with all the men screaming at each other. The women would stare at their laps in gloomy silence while this was going on.

I tried to intervene loudly when this happened, saying "No attacking in this group!" I also tried calmly reiterating the rules: no screaming in my group, no name calling. I reminded the group that the contract was to verbalize your thoughts and feelings toward others in the room, not to assault each other. These interventions would make things better temporarily, but even so, the primitive male aggression erupted regularly. So I decided to carefully study what was going on in my group just before these new and troublesome fights started, and what I observed was very interesting.

James had been a contented individual patient with a tendency to demonstrate an idealized transference to me in his sessions. In the group, he continued his idealization of me and often verbally admired interventions I made. He reminded the group frequently that, unlike many others in the room, he was in individual therapy with me. He also had a tendency to contact me at one point or another during the group session and say, "Lucy, I need your help." I would reply as I did in his individual sessions, "What kind of help do you need?" In individual treatment, James seemed to like this question, but in group, I was surprised to see that the question would usually make James angry. He would snarl, "Don't give me that therapy baloney! It's so formulaic! You're supposed to know what I need. That's what I'm paying you for!" I would reply, "You're paying me to understand you, but I can't read your mind. I can't understand you unless you talk." It was at this point that Michael would charge in angrily, "You're such an ass kisser, James. You're always telling Lucy how great she is, so that you can get special attention! You make me sick!" And we would be off and running.

Sometimes it was Michael who would ask for my help. But if I turned my gaze to him, James would complain loudly. I began to realize that my giving individual attention to either of these men was a mistake. It resulted in noisy wars between the men and depressed silence among the women. I decided to change my tactics. When Michael approached me for help, I turned to a female member of the group and said, "Ericka, what kind of help do you think Michael needs?" Ericka shrugged sadly and said, "I don't know. I just feel depressed when Michael and James go at it." I said, "Well, it is sort of depressing, but how about helping me out here. What do you think is going on?" Ericka thought a moment, and then said, "Brothers love, but they also hate." This made Michael laugh. He said, "You're so smart, Ericka. You really understand me." Then Michael turned to James and said, "Ericka's right, James. I do love you. And I wish you would talk to me instead of Lucy."

Sometimes when the men in the group would start to fight, I would intervene loudly and say, "You men are doing a wonderful job of shutting up the women in this group!" James would turn to me angrily and say, "Well, I feel like you're telling me to shut up!" I replied, "I'm not telling you to shut up. I'm telling you that you seem more interested in fighting than in talking to the women in this room." James said, "The women can talk if they want to. They can take care of themselves." At this, Rebecca spoke up energetically, "Oh good grief, James! You make me so angry! You and Michael are totally holding this group hostage with your stupid brawls. I'm sick of it!" James seemed stunned at this. I thought he would attack Rebecca, but he didn't. Instead, he said thoughtfully, "I don't mean to hold you hostage. Why don't you speak up when I do that?" I said, "That's an excellent question. What prevents you from telling James and Michael how you feel?" Rebecca shook her head sadly and said, "I just can't find my voice when James and Michael start screaming. I just feel depressed and oppressed." I turned to Eleanor, a member of the group who was a therapist and asked her, "Eleanor, why does Rebecca get depressed?" Eleanor said, "I'm just thinking of Psychology 101. Depression is anger turned toward the self. Who would you be mad at, Rebecca, if you didn't turn it on yourself?" Rebecca thought and said, "I'm angry at the men in this group. And I'm angry at you, Lucy, for letting the men monopolize."

Rebecca's expression of anger at me and the men seemed to have a positive effect on the other women in the room. They spoke up to admire Rebecca's courage in verbalizing difficult feelings, and they empathized with her feeling of depression. As the women began to talk to each other, the men began to talk to the women. They encouraged them to be more assertive and take their equal share of the talking time. When encouraged by the men, Eleanor said, "I just shut down when the men fight." I asked, "What shuts you down, Eleanor?" She said, "I don't know. It's so painful. It just feels like a lot of hungry babies and not enough milk to go around." I said, "So you feel the pain under the screaming?" Eleanor nodded, "And it just makes me feel so sad." I said, "The sadness is a feeling you feel with the men. What do you feel toward them?" Eleanor thought and then laughed, "Well, part of me wants to strangle all of them!"

As the women became more outspoken, they were pleasantly surprised to see that the men didn't punish or abandon them. Sexual feelings began to be expressed and the men were able to be less attacking of each other and more honest about their competitive feelings When the male aggression flared up again, the women began to intervene in therapeutic ways. They expressed anger toward the men, but they were also able to identify with them and understand what they were really feeling. "You know, Michael, " Ericka would say, "There's a lot of sadness and pain underneath all that yelling." A particularly satisfying moment came one day when Michael started attacking me, accusing me of being too incompetent to run a group. Rebecca intervened, saying, "I don't think incompetence is the problem, Michael. I think you're mad because you can't have Lucy all to yourself." Michael attempted to outshout her, "You're full of it, Rebecca. That's ridiculous!" Rebecca delicately held up her finger and pointed at Michael, "Just a minute," she said quietly, "I'm not finished."

Discussion

When I added a "new baby" to this group, particularly one who had been alone with me for many years and didn't mind bragging about it, it activated primitive hunger and rage at me as the treacherous pre-Oedipal mother. When James and Michael, psychic brothers, began to spar and attempt to create the symbiotic preverbal dyad with me by asking me to focus on helping them, I fell into the trap of acting out the excluding fusion of mother and infant, and the rage that resulted was primal.

The men in the group discharged this rage in words, but the words weren't really progressive emotional communication. They were the symbolic screams of hungry, angry infants. Their attempts to devalue me were actually defensive maneuvers to deny the primitive power of the preverbal mother. The women demonstrated how the feminine tendency to make obsessive identification with others can become oppressive. They became depressed, understanding and feeling the pain of the regressed male infants, while turning the anger they felt toward the men against themselves.

For many weeks after I added James to this group, I felt like a harried mother with too many children and not enough milk. I had to remind myself that a group is a family, not a mother/child dyad. It took my getting the member/siblings involved and interested in each other to resolve the primitive resistance demonstrated in my mother-led group. When that happened, the men were able to help the women become more assertive, and the women were able to help the men become more empathetic and connected.

Whether the leader's power and problem reside in the breasts or the penis, group leaders must be very careful; it can be a dangerous job. To be an effective leader, one must always be aware of the primitive aggression that lies below the surface in all of us. There are ways to mitigate that aggression. The cannibalism of the primitive horde and the competition for the breast are driven by toxic envy, by the idea that all goodness and power resides in the charismatic other, and that the only way to get that goodness and power is to devour the leader. If group members can be helped by the leader to believe that latent goodness and power lie within each of them, they are less likely to have to eat their leader. Good leaders, whether male or female, help their group members identify and develop their individual strengths. Unless they want to be eaten up or sucked dry!

References

Balint, M. (1949). "Early Developmental States of the Ego." *International Journal of Psycho-Analysis*, 30, 265–273.

Blos, P. (1984). "Son and father." *Journal of the American Psychoanalytic Association*, 32(2), 301–324.

Freud, S. (1925). "Some Psychical Consequences of the Anatomical Distinction between the Sexes." *Standard Edition, Volume 19*. London: Hogarth Press, 243–260.

Freud, S. (1939). "Moses and monotheism." *Standard Edition, Volume 23*. London: Hogarth Press, 81–122.

Gilligan, C., Lyons, N.P., and Hanmer, T.J. (eds). (1989). *Making Connections: The Relational World of Adolescent Girls at Emma Willard School*. Cambridge, MA: Harvard University Press.

Holmes, L. (2002). "Women in Groups and Women's Groups." *International Journal of Group Psychotherapy*, 52(2), 171–188.

Holmes, L. (2008). *The Internal Triangle: New theories of female development*. New York: Jason Aronson.

Holmes, L. (2009). "The technique of partial identification: Waking up to the world." *International Journal of Group Psychotherapy*, 59(2), 2.

Hurst, W.J. (2000). "What about Lacan?" *Modern Psychoanalysis*, 25(1), 91–108.

Lacan, J. (1977). *Écrits: A Selection*. A. Sheridan, trans. New York: W.W. Norton.

Mahler, M.S. (1968). "On Human Symbiosis and Vicissitudes of Individuation." *Psychoanalytic Study of the Child*. New Haven: Yale University Press, 1, 7–31.

McDougall, J. (1989). *Theaters of the Mind*. New York: W.W. Norton, 32–49.

Ormont, L. (1991). "Establishing Transient Identification in the Group Setting." *Modern Psychoanalysis*, 24(2), 143–156.

Ormont, L. (2001a). "Progressive emotional communication: Criteria for a well-functioning group." *The Technique of Group Therapy* (L. Furgeri, Ed.). Madison, CT: Psychosocial Press, pp. 373–384.

Ormont, L. (2001b). "Bringing life into the group experience: The power of immediacy." *The Technique of Group Therapy* (L. Fugeri, Ed.). Madison, CT: Psychosocial Press.

Yalom, I. D. (1995). *The theory and practice of group psychotherapy*, 4th ed. New York: Basic Books, pp. 13–15.

Part II
Psychoanalysis

Introduction

The following 11 papers, written between 2002 and 2019, chart my professional growth as a psychoanalyst, from learning to do psychoanalytic research as a student, to contemplating why the act of talking is so essentially therapeutic, to tackling the challenges of the repetition compulsion, to thinking about what we mean when we talk about cure in psychoanalysis.

The first paper that I had accepted for publication in 2002, "A Fascination with Death," is an abridged version of the final research project I did at the Center for Modern Psychoanalytic Studies in 1995. Creating it was probably the most important part of my analytic education. I was asked by the research faculty to study my patient, the boring "Mr B," and formulate a question about him. I had worked with him for four years when I started the final paper, and there were many things about him that I thought I understood. Now I was challenged to explore what I didn't know about him. What did I still not understand about Mr B? I had to formulate a question reflecting something that wasn't clear about the case. The question had to be simple, while focused on a dynamic that permeated the clinical material. The question that I settled on was: what is the unconscious meaning of the patient's fascination with death?

Memories, stories, and fantasies about death, as well as symbolic expressions of death, like boring the analyst, making her feel sick or breathless, and putting her to sleep, were Mr B's specialty, a sort of masterpiece he created in the treatment room to protect himself from primitive impulses and dangerous ideas. Now I was required to explore specifically why his unconscious had constructed the intricate, walled-off coffin he had put us in together in the analysis.

Of course, I had ideas about this, but I soon learned that my hunches and intuition, though valuable attributes in an analyst, were not enough to give my teachers the idea that my training had taught me how to do qualitative psychoanalytic research. To do that, I had to demonstrate that I could listen carefully and without prejudice to create and validate hypotheses. Every theory that I came up with about Mr B had to be borne out in what he actually said in each session.

I studied the theory of psychoanalytic research. I learned that Freud, the first psychoanalytic researcher, approached the creation of his theory in a surprisingly scientific way. He studied his patients the way a physicist would study atoms, using the reality of what his patients actually said to speculate on the unconscious meaning of their words. A theory, essentially a guess, would come out of listening carefully to all the diverse ideas and random thoughts of his patients. The theory that occurred to Freud was appealing because it promised to organize the clinical data, synthesize a large amount of information, and create relationships between seemingly unrelated material. In other words, the theory promised to explain the facts.

With his newly created theory in mind, Freud would continue to test its validity. Did his patient say new things that confirmed or refuted his theory? If new clinical material supported his speculative theory, could he find supporting evidence with other patients? Did the theory lead to a deeper understanding of the patient and human beings in general? Did it generate new and equally useful new theories as the treatment progressed? If so, Freud saw all of this as scientific evidence that his theory was correct (Mackay, 1989).

The demands of the rigorous, disciplined process demonstrated by Freud and described by Mackay (1989) generated tremendous growth in my professional self. I paid attention to Mr B in a new, focused way, completely absorbed in the journey we were both taking to understand him. My research project taught me how to really listen and how to really think, and these new skills have assisted me in the writing I have done since.

I was fortunate in the convergence of my interest in pregnancy and childbirth and my training in psychoanalytic research. I started my doctoral studies when I was completing my training at the Center for Modern Psychoanalytic Studies. When I decided to focus my PhD studies on the topic of pregnancy and childbirth as a developmental milestone in a woman's life, I knew, because I had recently learned how to do psychoanalytic research, exactly how to proceed. I developed my theory of the internal triangle by listening to what the women in my two groups actually said, developing hypotheses, and then testing them. Every paper I have submitted for publication since has been based on research done in the analytic session.

After the publication of my first paper, I was offered opportunities to participate in interesting projects and present papers at several psychoanalytic conferences. "Marking the Anniversary: Adolescents and the September 11 Healing Process," described one of those projects. It discusses a day I spent at a New Jersey high school on September 11, 2002, the first anniversary of the World Trade Center attack. The American Group Psychotherapy Association had provided a grant for therapists to go into schools that had been directly impacted in the attack to organize groups for adolescents to talk. The high school I was sent to was in a town in New Jersey that had lost

30 people on September 11, 2001. Many more residents of this community who had worked in the buildings had survived the attack but were forever changed by the event. The children of these victims and survivors were the young people we would be working with. The paper I wrote describing this experience offered not only clinical techniques about dealing with resistance and trauma, but also a reflection of the particularly malignant public health crisis 9/11 created for teenagers processing this terrible event while dealing with the developmental trauma of adolescence.

"Humor and Psychoanalysis," "Leadership and Psychoanalysis," and "Myth and Psychoanalysis" were presented before audiences of professional institutes and societies. They are certainly less scholarly than my research papers or any of my other papers where I endeavored to create theory or expand ideas about clinical practice, but I do think they illustrate the fact that psychoanalytic ideas can enrich our understanding of many aspects of our society.

"Humor and Psychoanalysis" makes the argument that psychoanalysis doesn't always have to be painfully intense. Including humor and play in the analytic session helps both analyst and analysand to deal with primitive impulses and negative emotions. Laughing with colleagues in supervision helps dissipate all the rage, grief, and despair that analysts have to tolerate and hold for their patients.

"Leadership and Psychoanalysis" and "Myth and Psychoanalysis" offer the idea that psychoanalytic theory has many applications outside the treatment room. We can use it to understand the earliest myths that human beings created and indeed, use Greek myth to validate Freud's theories. We can apply our ideas about the unconscious to organizations and understand and appreciate the fact that, whether they be analytic institutes or corporations, all human organizations have characteristics of Freud's primal horde.

When Phyllis Meadow, the founder of The Center for Modern Psychoanalytic Studies in New York died in 2005, I wrote "Becoming an Analyst: Learning to Live with Madness, Aggression, and the Unknown." Dr Meadow was one of my most important teachers, and this paper was a tribute to her. She was a passionate advocate of Freud and Dr Hyman Spotnitz, who was her analyst and the founder of modern psychoanalysis. Meadow was an unapologetic drive theorist and had little patience for the bleeding hearts of social work or the object relations theorists who described aggression as a response to frustrating and depriving objects which can be banished from the mind by a "corrective emotional experience" in therapy. Meadow had no interest in re-mothering her patients. Rather, she worked to get them to put all their thoughts and feelings into words. She saw the mind as a battleground between love and hate, sex and aggression, life and death. In its war with the primitive drives, the mind creatively develops repressions, resistances, and pathological repetitions, drafting them as intrapsychic soldiers to fight the war against the exciting and terrifying id. Rather than "curing" patients of their aggression, she urged them to put their drives into words. Meadow was a wonderful model in the creative use of aggression. I never met anyone who enjoyed her aggression more, and she used it constructively to become a brilliant scholar and to found her institute. When a student would present a patient, blaming all his symptoms on his toxic mother, Dr Meadow used to retort impatiently, "There is no mother!" Though I always thought that the impassioned statement told us all a lot about Dr Meadow's actual mother, I came to understand what she meant. She believed that the reality of the actual maternal object was less important than the intrapsychic mother we create in fantasy at the beginning of life to quiet our drives. Meadow was responsible for my learning to tolerate and even enjoy and exploit my anger, secret insanity, and ignorance. For that, I will be forever in her debt.

As I gained more experience in the treatment room, new research questions sprouted in my mind. I wondered how patients get better. After 20 years of listening, I saw clearly that the people in my practice who improved were the ones who had no resistance to talking. They were a very diverse group. They included depressives, people with anger management problems, women seeking marriage, and men wanting a divorce. There was even one schizophrenic, who became a fully functional, if slightly eccentric individual. The only common denominator between my diverse success stories is that they enjoyed talking and seemed to know unconsciously that words in abundance were the road to cure. They didn't want me to tell them what to do; most of them gabbed on with very little awareness that I was even in the room. Slowly, they all made remarkable progress. This was an objective reality, but I had no idea why it was so. How did talking cure? Why was it so essentially therapeutic?

One day in 2005, I read an article by Dr Mary Shepherd in *Modern Psychoanalysis* which described the new research that was going on in neurobiology. A light bulb went off in my head, and I felt terribly excited. Shepherd's description of the structure of the brain gave me an idea about why talking changes people. Spotnitz had speculated back in the 1960s that talking had the power to deactivate neural pathways in the brain and activate new ones, but the new neurobiology was actually looking at the structure of the brain and proving Spotnitz right. I began to have new thoughts about exactly how talking cures. My 2008 article "Why Talking Cures" addressed those ideas.

Most of those enthusiastic talkers that psychoanalysis actually helped have stayed with me for 20 or 30 years, and they show no signs of leaving anytime soon. I myself have been in analysis for over 40 years, and my addiction to talking has been invaluable in my ability to tolerate my patients, find a loving partner, raise my children, treasure my grandchildren, and enjoy a satisfying and intellectually stimulating life. I considered myself "cured" long ago. My

2012 article "Beyond Cure," argues for the value of the psychoanalytic experience as a healthy and ongoing mental health practice – not just a cure for psychopathology.

I then turned my attention to that behemoth of all psychoanalysts, the repetition compulsion. It is a dynamic that often proves intractable, and most of the people who left analysis with me with almost no progress being made were its victims. In every case, I had failed to help them give up their toxic patterns and try new behaviors. I knew it wasn't impossible. I myself had been able to overcome my personal repetitions after years in analysis, and I searched my memory for how my analyst and I had done it. The idea I came up with is that my successful treatment involved the analyst adhering to the modern analytic techniques of mirroring, joining, following the contact function, and limiting her talking to three to five object-oriented questions in each session. This disciplined, non-stimulating environment was maintained for many years until I, the patient, had said everything. The repetition compulsion had been explored and understood at length by both analyst and patient. We came to a point in the treatment where I knew all the old feelings to the point of boredom with myself. There was only one thing to be done at this point. I was going to have to make a decision to change my behavior. But why would I do that? Repetitions are unpleasant and toxic, but they are so gratifying and familiar, while new behaviors seem terrifying. One of my patients described giving them up as "matricide," the death of the earliest and crucial object. Another patient reported that trying to give up repetitions is like standing on a high cliff gazing at another cliff a quarter of mile away and wanting to get to it, but seeing nothing between the points but empty space. He said, "Even thinking about giving up my destructive behaviors feels like taking the first step when all I see is thin air."

My analyst found a way to break the spell of my repetitions in an intervention that was exquisitely timed after all those years of quiet acceptance of my thoughts and feelings. It was not an intellectual or didactic interpretation. It was a highly emotional communication, charged with both love and hate and the threat of the loss of a valued and trusted object. In the moment of my analyst's dramatic intervention, I could feel my brain rewiring, creating a new neural pathway that enabled me to change my behaviors and my life. I describe this intervention in my 2014 paper "Reaching the Repetition Compulsion."

The final paper in this section is titled "The Analyst in Winter," published in the journal *Modern Psychoanalysis* in 2020. Like my early papers, it was inspired by my personal life. Just as I used my own pregnancies many years ago to inspire my exploration of childbirth and how it serves as a developmental milestone in the female life cycle, I am now focusing on old age, its many challenges and scant pleasures. I was aided in the research for this paper by more than a few long term patients who, like me, have now reached an advanced age that can objectively be called "old." As was the case with almost all my papers, researching it has expanded by consciousness and helped me find ways to cope with the greatest challenge of all: human mortality.

References

Mackay, N. (1989). *Motivation and explanation*. Madison, CT: International Universities Press.

Shepherd, M. (2005). Toward a psychobiology of desire: Drive theory in the time of nueuroscience. *Modern Psychoanalysis*, *30*(1), 43–59.

Chapter 9

A single case study of a fascination with death

Mr B came into treatment because he was "having trouble dealing with" the death of his stepmother who had died three months earlier. It worried him that he hadn't been able to cry, that he had gained weight, and that he ate out every night because he "couldn't be home alone." He had bought a book about mourning but discovered when he got home that it was a book for children who had lost a parent. His biological mother had died of cancer when he was three years old. He had no memory of her, even when looking at a photo. His mother became ill when Mr B was two, and the family decided it would be better if he went to live with his paternal grandmother. Two older brothers, aged five and nine, were allowed to stay home while their mother died. Mr B did not return home until he was five, after his father remarried.

The first thing Mr B said to me was, "I'm gay. I've always been gay. I'm very comfortable with it. My family is comfortable with it." He said he didn't want a "gay analysis," which seemed to mean one that would "reform" him of his homosexuality.

One of the most interesting aspects of this case, which is hard to replicate on paper, was the discrepancy between the stimulating material verbalized by Mr B and his deathly dull delivery. Affect was totally split off from ideation. Mr B talked with absolutely no feeling and spoke in a soft monotone from the back of his throat. Calling himself the "king of bland," he said, "I could be a creative person if I could connect to my feelings. I have no ability to be extreme. When my real mother died, I died with her." I felt bored, pushed away, put to sleep, and I began to doze.

Unfortunately, Mr B had the habit of occasionally startling me by unexpectedly jumping off the couch and saying something sarcastic, like, "Well that's that. That's all I have to say!" Then he would laugh maniacally, resume his position on the couch, and continue his flat monotone. I began to feel that it was "dangerous to sleep with him." I decided to solve my problem by taking notes during the session to keep myself awake. Mr B was delighted. He asked, "Are you writing? What are you writing?" I told him I was writing down what he said and asked him his thoughts about it. He said it made him feel important. He told me that the sound of my pen on the paper was the only contact he needed or wanted from me. So, we found our rhythm. I wrote and he talked in his boring way. I felt like we were floating together in separate bubbles.

When Mr B was not boring, he was overstimulating. He had dreams of angry little animals with sharp teeth that he had to take care of. They often ended up being run over by trucks or burned to death. He dreamed his stepmother was shot in the chest, and he had to nurse her, but she died a painful death anyway. He dreamed a man with a long knife stabbed him repeatedly in the chest. He liked to "invent horrible scenarios, fantasies that allow me to get upset" and imagine an old boyfriend mugged or run over by a car. Part of the pleasure of these fantasies was imagining all the attention and condolence he would get. He described at great length and in minute detail a movie in which a woman got hacked to death with a machete. He told me that I looked like the actress Glenn Close and brought in a fantasy, based on the move *Fatal Attraction*, in which I repeatedly stabbed him. He related a dream in which an icicle had fallen off a building and penetrated my body. Both of these were reported in a flat monotone, totally devoid of the sexual and aggressive feelings that they seemed to convey.

About a year into treatment, Mr B had a long rambling dream. He was looking for his mother. Finding she was dead, he became hysterical, throwing his arms around the knees of his older brother. The brother pushed him away. At that point, Mr B noticed some mums behind him and buried his face in them. Their fragrance soothed him, and he thought, "This is what my mother smelled like." I was bored and confused by the dream, but while he was telling it, I had a somatic reaction. I felt dizzy and nauseated. I started sweating. I realized I had some feelings about being the "mum behind him." It felt like a huge responsibility that I didn't want. There was such a bleakness and emptiness about him that made me think he had been a wantonly neglected child. I felt that mothering him could kill me. Each time Mr B mentioned that he would like me to be "a replacement for my various mothers," I felt physically sick and worried that I had cancer. I began to have the conviction that Mr B had the unconscious idea that his love and neediness were lethal, that they had killed his mother.

Klein (Klein and Riviere, 1967) discussed the destructive fantasies infants have toward their mothers which makes them feel that they have destroyed the object and continue destroying it. The conflict between these aggressive fantasies and feelings of love give rise to guilt and a need to make reparation. The most important thing a mother can do for the infant's continued constructive mental development, according to Klein, is to survive these early sadistic fantasies. Mr B's mother failed to do this. Would I be able to survive Mr B's attempts to sicken me with his ruthless needs or bore me to death?

Primitive object relations and the defenses erected around these relations are repeated in the transference rather than remembered (A. Freud, 1966). They wipe out the memories of early objects by externalizing primitive impulses to a figure in the current environment. Studying this process in the "here and now" should take precedence over elaborate attempts to reconstruct their history (Spotnitz and Meadow, 1976). The somatic symptoms I experienced in many sessions with Mr B acted as a powerful nonverbal communication about the trauma he experienced with the separation from and loss of his mother. Bollas (1987) described a patient's recollection of his earliest pre-objects as a "psychosomatic fusion." My responsive bodily identification with the mother's suffering was most likely experienced somatically rather than ideationally because the patient was communicating what Bollas called the "unthought known," that is, something that Mr B was painfully aware of long before he used speech or rational thought.

Death permeated most of what Mr B talked about in the treatment. He told me about a friend who had developed AIDS and suffered terribly. Shortly before this friend died, Mr B stopped seeing him, never giving any explanation and never returning his phone calls. Mr B next volunteered at an agency that paid home visits to people with AIDS. Once a week he would visit a family where both the mother and the father were dying. Mr B said the family reminded him of his own, in that there were three young children who were witnessing the slow, painful death of their parents. Mr B seemed to enjoy telling me in excruciating detail about the misery of the parents' horrible suffering. I couldn't breathe, and I felt nauseated and sweaty – a now-familiar countertransference. A few weeks before the father died, Mr B left this family and never went back.

In the third year of treatment, Mr B began a series of "confessions" to me about his self-neglect and abuse. He started by saying, "I want to confess all my sins to you. I ought to be confessing." He told me that because he owed $ 40,000 in back taxes, the IRS had put a lien on all his property. He admitted he had a drinking problem, and that his last relationship, which had been "based on alcohol," ended when his lover went to AA. He confessed that he hadn't been to the dentist in years, and his teeth were falling out. He neglected his car to the point of making it dangerous to drive. He said, "Maybe at bottom, I'm just a bad person, a criminal. All of these situations are of my own making. I'm building up a huge tragedy, so that someone will have to take care of me. When I was a little kid, I covered myself in a plastic dome, as if I didn't need anything. Now I'm creating upsetting things to get me to express something in my life around death. If something bad happens, people will have to take care of me." I asked if I should be taking care of him. He said, "You are – by letting me talk."

A tendency toward self-punishment and neglect, such as we see with Mr B, is a reversal of the hate and sadism that was initially associated with an early object but has been turned toward the self. By this circuitous route, the patient succeeds in taking revenge on the original object and in tormenting present ones (such as the analyst), all to avoid the open expression of hostility (Freud, 1915; 1917), Self-destructive reactions are organized reactions originally intended to master tension. Libidinal energy redirects aggression toward the self to protect the beloved and needed object (Spotnitz and Meadow, 1976). Wolfenstein (1956) presented a patient who had lost a parent and had the unconscious fantasy that her compulsive self-punishment and intense suffering would force the dead parent to return.

Another confession involved Mr B's feelings about his homosexuality. He told me about a story he had written about a convict who was "executed for his sins." Mr B implied that this convict was being put to death for his homosexuality. Before the convict went to his death, he had to "take care" of the man who was executed before him. Later, Mr B told me that "homosexuals are worthless. Being heterosexual is much more worthwhile." When he reported that he had gone out drinking and then to sex clubs, he said he felt, "guilty, less than, weird." He told me that his homosexual acting out "gives me something tangible to feel guilty about. I do these things to feel horrible and shameful, to remind myself that I'm not good. Being gay is self-obliterating and degrading." When I asked why he wanted to feel this way, he replied, "because my mother died." He seemed to be telling me that his automatic and intrinsic guilt preceded his homosexuality; that his homosexuality served the purpose of perpetuating his guilt; and that the guilt involved his mother's death.

Socarides (1978) wrote that in homosexuality there is a fusion of the aggressive and libidinal drives, along with an intensification of the aggressive drive. Aggression is expressed in guilt and a compulsive need for self-punishment. Homosexuals in particular search for replicas of the mother to whom they can make reparation in an attempt to alleviate guilt. The homosexual has been unable to negotiate successfully the separation–individuation phase of development. There is a failure to make a proper separation from the mother, along with insufficient self–object differentiation. Therefore, when Mr B attacks himself, I can understand that he is also attacking the mother/analyst. Spotnitz and Meadow (1976) advised that it is the analyst's job to study to what extent the patient is dominated by libidinal defenses against aggression or aggressive defenses against libido. Looked at from this perspective, Mr B's homosexuality can be seen as a particular manifestation of the narcissistic defense. Mr B's guilt about his homosexuality, his sense that he is "horrible" and "shameful," protects the mother/analyst from his wish to destroy her. McDougall (1992) described homosexuality as a defense against a double polarity of terror: that of losing one's psychic and bodily limits and dissolving into the primitive oral or anal mother, and that of desiring this fusional form of psychic death. This theory provides a more plausible explanation of how Mr B's homosexuality and his fascination with death are related in the unconscious.

Joseph (1982) wrote that when powerful masochism (the death instinct) expresses itself in an addiction to death, the patient obtains significant libidinal satisfaction from the drive toward death. As the treatment progressed, Mr B's tendency to eroticize death became more and more apparent. The first time I ever experienced him as animated and alive was when he told me about his friend's mother who had been brutally murdered. For weeks, he talked about the details of the bloody crime. He spoke at length about the eyes of the dying, "They're so beautiful, deep, and bottomless. The eyes of the living have a door behind them, but the eyes of the dying are totally open. When you die you go to Jesus, into the light. You become an angel."

In the weeks that followed, he began to speak with more affect and passion, but his passion was about death. At the beginning of one session, he got on the couch and said, "What a week! The most intense since I've known you!" The occurrence which had filled him with all this feeling was the death of a friend from AIDS. Mr B had been present at the moment of death. He described it as "the most intimate thing I've ever experienced." He talked about the "miracle of death, the same as a baby being born. I've never felt so alive!" He went on to describe the death in agonizing detail that I found almost unbearable. Though my patient was euphoric, I wanted to get up and leave the room.

These periods of heightened feeling for both patient and analyst were relieved with the now-familiar more boring Mr B. He would talk about "zoning out" and "feeling detached." He described the "glass partition" that separated and shielded him from life and the world. He took a night job at an insurance company. It was in the basement of a building, and there were no windows. Mr B described it as

> very restful. There's very little stimulation. It's so soothing to be down there underground. Working at night in a basement is better than all the aggravation I experience at my day job. I'd like to give it all up. I like being down there all by myself. It's so quiet. It opens a gateway to feeling.

The details of this coffin of a job killed me by putting me back to sleep.

On the third anniversary of the beginning of treatment, this case took a dramatic turn. Mr B reported that he had met a man, X, who was HIV positive and with whom he had had sex twice. He felt a "powerful, passionate connection" with this man. He was attracted to taking care of X while he died. He said, "I would be repeating my father's life." He fantasized about his own death from AIDS, his body lying in a casket, "but alive, so I could watch everyone crying over me." He described sex with X as "very daring. He's into giving and receiving pain. It's very cathartic – a gateway to emotion." Mr B said the idea that "If X dies, I'll still be alive" kept going through his head. He felt that going through X's death would

> bring me to a new place. I would change, develop, become intensely passionate. When my mother died, I felt nothing. I just put it away. I feel a need to incorporate that experience, delve into it somehow. I loved the surge of feeling that came from meeting X and watching my friend die.

There seemed to be several reasons why the patient chose during the course of treatment to begin a relationship with a sick lover threatened with impending death. Certainly this relationship was in the service of the repetition compulsion. Freud (1920) discussed the repetition compulsion as an attempt to be active in a situation in which one was originally passive; patients use it to master what is repeated. The repetition compulsion is based on the death instinct, in that it is ultimately a wish to return the organism to an inanimate state, free of tension. Loving someone who is dying allowed Mr B to repeat his history, this time in the role of "spouse" rather than the helpless child. He told me that the death of a spouse is the only "legitimate" reason that a person can be expected to be comforted and cared for. By repeating his history, Mr B would finally be allowed to grieve and be consoled.

X provided my patient with a "gateway to emotion." Watching someone die gave him a "surge of feeling." Whenever X's condition deteriorated or his T-cell count went down, Mr B experienced a period of "heightened sexuality" with his lover. Death and X were fascinating because they provided an opportunity to finally have feelings.

The choice of X was particularly significant in terms of the transference. Mr B had consistently demonstrated a narcissistic defense in the treatment, protecting the analyst from his hostility by neglecting, abusing, and "deadening" himself. But when a patient is ready to give up their narcissistic defense, there is often a tendency to engage in particularly self-destructive acts (Spotnitz and Meadow, 1976). When hostile feelings toward the analyst threaten to erupt, the patient must compensate by heightening the attack on self. After three years of being merged in a deadened state with the analyst, Mr B seemed to feel safe enough to experience primitive pre-feelings toward the analyst. But those impulses, lethal to his own mother, were experienced as highly dangerous, and Mr B responded by bringing himself even closer to death. Since he seemed to have the unconscious idea that his ruthless needs had killed his mother, he had to protect me from his intense wish to be taken care of. In the relationship with X, he seemed to be telling me that he had found a solution to his conflict. His dangerous actions would induce feelings of care and concern in me, but I would not risk death in this situation. He would risk it for me. As long as he keeps himself perilously close to death without being consumed by it, he expresses his wish to merge with and be saved by the analyst without putting her at risk.

A few months after meeting X, Mr B announced that he was thinking of taking a break in treatment. I asked him what put that thought in his head:

B: All the silences. You're so quiet. I say to myself, "Well, by being quiet, she's reflecting all the women in my life. She's trying to get me angry by neglecting me." I know what I should feel is anger, but I don't. I just feel detached.

L: So you're not going to be angry at me. You're just going to leave.

B: What's the point of being angry? They're all dead.
L: Well, it's true that your mothers are dead. But am I dead?
B: It isn't fair to you to be angry unless I've been clear about what I really want or need from you.
L: What do you want from me?
B: (*With astonishing affect*) I want you to leave me alone!
L: That's been my impression for three and a half years.
B: I get annoyed when people show an interest in me. I get bratty. I want to scream, "Leave me alone!" So now that I've told you that, can I have the summer off? Please, Mommy, can I go out and play alone?

Mr B had rented a summer house with X and his friend J, who was in the last stages of AIDS. I was concerned about him taking the entire summer off, and so I said to him, "It's fine if you go play alone for a while, but how about checking in with me from time to time? What if we scheduled a monthly session in July and August?"

B: You're muddying my mind with the things I have to do instead of relaxing. Therapy is an intrusion on my rest.

Mr B wanted to end the treatment that day, but he realized he "forgot" his check for me, and he agreed to come back for one more session to pay me. When he came back the following week, he said:

B: I've been thinking about your suggestion of us meeting once a month this summer. That's probably a good idea. Things are very stressful out there. J is very sick and wan. He has an incurable virus which attacks the eyes, and he's going blind. (*Laughing*). Death is a part of life. It's so peaceful and restful out there. J will kill himself if things get very bad. I can see him doing that. He has a constant fever now. He'll overdose on valium. He saw his lover die. He wants to be more graceful at the precipice. I watch X watching J, and it's very pleasurable. X and I talk about J as if he was our kid. It's sort of odd, but I'm glad to be around J at this moment in his life. We work in the garden together out there. We're getting our roots entangled under the dirt. I think while I'm gone, it will be like a garden going through a fallow period. The roots of our work will be waiting underground till the fall. We can put up some new sprouts then. I bet you're pretty upset by all of this. Will you still be here in September?
L: Will I? Where am I going?
B: I've never really brought you in. I'll miss you, but I need to take myself away. I guess I'm isolating myself, withdrawing from the world. It's so great to be out there. Everything is amazingly calm.

In telling me there is no point in being angry at the dead, Mr B seemed to be telling me what is so attractive about death. Proving that contradictory ideas can simultaneously exist in the unconscious, Mr B was fascinated with death not only as the "gateway to emotion," but also as a useful way to kill off dangerous feelings like rage. He preferred to kill me off by leaving treatment rather than telling me that I deserved to die because I had neglected him with silence as his mother had. Being close to people who are dying at the summer house made it easier to repress rage.

Though Mr B was clear in his wish to kill both the therapy and the analyst, there were also indications that he wanted me and the therapy to live. When he came back for his summer session, he remarked, "Something new happens here every week. Oh well, I guess that's what keeps us alive." Though I was intruding on his death wishes, the conflict between therapy and the summer house, where he would spend his days with the dying, was a clear manifestation of the struggle between life and death. In the session that was supposed to be his last, Mr B vacillated between the wish to separate from me and his fear of severing his connections, but ultimately life seemed to win out; he forgot his check and had to return. His horticultural images of underground roots and new sprouts reflected the life and death struggle active in his unconscious. His anxious query about whether I would be here in September demonstrated his wish to kill me and his fear that it would really happen.

When Mr B returned for his August session, he reported a dream:

B: I was living in Little Italy. I went to pee in this big public bathroom, and there were lots of men around. It was a homosexual scene. These guys were gangster types. I was in a stall, and they pulled out guns. One guy had a shotgun. He shot the guy in the stall next to me. Then he pulled out a machine gun and shot everyone. I hit the floor. The guy was going to get me. He was stabbing everyone. It was a beautiful bathroom with beautiful tiles. I think this dream is about AIDS.
L: How does that work?
B: All those guys with guns are the different ways you can contract AIDS. I didn't get hit because I was playing dead.

This dream in which Mr B survived by playing dead struck me as an expression of the magical idea: my fascination with death will save me from actual death. I had heard this expressed before when Mr B kept repeating, "If X dies, I'll still be alive." He also said over and over, "X and I are just alike." The obsessive reiteration of this idea made me begin to suspect that its opposite was in Mr B's unconscious: X and I are not at all alike. Because he is dying, therefore, I am not. He described his relationship with X as "unreal in some way, as if I was playing a game." By flirting with death, he warded it off.

Mr B very much wanted to tell his father that he was gay and in love with X, but though he kept setting up meetings with his father to have this talk, it never happened.

B: There's a process that goes on between us. I put a veneer over everything. I avoid, gloss over. I put a polyurethane coating over everything that keeps me from breathing. With my father, a glass partition separates me. There's a conscious lowering of the partition to detach.
L: What makes it hard to talk to your father?
B: When I was 20, I wrote a complimentary letter to the editor of the local paper after the paper had printed a positive article about homosexuality. They printed the letter. The day the letter came out in the paper, I watched my father reading the paper. I wanted to see if he would react when he saw the letter. He didn't react as he was reading, but that night he had an angina attack. I'm afraid he'll keel over if I tell him I'm gay.
L: You'll kill him?
B: (*Laughing*). I was telling X that my father and I are planning a trip to the Statue of Liberty. I said, "Maybe I'll tell him on the ferry. That way he can fall right into the harbor, and we won't have to bury him. Or maybe I should tell him on our next trip to the cemetery. Just stand him right by an open grave and push him in." He's like me; he's just so bland. I was glad when my stepmother died to hear his voice shake a little when he was telling people on the phone. At least he was alive after 80 years of polyurethane. By the way, there's something I've been meaning to talk to you about.
L: What is it?
B: Lately, I've had this phobia about walking into shards of glass. My friend R and I were in San Francisco when they had the earthquake, and afterwards, we were walking down the street, and a jagged, broken plate glass window swung out and nearly hit R. He could have been killed. Since then, I walk down the street and all of a sudden, I get the split-second feeling that glass is going to swing out and cut my body open. It happened on the way over here. I was looking at a cute guy, and all of a sudden, it happened. It happens when I'm looking left or right, and suddenly I feel I'm not watching where I'm going, and I quickly look to center expecting to see the glass. If I don't watch where I'm going, I'm going to get cut. When X and I were in the kitchen this summer with knives, I kept worrying I was going to cut him. If X were dead, I wouldn't have to worry about his illness. Sometimes, I envy guys whose lovers are already dead. Everybody has to feel sorry for them – they're like orphans. I'm always wishing something awful would happen so people would have to take care of me.

When Mr B stood to leave the session, he stared at my breasts with a look of anxiety for a long moment, blushed, and said, "That's a beautiful blouse."

The fear/wish to kill the father expressed in this session illustrates that Mr B's father is unconsciously experienced as an extension or continuation of the primitive mother on whom the patient is fixated. The same unconscious psychic fusion of self and object which characterizes the relationship with the mother/analyst, permeates his other relationships as well. Mr B vacillates between the idea that his homosexuality will kill his father or himself, that he will get cut or cut X, and that he will kill or be killed.

In the next session, Mr B reported the following dream:

B: I was in a public restroom, and men were having sex everywhere. A middle-aged man came out of a changing room. He was with a little girl. He put her in another room. I thought, "Why did he bring his daughter here when he's having sex with other men?" The little girl had blonde, curly hair. [The analyst has blonde, curly hair.] Men were having sex right in the doorway. I'm used to that. I've surrounded myself with that kind of sex-charged environment. It was fine for me to be standing and watching, but it was peculiar for the little girl to be watching. Who was she? I mean, I could go for the obvious: she represents innocence, sweetness, and light. I can't figure what she was doing there. Any ideas?
L: What's your idea?
B: Have you read *The Alienist?* Do you know what the term means?
L: Tell me.
B: You're one.
L: What is it?
B: Oh, a little blonde – ha ha! No, it means a psychologist. The book is about a serial killer who kills little boy prostitutes. Teddy Roosevelt hires an alienist, a woman, to help him figure the case out. They make a psychological profile of the killer. He only kills young boys; he cuts out their eyes and mutilates their bodies. At one point, he kills a little girl. Maybe that's why the little girl was in my dream. I don't know what else she could be.
L: What was the little girl feeling in the dream?
B: She was a prop. She wasn't agitated or excited. The little girl was playing with something on her lap.

This dream clearly brought the analyst into Mr B's unconscious. He denies any feelings toward the analyst when he described the little girl as a "prop," but he seems to like the idea that she isn't agitated or excited by the homosexual, sex-charged atmosphere. She sits and plays with something on her lap, just as I write in my notebook. It is a woman in *The Alienist* who "figures out the case" and saves the little boys. But a little girl is murdered too. Will I be able to save Mr B from death? Maybe I will be killed too.

Mr B announced his plans to move in with X.

B: Here I am moving in with someone who's positive, who may get sick and die within the year. Whatever makes him attractive to me, HIV is a part of him, and I think that element has a draw for me.

L: What is it?

B: I have these little imaginings that something bad will happen, and people will have to take care of me. Everyone will pay attention. When my stepmother died, Dad got all the attention. But this time, I'm the spouse. I can be comforted.

L: Why can't you be comforted without someone dying?

B: This time it's legitimate. I can't say, "My mother died when I was three." I can't be comforted for something that happened 35 years ago.

L: Why can't you be comforted for something that happened 35 years ago?

B: When we were little, no attention was paid to grief and mourning. My father remarried quickly. She died on August 25, and school started a week later, and my older brothers went back, and that was that. I think of myself as a kid, still waiting for the release from that trauma. I'm waiting to release the angst I've been carrying around all this time.

In this session, I understood that Mr B's fascination with death reflected the unconscious wish, not only to merge with his mother in death, but also to master the trauma of her loss.

Discussion

Mr B's mother died when he was just three. The boundaries between self and object are not clearly differentiated in the pre-Oedipal mind (Mahler, 1967). This lack of separation and individuation means that the destruction of the beloved object can also be experienced as the destruction of self. Moreover, the destructive fantasies against the mother which all young children experience from time to time (Klein and Riviere, 1967) were seemingly magically fulfilled in Mr B's case.

Mr B expresses the idea that he is one with his dead mother by being the "king of bland," killing off all his feelings. Like her, he is dead. Being boring also has the advantage of expressing retribution for the murder of his mother: I will make myself dead as a punishment for the murder I have committed. My ruthless, lethal needs will be transformed into the death of no needs.

Mr B's blandness in the treatment room induces deathlike states of boredom and detachment in the analyst. She feels she will die, just as his mother did, if she has to take care of him. Alternately, she feels merged with her patient in a state of feelingless ennui. The simultaneous symbiotic murder of and merging with the object that Mr B's fascination with death creates in the analysis, allow him to discharge both the life and death instincts in an atmosphere of relative safety.

Mr B has created an environment within the analysis in which he feels safe by "playing dead." His "boring" defense has enabled him to master tension from both the life and death instincts and exist with the analyst in an objectless state of symbiotic merger. The analyst has joined him in this deathlike state by detaching and sleeping. In this narcissistic merger where self and object are one, libido has been used to kill off his primitive sadistic feelings, thereby protecting himself and me from the aggression which would destroy us both. By killing me and himself, he also uses aggressive defenses against his libidinal impulses; making us both dead expresses the unconscious libidinal idea that we are merged in primitive union. Using death as an aggressive defense against libido and as a libidinal defense against aggression has permitted Mr B to exist in the presence of the analyst with very little disturbing tension or excitation.

Sometimes Mr B gets angry at me for being dead "like my two other mothers," or for being too lively by talking too much or making an interpretation. Then his libidinal defenses fail and primitive sadism toward the analyst threatens to erupt. Mr B neglects and punishes himself, rather than telling me he would like to kill me for joining him in his deathlike state or for demonstrating that I am alive. He "murders" me with horrible descriptions of death bed scenes, of illness and suffering. He brings himself to the edge of death by becoming involved with a man who is HIV positive and forbids me to feel anything but detached about it. If, by my silence, I convince him that he has really killed me off, he will threaten to leave the analysis rather than experience the primitive rage that abandonment by death induces in him.

At other times, Mr B's aggressive defenses fail, and dangerous libidinal longings threaten to emerge. He dreams that an icicle "penetrates" the analyst. He wants to use her breasts as objects of gratification and tension reduction. He wants to "delve into death" in her presence, which she understands as a wish to lose his psychic and bodily limits and dissolve into her body. His dream tells me that he wants to bring me into a "sex-charged" environment, and that he has a wish that this environment will not excite or agitate me. I will be able to survive his sexual wish to achieve primitive union with the object.

These libidinal longings are extremely dangerous, because in Mr B's unconscious they are equated with the death of self and object. Throughout the analysis, a pattern emerges. For a while, analyst and patient exist comfortably together in a deathlike state of primitive merger. In this state of safety, meager impulses toward life begin to assert themselves. Mr B experiences a pre-feeling, an impulse toward the analyst. He wants to "confess" all his sins to her, thereby relieving himself of the tension of his self-destructive wishes. If he demonstrates enough suffering to her, she may "come alive," take care of him, and save him from an early death at the hands of his lover. But these longings arouse intense anxiety. If the analyst is indeed there and not dead, she may penetrate his deadness, causing painful sensations. He will experience the therapy as "intrusive," which may in turn produce a desire in him to intrude upon the analyst, to penetrate and destroy her body. Her destruction means his. Therefore, he returns the analysis to a state of merged non-tension, dead but safe.

The life instinct can emerge safely only when Mr B is sure there is no living external object to receive it. His sexual passion is aroused when X's T-cell count goes down or someone has died. He can return to the analysis and quit his underground job when he has decided to live with his dying lover. As long as he is fascinated with death and compulsively talking about it, and as long as he can keep himself perilously close to death without being consumed by it, he can express his wish to merge with and be saved by the analyst without putting her at risk.

Throughout treatment, Mr B has "bored" me. But "boring" someone can have two meanings, and one of them is sexual. I have not allowed myself to consider the other way my patient could "bore" me, because I have the idea that penetration by Mr B would kill me. This mirrors Mr B's unconscious conviction that the desired union with mother/analyst means death for both. Mr B fears penetration by the analysis, as I fear penetration by him.

In the end, Mr B's fascination with death keeps him alive. Ironically, the "delving into" death, the boring delivery, the self-neglect, and the love of death beds and suffering express the unconscious wish: I want to live. This wish is originally and primarily an intrapsychic expression of the life instinct, but from time to time in the analysis, it threatens to erupt as an impulse toward the object. Then the wish becomes directed at the analyst. As the analyst, will I be able to save him from death? Can I, as the preverbal object, muster up enough libido to keep him alive? This wish is experienced by both patient and analyst as highly dangerous. The task of keeping him alive could kill me. Better that we go back to "playing dead," merged in primitive union.

Now Mr B tells me that the analysis "depletes" him. It is the analyst and not he who is responsible for the deadness of the treatment. Is he telling me that I am dead, and, therefore, he is not? Is he once again using his magical idea as a defense against merger; or is he finally projecting his whole conflict around death out of his unconscious and into the analysis? Perhaps it is both, but if it is the latter, we are making some progress.

Conclusions

Mr B's fascination with death is a fascination with the primitive, all-encompassing, symbiotic mother. All the unconscious themes lend support to this hypothesis. This "mother" is not Mr B's actual mother. She is not an object at all. She is rather the earliest perception of mother as an external port for the discharge of tension and excitation. Looked at from this perspective, it becomes clear that mother and death both represent states of non-tension.

The core conflict which manifests itself in the fascination with death is that Mr B longs to merge with the primordial, oceanic pre-object, but that merger means death. This conflict can be reconstructed historically and understood in terms of object relations theory. It can also be shown to be present in the "here and now" of the transference as a unique organization of defenses against early drive states reenacted with the analyst. Mr B has a wish to return to a state of symbiotic union with a pre-object, thereby ridding himself of all unpleasant stimulation and tension, but that return risks death to himself and the needed pre-object. Mr B attempts to protect the needed pre-object from this deathlike merger with his compulsive self-punishment. His magical idea that he can live and be separated by killing the object is his attempt to protect himself from this desired but dangerous union.

For most of the treatment, Mr B's fascination with death has succeeded in keeping him in a state of relative non-tension. He has protected himself from his drives and eliminated the dangerous presence of the analyst by making death and merger interchangeable in his mind. He has played dead to stay alive.

Now he talks about his wish that the analyst "help" him by talking. He wants to know she is there, but when he does, it gives him a feeling of unpleasure. He talks about "thrashing about," "treading water" in the treatment, but if I say anything, he gets a "sinking feeling." I see him thrashing about in the uterus, waiting to be born. The image of treading water seems halfway between swimming, which is pleasure, and drowning, which is death. When he thrashes, I say, "How should I feel about it? What should I do about it?" The analyst is in conflict. Should I save him or let him drown and return to that blissful state of merged non-tension that is so safe and familiar?

I don't want to know that he wants to live and that I should be the person to help him do it. The idea enrages me; I feel he will kill me. I experience the primitive sadistic wish to eat me up and destroy my body implied in his wish. It feels like too big a job. Why should I be responsible for him? Let him die.

On the other hand, I have spent the last several years studying him. He has been a cooperative patient and has an earnest commitment to the analysis. My intense wish to understand his unconscious motivations and the defenses he has erected against them has yielded a rather profound knowledge of his character which I now experience as intimacy. I feel connected to him. I want him to live. I would like to save him.

But how to do it? I think the most crucial thing I can do is to continue to live and be present in the analysis. I must survive all his wishes to kill me and to dissolve into my body. My plan is to continue to offer myself as an object which Mr B can use to express his wish to be saved and to live. I will do that by asking him what he would like me to feel or do about the fact that he is "thrashing." If he asks for help, I will explore what kind of help he needs. If I see that he returns to his "boring" defense, I will understand that I am over-stimulating him and return to my deathlike invisibility.

Cautiously, I will make my presence known with the hope that it will occur to Mr B that I might be a useful object for the discharge of his drives into words.

Several questions for study remain in this case. I want to understand whether the fascination with death preceded and provided a motive for Mr

B's homosexuality or whether it was the reverse. This case also stimulates the question: what activates libido? I believe, as do most drive theorists, that hate comes first, that babies are born without much will to live. Infants, like Mr B, are more interested in avoiding unpleasure than in seeking pleasure. Mothers get babies interested in living by lending the infant their libido. But intrapsychically, what makes a baby decide to become interested in his own fingers or his mother's eyes? What will stimulate curiosity and a drive toward pleasure in Mr B?

My last question deals with the construction of the defenses. Certainly, Mr B's life history played a part in the creation of his fascination with death with its multiplicity of dynamics. Object relations theory would probably say that all Mr B's deadness could be explained by the trauma of losing his mother to cancer at age three. But this explanation denigrates the work of art that Mr B himself created with his fascination with death. His elaborate, personal construction occurred internally and intrapsychically. The creation involved objects, certainly, but the objects were not true others; rather they were fantasied projections of parts of Mr B which he used to express his own idiom. More research needs to be done to unearth how the mind creates these intricate defense structures using fantasied ideas about external objects to create a unique character. Such research could finally integrate object relations and drive theory.

Mr B's fascination with death proves again that the unconscious is a genius. It is a brilliant solution to a complex problem. It accomplishes several tasks in an economical and elegant fashion. It protects Mr B from dangerous states of tension produced by the drives. It allows him to experience the pleasure of male and female discharge and aggression in an atmosphere of relative safety. He gains enormous voyeuristic satisfaction from watching death and dying. And ultimately, his fascination gives him the delusion that he is immortal and will escape death by courting and controlling it.

In the last session, Mr B told me that he had a fantasy of being on a park bench as an old man, long after X, his friend J, and his father have died. What I want to know now is: will I be there with him?

References

Bollas, C. (1987). *The Shadow of the Object*. New York: Columbia University Press.
Freud, A. (1966). *The Ego and the Mechanisms of Defense*. New York: International Universities Press.
Freud, S. (1915, 1917). "Mourning and Melancholia." *Standard Edition*, Volume 14. London: Hogarth Press, 237–260.
Freud, S. (1920). "Beyond the Pleasure Principle." *Standard Edition*, Volume 23. London: Hogarth Press, 3–64.
Joseph, B. (1982). "Addiction to Near Death." *International Journal of Psycho-Analysis*, 63(4), 449–456.

Klein, M., and Riviere, J. (1967). *Love, Hate and Reparation*. New York: W. W. Norton.
Mahler, M. (1967). "On Human Symbiosis and the Vicissitudes of Individuation." *Journal of the American Psychoanalytic Association*, 15(4), 740–763.
McDougall, J. (1992). *Plea for a Measure of Abnormality*. New York: Brunner/Mazel.
Socarides, C.W. (1978). *Homosexuality*. New York: Jason Aronson.
Spotnitz, H., and Meadow, P. (1976). *Treatment of the narcissistic neurosis*. New York: Manhattan Center for Advanced Group Studies.
Wolfenstein, M. (1956). "Analysis of a juvenile poem." *Psychoanalytic Study of the Child*, 11(1), 450–470.

Chapter 10

Marking the anniversary

Adolescents and the September 11 healing process

In the summer of 2002, I got a phone call from the director of an organization called Adventures in Teaching and Counseling (ATC). She told me that ATC had received a grant from the American Group Psychotherapy Association to help educators and children traumatized by the events of September 11, 2001. Along with three other clinicians trained in the methods of modern group work, I was invited to spend the first anniversary of September 11 at a high school in a small town in New Jersey, a suburb of New York City. This town had a large population of New York City police and firefighters, as well as many white-collar workers who had worked in the World Trade Center. Altogether, the town had lost over 30 people in the tragedy, and all of the young people at the local high school were affected, either directly or indirectly.

New Jersey educators realized that students might be dealing with intense feelings on the anniversary, and that helping them work through these feelings took precedence over studies on this difficult day. The high school had arranged to have three performances of *Finding the Words*, a play by a group called ENACT, which was based on the actual statements of children who had lost someone on 9/11 or whose schools were close enough to the towers to be impacted by the disaster. This performance was to be presented to the senior, the junior, and finally, the sophomore class at the high school. My three colleagues and I were there to organize groups with the senior and junior classes after the performances to help the students process their feelings.

One dynamic that makes the events of September 11 so different from other traumas is the fact that it happened to all of us. Therapists who had years of experience in the treatment of trauma, suddenly found themselves with little of the emotional insulation that is so vital in this work. Group therapists trying to work with young people impacted by 9/11 are often dealing with their own post-traumatic stress symptoms. Though I have worked extensively with incest survivors and recently bereaved clients, I came to 9/11 groups with a much more fragile insulation barrier than usual. I am a New Yorker and I knew people in the towers, though no one I knew lost their lives. I was very grateful and excited that I had the opportunity to spend the anniversary of 9/11 in this special way, but I was also amazed at the resistances I was experiencing on my way to New Jersey that morning. It seemed I had forgotten 30 years of training in social work, psychoanalysis, and group studies. I was sure I didn't have a clue about how to help these young people, since I myself was feeling anxious, sweaty, nauseous, teary, and hopeless. I told myself that experiencing these challenging feelings would only help me understand the resistances I would confront in the students.

What I did find when I arrived at school that morning was that none of the high school students seemed to share the emotions that had made me want to stay home with the covers over my head. Indeed, none of these teenagers appeared to be suffering at all. Throughout the day, the emotional climate in the school halls seemed to vacillate between raucous, manic hilarity and dreamy, "ultra-cool" indifference. Though I was quite sure that these two stances were defenses against some of the discomfort I was experiencing, I was also careful to stay neutral rather than assault these resistances. Rosenthal (1987) described resistance as an instrument necessary for preserving emotional equilibrium. He recommended supporting and joining the defensive stance until the resistor has developed the ego strength to master and outgrow the need for it. Being in touch with all my own painful feelings gave me a deeper respect for these students' need for their defenses.

The senior class, the first audience of the day, seemed most in touch with their feelings. They watched the ENACT program with a silent intensity. Afterward, when they were invited by the actors to give feedback, they commented that an important feeling that was left out of the performance was anger. Several of the students were quite forthcoming in verbalizing that anger. One student said, "I've never thought of myself as a killer, but I would like to kill Osama Bin Laden. I realize I would enjoy killing him." Another said, "How could our government let this happen to us? It's their job to keep us safe. I don't think I'm ever going to feel safe again, and I'm mad about that." Roth (2002) discussed the psychic vulnerability that trauma affects. It brings into question whether our significant objects, beliefs, and institutions can really offer us adequate protection. This is particularly prevalent in adolescents who have their superego identifications threatened at a time when the superego is in formation. Verbalizing the disappointment and rage these students felt at the failure of authority figures became an important part of the process.

When the four of us from Adventures in Teaching and Counseling invited any senior who still felt the need to talk to join a group with one of us, I could see that many of the students were attracted to the idea, but they didn't want to appear "uncool." They gathered together in the hall outside the auditorium in sullen little groups. A female colleague and I followed the students out of the auditorium and approached several groups of girls who were "hanging out" in the hall. My partner asked them what they thought of the play. When she got them talking, she said, "Why don't all of you come on upstairs to the library? We're going to have a conversation about the performance." Getting the girls to agree as a clique to come and talk seemed to resolve the resistance of peer pressure. We ended up in the library with a group of 30 senior girls and two leaders. Though I had concerns that the group was too large, I resisted suggesting we break up into two groups. The willingness to be there was so fragile, I didn't want to ask anyone to make a move.

As it turned out, the process was very meaningful, and my colleague and I worked well together. She focused on helping people identify their feelings, while I tried to help every member to talk and build bridges between the talkative and silent members. Ormont (1990) delineated the importance of using bridging techniques in the very early stages of a group to strengthen emotional connections or build connections where none existed before. By asking a group member about the interaction of two other members, or by inviting a quiet member to speculate on why another member is not talking, we strive to achieve full group participation and to build a community of support.

One young woman told the group that she had seven close family members in the towers. They all got out alive. The problem she now has is that, on that day, she had wished that her new stepmother, who was then pregnant with her stepsister, would die. She wept, saying that she feels guilty that she could have been so wicked. Now that she knows her new stepsister, she can't imagine life without her. The other girls in the group rushed to reassure her. One girl said, "Gosh, everyone hates a new stepmother. It's like Cinderella!" My colleague pointed out that we can't control our feelings, and after all, they're just feelings.

A black girl talked about the difficulty she was having with feelings of prejudice. She said, "I've been a victim of prejudice all my life, but here I am checking out every crowded place for an Arab." Kauff (2002) reminded us that the disconnect between self-image and actual behavior in response to a trauma can be traumatic in itself. Several of the other group members spoke up about how hard it is not to group all Islamic people with the terrorists. My colleague and I talked about how prejudicial feelings are very human, and that in terms of prejudice, actions are more important than feelings.

Both these young women were having trouble dealing with the shame they felt at their response to a traumatic situation. Developmentally, adolescents are in a struggle to control their internal impulses, a struggle between the ego and id. Some of the most disturbing fluctuations of feeling in this period have to do with self-feelings, feelings of identity. Strengthening the ego ideal, the positive sense of self, is a major aspect of growth in teenage years (Jacobson, 1961). Trauma can induce feelings that threaten the ego's basic sense of worth, and for an adolescent, this can be a crisis of enormous magnitude. The World Trade Center disaster presents a major disruption in the process of normal adolescent development to a whole generation of young people.

All the girls in the senior group were concerned about Jessica, who lost her father in the towers. Most of them had stayed away from Jessica since the tragedy. They were all worried about "saying the wrong thing." We explored what the "wrong thing" might be. They all were afraid they would cry if they talked to Jessica. They felt they have no right to cry, since they didn't lose their fathers. If they started crying, they feared they might never stop. I asked if Jessica might be comforted by a friend's willingness to cry with her. My colleague asked how Jessica might be feeling on this day, with all her friends keeping a protective distance from her. One girl said, "I didn't think about the fact that she might feel isolated and lonely on top of the sadness about her dad."

I was very focused on helping everyone talk. In fact, the only girl I was really concerned about when it was over was a girl who was drumming her fingers and feet through the whole group but couldn't seem to speak. Spotnitz (1987) wrote about the resistances of the non-communicating group member. He emphasized that silence is a very potent form of communication. The silence is saying something, but before the leader can make an intervention, he must begin by understanding what the resistance to talk is about. I tried bridging, asking another quiet girl why she thought Angela was silent. I also tried to build a bridge between more talkative girls and Angela. Angela was never able to speak, and in the end, I realized she was not ready to deal with her feelings. I think she is an example of how pervasive the resistances of numbness, denial, and silence can be in trauma. Helping young people deal with the events of 9/11 is going to take years of support and outreach. A year after the event, many therapists report that a number of their clients who were directly affected on September 11 are still reluctant to talk about the event. Numbness is pervasive.

At the end of the group with the senior girls, one of the strongest girls who had done a lot of talking said, "This has been so interesting. Here I am sitting with my own little clique, and I don't even know the rest of you that well, except to know who belongs to which clique. But after this talk, I just love you all." To me, this statement is the strongest argument for what group process can offer a school, a community, and even the world. Though we had only made a tentative beginning of the healing process, I felt good about the fact that these girls came away with the sense that they were not isolated. They all were experiencing powerful feelings, some of which were very uncomfortable; but they could use each other as resources of support.

The 11th and 10th grades had a totally different energy. They talked, kidded, and hooted through the performances of "Finding the Words." The principal constantly had to stop and call for order and good manners. It seemed these younger students were having a difficult time dealing with their feelings and were defending against them by being noisy, rude, and rambunctious adolescents. The 11th grade left quickly after the performances and our technique of enlisting cliques did not persuade them to come and talk in a group. My colleague and I went to our designated room and waited without too much hope that we would be able to run a group. After about ten minutes, an 11th grade girl came in and sat down. She said she was worried because she was "having no feelings." She had been disturbed by the noisy crowd during the performance. She told us that she had lost six close family members in her 16 years, but that she felt "absolutely numb" about 9/11. The three of us talked about what numbness means and what it feels like. My colleague and I related incidents in our own lives when we had felt numb. The atmosphere was quiet, depressed, but soothing because it felt real after the forced hilarity in the auditorium.

A few minutes later, a boy came to join us. He was also feeling numb, but what he came to talk about was that he had been "confused" during the performance. Because it was so noisy all around him, he hadn't been able to "concentrate" on what was going on. He said he wanted some "quiet time" to process what had happened. He fit right into the mood in the room, which was very still and reflective. Although our group was so small that it was difficult to define it as a group, I felt that this encounter may have been just as healing and important to these two young people as the first. It certainly helped me understand and experience some of the feelings that the rowdiness in the auditorium had masked. My colleague and I made no attempt to attack the "numb" resistance of these two young people. I felt particularly protective of the girl, realizing that she had come to the events of September 11 already traumatized by familial losses unusual in one so young. We knew we would probably not be seeing either of these teenagers again, and it would have been a breach of empathy to confront their defenses and then leave just as they became vulnerable to the feelings those defenses were concealing. We did tell the two that numbness is a common reaction to trauma. We reminded them that Middletown has a team of guidance counselors who are ready and willing to talk to any student, and we stressed that talking helps. Again, I was struck by the fact that there will be no quick fix in helping young people deal with 9/11. A full year after the tragedy, many of these children were still utilizing rigid defenses, which need to be respected. What is needed now is ongoing group process to patiently work through and resolve these resistances.

This girl and boy hardly knew each other, but when our little group was over, they decided to have lunch together and walked off talking up a storm. I realized again that one of the most helpful things that group process can do is build bridges between people who have felt isolated. So many of these young people seemed to believe that the feelings they were experiencing were crazy, wicked, weak, or just wrong. To the extent that we were able to give them the idea that these "bad" feelings are not only acceptable but normal, and that all of us are experiencing them, we began the process of recovery.

Since spending the anniversary of 9/11 in New Jersey, I have watched the actress Susan Sarandon on television inviting New Yorkers to "Feel free to feel better." Though I am heartened to see these public service ads, I only wish the recovery from our national trauma could be that easy. It seems to me that the first step toward healing is, "Feel free to feel worse," or even, "Dare to feel." Dissociation and numbness are an almost universal reaction to the World Trade Center disaster, but they are particularly prevalent in adolescents.

Adolescents, like the teenagers in New Jersey, are immersed in a developmental process that is challenging in the best of times. The primary task of adolescence is separation from the primitive identification with early parental introjects. Residual traumas from injurious experiences as an infant must be socialized and put to use as organizers of the adult personality. Adolescents are in a kind of mourning at the loosening of childhood ties, and are working hard to establish a personal view of past, present, and future that is not simply an extension of their parents (Blos, 1958; 1976). Young people are striving to distance themselves from all the primitive feelings of the family romance and turn outward toward reality and the world. This process involves repression and dissociation from early feelings. It is hard work and can sometimes leave the ego depleted and particularly vulnerable to stressful events. The tendency for teenagers to dissociate from their childish self makes it extremely difficult for them to deal with trauma. Because adolescence is a time when the superego is alternately harsh and weakened, teenagers can experience intense shame, inferiority, and guilt conflicts. This means that some of the turbulent feelings that 9/11 induced become extremely unacceptable and painful. If things go well in adolescent development, the ego ideal bridges the ego and superego; but this process is totally disrupted when the traumatized self is experienced as toxic and full of "bad" feelings (Jacobson, 1961). A disaster of the magnitude of September 11 is going to have a profound effect on a whole generation of American children who were trying to establish their personal "view of the world" at the moment the world became such a dangerous place.

Our adolescent children have had the "safe enough" environment where growth and maturation can occur wrenched away from them. Group process will be, I believe, extraordinarily important in the recovery of these adolescents for several reasons. First, a well-run group provides that safe place where trust in the world and the people in it can slowly be rebuilt. Second, a group builds a sense of community. Over and over, I have heard group members verbalize the idea that in these difficult days in which all of us are coping with feelings of anxiety, fear, rage, and grief a particular kind of community can provide solace. To have a place to talk honestly with others, where any feeling no matter how seemingly "crazy" or "bad" can be verbalized and resonated with, will be healing. But this process is not going to be a quick fix. The extremely rigid dissociative defense that adolescents manifest is only the gatekeeper to underlying distress that must be worked through in the years ahead. This process of healing our children should be a public health priority.

September 11, 2001, offers a rare opportunity to do research on post-traumatic stress syndrome in adolescents. September 11, 2002, drove home to me that the road to recovery, particularly for adolescents, will be arduous and slow. Through trial and error, we can collect data about how best to get traumatized children into the room to talk, and about how to deal with rigid defenses, such as numbness and manic behavior. Ongoing clinical data will be a valuable resource in understanding the path to healing in trauma.

References

Blos, Peter (1958). Pre-adolescent drive organization. *JAPA*, 6, 47–56.
Blos, Peter (1976). When and how does adolescence end? Structural criteria for adolescent closure. In S. C. Feinstein and P. Giovachinni (eds), *Adolescent psychiatry*, vol. V. New York: Jason Aronson, pp. 407–422
Jacobson, Edith (1961). Adolescent moods and the remodeling of psychic structures in adolescence. *Psychoanalytic Study of the Child*, 16(1), 164–183.
Kauff, Priscilla E. (2002). Analytic group psychotherapy: A uniquely effective crisis intervention. *Group*, 26(2), 137–147.
Ormont, Louis R. (1990). The craft of bridging. In L. Furgeri (ed.), *The technique of group treatment: The collected papers of Louis R. Ormont, PhD* (pp. 263–278). New York: Psychosocial Press.
Rosenthal, Leslie (1987). *Resolving resistance in group psychotherapy*. Northvale, NJ: Jason Aronson, Inc.
Roth, Bennett E. (2002). Some diagnostic observations of post-September 11, 2001 crisis groups. *Group*, 26(2), 155–161.
Spotnitz, Hyman (1987). Resistance of the non-communicating patient in the group. *Modern Psychoanalysis*, 12(1), 17–23.

Chapter 11

Humor and psychoanalysis

I have always had the idea that what separates the truly great analysts from the merely competent is a talent and appreciation for laughter and play. People criticize psychoanalysts sometimes for being too focused on aggression and primary process, but I think what our critics don't appreciate is how much fun modern analysts and their patients have playing with the most primitive ideas. In fact, laughing and playing help us bear and cope with all that is miserable and brutal in the world and more importantly, within ourselves.

Anna Freud (1960) described the maturational sequence of play in young children. Originally, play is parallel; very young children may play side by side, but they play alone. When young children become aware of other children, they usually treat them as a toy that can be used, mistreated, and then pushed away. By the end of the second year of life though, most children are capable of seeing others as playmates who can be helpful in building or destroying something together in a cooperative, give and take manner. In play, therefore, we trace human development from inner reality to shared reality, from egocentricity to companionship.

This progression of play from narcissism to object relatedness is usually reflected in the analysis. Early in treatment, we often see a patient who simply wants to play alone. She has a "story" to relate, usually focusing on the way the world and the people in it have been a source of disappointment or pain. She wants to play with her story/toy with very little awareness that there is another potential playmate in the room. In the narcissistic transference, the analyst is perceived not as a real and separate object, but as a toy to be used. As the analysis progresses and the transference becomes more object-oriented, together the analyst and the patient can create a third party in the analysis, which is the play space between them.

The analytic play space is an intermediate area between fantasy and reality, between the "me and not me" where analyst and patient perceive each other as both outside omnipotent control and yet willing to receive and play with the various projections and fantasies of the other. After the resolution of the narcissistic transference, the analyst is free to play by putting forth ideas as objects that exist, not in the patient, nor in the analyst, but in that potential play space between the two.

The patient plays with the analyst by projecting early objects onto and into her. The analyst identifies and attempts to understand these projections, but inevitably through the filter of her own subjective experience. What the analyst gives back to the patient is the patient's projection altered and played with by the analyst's ideas. It's sort of like a ball being tossed back and forth. The fluid process of lively interchange between the inner and the outer world, the continual bounce of projective and introjective identifications liberate feelings and help the patient say new things.

Of course, to play well a patient must have developed a capacity to recognize and use objects. Play in analysis becomes a crucial part of the transition from the primary process of narcissism to the reality principle.

How does the analyst encourage this play? Well, first of all by being very, very patient with the process, allowing the patient to be alone and then to use the analyst as a toy in the narcissistic transference. After 10 or 20 years of this, the patient may be ready to play with the analyst, and at that point the story/toy may become less important than the here and now of the analysis. The patient is ready to tell the analyst thoughts and feelings in the moment about the analysis and the analyst. In this playful atmosphere, both the analyst and patient can toss around themes, metaphors, and dreams.

In one of my groups, the members played with the theme of water. After Jane compared her relationship with her boyfriend to scuba diving – exhilarating as long as you can come up for air – members began to use water metaphors as a method of communication. They felt engulfed and drowned by their children, their mates, and their careers. They encouraged each other to just go with the flow. A quiet group member said she was standing on the beach holding her towel, watching the others swim. The other members encouraged her to just "jump in." She couldn't. The water was too hot and turbulent, and she was afraid she would never get out again. Someone suggested that I, as group leader, should play lifeguard. On evenings when the group was muted and overly intellectual, someone would remark that the water was too cold tonight. Playing in the water was a step toward helping group members become more articulate about their feelings.

Dreams can be wonderful toys in analysis. Classical analysts would feel compelled to analyze the dream. A modern analyst will do better to treat the dream as a toy to be shared. No longer the exclusive possession of the dreamer the dream can receive myriad fantasies, projections, and identifications.

I had a patient Mary who was terrified of aggression, especially her own. After several years of sitting with this gentle fairy and joining her resistance by being very nice, I began to get impatient with her defenses. I started to make some provocative interventions to see if I could move her along and make her get in touch with her anger. In response to this change in my treatment plan, she came in with a dream. She was with a black woman who was speaking softly and supposedly lovingly, touching her in a pseudo-gentle way. But this woman had a needle in her hand. She stuck it in Mary's leg and screamed, "You must have an orgasm." Mary screamed, "I can't! I can't."

Mary's association to the dream was that I was the pseudo-gentle black woman who was demanding orgasms. I agreed that I should stop needling her but silently thought that this pseudo-gentle black woman might also represent a part of Mary.

That night, I dreamed Mary and I were taking a test, and we were both having difficulty with it. Mary created the test, but neither one of us could answer the questions. There was a woman in the dream who had already finished the test, and she was very harsh. She told us that we only had a half hour to finish, and if we weren't able, we would both fail. While Mary and I struggled to answer the questions, the other woman was talking and talking much too loudly, and it was impossible to concentrate. I said to the woman, "Please be quiet! We will never pass, if you don't stop talking!"

I played with these two dreams for many weeks in my own head. While Mary talked on the couch, I thought about the test that we both might fail, about how much she induced in me the desire to be noisy and say "hurry up!" I thought about the part of Mary that likes to create tests so difficult that we both struggle.

Freud (1905, p. 164) characterized humor as man's "highest psychical achievement." Jokes and humor give us a life-affirming way of discharging primitive sex and aggression while preventing the acting out of these feelings. They allow us to have our cake and eat it too.

Freud's remarks remind me of a supervision group I'm in where we all tossed some primitive aggression around. An analyst, I'll call her Martha, was talking about a male patient she was having difficulty with. "The problem is I'd like to kill him. He reminds me of my ex-husband. Truthfully, if I thought I could kill them both and get away with it, I would." Martha blushed and added, "I can't believe I could even entertain the idea of actually murdering someone."

Anne, another analyst in the group said, "Martha, you need to go see my Bubala. She's my Russian grandmother and she casts spells on people." She went on,

> Bubala went to a family wedding and she didn't like the way my cousin was dancing with this young woman in a very short skirt. She said it was unseemly. So she went home and put a curse on the young man. Sure enough, my cousin began to get sick. He lost weight and couldn't eat. He went to the doctor, but they couldn't find anything wrong with him. His mother called my Bubala and said she didn't know what to do, she was at her wits' end. Bubala said, 'the only thing wrong with him is that I put a curse on him, and now he sees what happens to young men who behave in brazen ways to disgrace our family!' My aunt said, 'Bubala, stop it! Take the curse off.' My grandmother said, 'I won't! He's only getting what he deserves!' Well, my cousin got sicker and sicker, and his mother called my grandmother back and said, 'Bubala – are you trying to kill him? He's

very sick.' My grandmother said, 'Oh, all right. I guess I don't want to see him dead. I'll take the curse off.' And she did, and my cousin recovered. You need my Bubala, Martha.

Martha's eyes got very wide with pleasure and anxiety, and she said, "You mean your Bubala could put a curse on my ex-husband, and he would *die?*" Anne said, "I'm pretty sure she could do it." Martha said, "This is terrible. I can't believe I'm entertaining this idea. Would she see me?" Anne said, "I'm sure she would do it if she knew you were a good friend of mine." Martha giggled nervously, "Oh my God, I could really arrange my ex-husband's death and actually get away with it? Oh God, I can't believe I'm talking like that. I couldn't do that. I would feel so guilty. No, it would never work. I would probably have to give myself cancer in punishment for being a murderer." "Don't be ridiculous," said Anne, "you would have no reason to feel guilty at all. All this black magic is a bunch of hocus-pocus bullshit anyway!"

At this, the other group members began to giggle and chortle, and then Martha started to laugh. She laughed and then she cried. Her laughter and tears seemed to me to be a release of all the toxic primitive feelings that were overwhelming her: the wish to murder, the self-destructive guilt, the shame at her own aggression, the horrible feelings toward her patient. She was able to laugh at and let go of all of this. The laughter helped her understand that all the horrible stuff within her is all just feelings. Martha could laugh about it, share it with friends in a playful way, and then decide how she wanted to operate in the world vis-à-vis her patient and the father of her children. She could face the primitive feelings and forgive herself; and this in turn could help her to understand and forgive her patient and her ex-husband. If we use humor and play, we can both face and cope with our primitive aggression, and use it, like the cayenne pepper in the stew to enliven our life and increase its savor.

References

Freud, A. (1960). Entrance into nursery school: The psychological prerequisites. *The Writings of Anna Freud, Volume 5 (1956–1965)*. New York: International Universities Press, pp. 315–335.

Freud, S. (1905). *Jokes and their relation to the unconscious. Standard edition, volume 8.* London: Hogarth Press, pp. 3–248.

Chapter 12

Leadership and psychoanalysis

When I was a little girl, I wanted to grow up to be someone very important and accomplished, a great leader. I wanted this because when I accomplished important things and got good report cards and awards as a child, my father loved me and gave me lots of positive attention. This gave me the childish idea that if I did great things, everyone would love me. Along the way, I met some great examples of what Maccoby (2002) called charismatic "productive narcissists" (though I certainly wouldn't have identified them as such at the time). They were wonderful role models for me and I idealized them. With their encouragement, I worked very hard. After many years, I accomplished some things that I thought were pretty great, and after a while, I began to become a leader. But I was very disappointed, indeed I was horrified, to find that this didn't have the desired result. Everybody didn't love me. In fact, I began to see that the more I accomplished, the more people hated me. What a dilemma! I wanted to be loved, but I also wanted to be the big boss!

In 1998, I was asked to become the director of The Center for Group Studies in New York City. Like most institutes, this one was organized around a beloved and charismatic leader. The long-term patients of this wonderful man had created a center where his techniques, which had helped so many of us, could be taught and perpetuated. I too love this man, and I was excited to be chosen by him to lead his institute. Still deluded, I was sure that when everyone saw how hard I worked and what good ideas I had, they would all love me too. So, I was once again astonished to confront the fact that the major problem I had to deal with every day as director was primitive aggression. Most of the faculty resented me, and though they gave lip service to the idea that they wanted to help me, in actuality, many of them did everything they could to undermine me. Even more amazing was the realization that, though everyone adored, even worshiped our charismatic leader, they made his life a living hell. Each of his followers wanted special privileges and recognition, love from him and only him. If they didn't like what I said to them, they went over my head to God. God was expected to settle disputes, and there were always disputes. I began to realize that the constant squabbles that made a smooth-running organization an impossibility were a kind of pleasurable game, an opportunity to get special love and attention from God, while insuring that God's work would not succeed. Though the faculty declared their devotion to the charismatic leader's techniques, when teaching they focused on spirituality, hypnotism, or behavior modification – anything but teaching modern analysis, which was what they were there for. They criticized God to the students. They tried to steal God's patients. They tried to steal each other's patients. Boy, was this an eye-opener!

I went back to my books and found a book titled *Unfree Association* about the history of analytic institutes. I was disheartened to read that institutes seem to be organized like primal hordes, and that the vast majority of institutes in the United States had not survived the demise of their charismatic leader.

I consulted Freud's *Totem and Taboo* and *Moses and Monotheism* and read about primal hordes. What he wrote was enlightening. It also sounded very familiar. According to Freud, the first human communities were organized around a powerful father who was worshipped and feared by his sons. This father alone had sexual access to the women in the group, and though the sons venerated the father, eventually they killed him and ate him, thereby incorporating his power into themselves. To atone for this patricide, the sons set up totems to worship and began to sacrifice animals in religious services to re-enact the original crime. They also set up laws against incest and murder to protect themselves from their father's fate.

What can this story tell us about institutes and leadership? Well, I think the first lesson is that behind all idealization hides primitive rage. We love our leaders, but we also envy their power and want to devour them and get the power for ourselves. I see now that my wish to eat up God and take his place drove my enormous pleasure in being his chosen one. I also realize that, in my role as the chosen child in the primal horde, I could have been killed. It is notable in the Freud story that no single son is chosen. They all collaborate to kill off the father, and then and only then, they establish order and morality.

So where does that leave those of us who want to be leaders? Is the choice crushing our natural drive to lead or be killed? Well, I hope not, and I don't think so. But leaders must be very careful; it can be a dangerous job. It seems to me that to be an effective leader, one must always be aware of the primitive aggression that lies below the surface in all of us. The more that leaders can understand and accept that aggression in themselves and in their followers, the less it will have to be acted out in all sorts of sneaky ways that undermine institutions.

And there are ways to mitigate the aggression. The cannibalism of the primal horde is driven by a toxic envy, by the idea that all goodness and all power reside in the charismatic other; and that the only way to get that goodness and power is to devour that other. If followers can believe that latent goodness and power lie within each of us, they are less likely to have to eat their leader. Good leaders help their followers identify and develop their individual strengths. Maccoby discussed the three character types Freud described: the erotic, who needs to be loved and wants to take care of people; the obsessive who has tremendous organizational energy and wants to make things run well; and the narcissist, who is the charismatic visionary. All three types are needed for an organization to run smoothly. It is noteworthy that in the primal horde story, after the charismatic father was killed, his children were able to work together to establish social structure and governance. This is the team model that Maccoby described. For these teams to work, leaders must collaborate with their peers to encourage the unique style of leadership in each member of the group. We are all a fascinating mixture of the erotic, obsessive, and productive narcissists. I want to be loved and take care of people like the erotic narcissist. Though I would like to be a charismatic narcissist, I lack a great vision and the constructive ruthlessness to carry it out. I guess I am more of a hard-working obsessive, and I know I need to work with visionaries to get the job done. Leaders need to know that they need others and how to identify and harness the leadership strengths in others to achieve a goal – unless they want to be eaten alive!

References

Freud, S. (1913). *Totem and taboo*. The standard edition of the complete psychological works of Sigmund Freud, Volume 13, pp. 1–162.

Freud, S. (1939). *Moses and monotheism*. The standard edition of the complete psychological works of Sigmund Freud, Volume 23, pp. 3–140.

Kirsner, D. (2009). *Unfree association*. New York: Jason Aronson.

Maccoby, M. (2002). Toward a science of social character. *International Forum of Psychoanalysis*, *11*(1), 33–44.

Chapter 13

Myth and psychoanalysis

When I was asked to present a paper on this cruise of the Greek Islands with the Society of Modern Psychoanalysts, I was told I could speak on anything that interested me. This, of course, is a very difficult situation. Too many choices can make one feel as paralyzed as no choice at all. But I decided that, since we are cruising in the beautiful Greek islands, it might be fun to take a look at the Greek myths that originated in this part of the world from a psychoanalytic perspective. Certainly, psychoanalysis should have something to say about stories where sons marry their mothers and castrate their fathers. Freud found the ancient world and its myths fascinating. He said that he derived his ideas about conflict and duality from these ancient tales. The founder of psychoanalysis was a great collector of antiquities, and we find the names of Greek gods and heroes like Oedipus and Narcissus linked to various complexes and pathologies in Freud's theories. Greek myth is often the story of a hero in search of meaning, and this search is also the cornerstone of psychoanalysis. As the mythical struggle of the hero is an emotional voyage, so psychoanalysis is the re-experiencing of old truths (Spotnitz and Meadow, 1976).

I remembered from my high school reading that Greek myths are full of murder, incest, rape, and heroic confrontations with all sorts of scary monsters. But what surprised me in re-reading these stories 40 years later is how completely delightful they are. They are delightful in the same way that a small child is delightful: primitive, innocently barbaric, and much closer to the unconscious than we adults are. They are also very funny. Unlike Judeo-Christian religion, which can be deadly serious, Greek mythology is rendered with humor.

The word myth is sometimes used as a synonym for a lie, though in fact myths help us understand deep truths about the experience of being alive. Some people consider myth irrelevant in our modern scientific world, and yet the great themes of myth line the walls of our unconscious like pieces of broken pottery in an archaeological site. Indeed, I believe that it is because Greek myth expresses primitive but universal unconscious ideas or conflicts in fantasy and symbolism, that these stories have been able to speak to people for thousands of years. Myth gives us a road map to cope with the most unsettling facts about being alive: that we must kill other living things to eat and hurt people we love to get what we desire; that we routinely suffer pain and anxiety; and that ultimately, we must die. Being alive means that we often experience the things we are compelled to do as repulsive, difficult, frightening or sinful. This is when we begin to get in real psychological trouble. Myths provide fundamental instruction on these matters. In myth, all human suffering is shifted away from the reality level and concentrated in a symbolic sphere. The story creates group solidarity by helping a society experience and then overcome this symbolic anxiety. Frightening repressed ideas become acceptable in myth because they are disguised and transformed in a way that links them to the gods rather than to human psychopathology. In sanctioning the outrageous behavior of Zeus and his cohorts, society tells its members that primitive impulses can be acknowledged and dealt with.

Myths have often been compared to dreams, in that both myth and dream maintain psychic health and stability through the allowable expression of repressed ideas. Individuals must dream their own idiosyncratic dreams and perform their private rituals to prevent anxiety, and societies, which are groups of individuals, need shared myths and public rituals to maintain the emotional integrity and public health of the group.

A Greek myth is a traditional story handed down over generations about gods or heroes and their families. What is a god? A god is the personification of a motivating power or a value system in human life. Gods most often represent the power of nature, while heroes reflect the power of the life force in human beings. Greek myths are set either in the remote past during the time of creation or in the more recent past, including the quasi-historical time of the Trojan War. Robert Graves (1955, p. 17), probably the most esteemed collector of Greek myth, believed that most myths were generated by actual historical events, with gods and goddesses standing in for real military leaders or kings and queens of ancient kingdoms. History is used in myth the way the day's residues are used in dreaming: as the raw material for the expression of an unconscious idea.

Graves (1955, p. 13) maintained that prehistoric Europe had no gods. Joseph Campbell (1988 pp. 209–213), another great scholar of myth, asserted that male gods existed where societies were based on hunting, while agricultural communities worshiped the great goddess, Mother Earth, who was regarded as immortal, changeless, and omnipotent. Both theories are speculation, since we have no real written record of European history until the eight century BC. Before this, myth was a fluid oral history, organic, and amorphous, with the story changing and being modified by every storyteller and community to suit psychological needs. Graves uses the first written records to theorize that early man worshiped a female goddess. The concept of fatherhood was not introduced into the religious thought of early human beings. Wind or rain was given credit for impregnating women, and the goddess took male lovers for pleasure, not to procreate. However, once the relevance of sexual intercourse to child-bearing had been established, man's religious status gradually improved. The tribal queen chose an annual lover from her entourage of young men, a king to be sacrificed at the year's end, making him a symbol of fertility. When the shortness of the king's reign proved to be a bit irksome for potential lovers, it was agreed to prolong his reign to 100 lunations or months – note that the 28 days of these lunations mirrors the female menstrual cycle. Later, young boys were sacrificed in place of the king, and finally animals were substituted. Early Greek mythology is concerned with the changing relationships between the queen and her lovers. The sacred king continued to hold his position only by right of marriage to the tribal goddess, until some daring king at last decided to commit incest with his daughter and thus gain a new title to the throne when his reign ended. By the time the *Iliad* had been composed, the goddess had been eclipsed by an unlimited male monarchy (Graves, 1955, pp. 18–19).

The first written account of Greek mythology appeared toward the end of the eighth century BC when a Greek named Hesiod wrote a poem of about a thousand lines on the beginning of the world, the emergence of the gods, and the conflicts between generations which resulted in the permanent seizure of power by Zeus, ruler of the world and king over gods and man. This poem is known as the *Theogony*, which translates as the birth of the gods. Homer's *Iliad* and *Odyssey* may have been composed somewhat earlier than the *Theogony*, though this is by no means certain. There is no hard evidence that Homer or Hesiod knew the works of the other. Similarities between the two were probably not borrowings or references, but rather evidence that both writers were composing from the same long-established oral history. Greek history can be said to have begun in the eighth century BC. Everything before this time is prehistoric in the sense that all we know about the way people lived, including their religious beliefs and myth, is based on physical remains and not on written records.

Greek mythology is in large part the saga of the conflict between men and women presented from the point of view of male fantasy. Father–son conflict and mother–son and brother–sister incest are primary motives. Women often appear as dangerous and evil. Possibly to confront earlier strongly matriarchal religious systems, the Greeks admitted into their own myths a female principle which could be a formidable enemy to both her husband and her sons.

The Greeks don't seem to be too interested in the appearance of the first human beings, but the Greek story of the creation of the world mirrors the psychosocial development of each human being in an uncanny way. Let me tell you the Greek story of the creation, as told by Hesiod, and I'm sure you will be able to find similarities in human development.

The story of the world begins with the spontaneous emergence of four uncaused entities. The first is Chaos, which signifies unlimited space, infinite darkness, and unformed matter. Next comes wide-breasted Gaia, the earth and mother of us all. Tartaros and Eros follow Gaia. Gaia and Tartaros are both locations and anthropomorphized beings, who mate and produce offspring but have no real personality or career. Tartaros is a place of punishment, a place where losers in generational conflict suffer eternal punishment. Immediately after the appearance of Eros, the first suggestion of mating and coupling appears. We might think of Tartaros as the frustration of desire, and Eros as the emergence of desire. It is interesting to consider why Tartaros comes first. If Tartaros is the death instinct and Eros the life instinct, the Greeks have placed aggression before love. And certainly, modern analysts believe that in human development babies hate before they can love. Chaos and Gaia were both able to produce many children without the need of a sexual partner. But after the appearance of Eros, Gaia marries her son Uranus. The world begins with the marriage of Gaia and Uranus

If we think of this myth in terms of human psychology, Chaos, a state prior to perception, represents the child in utero and in the symbiotic state of undifferentiated fusion with the mother, a place where "I" has not become "I." Symbiotic memories appear prominently in all the Greek myths that have to do with a primal paradise where there is no desire because there is no lack of gratification. Like the Garden of Eden, these myths are a fantasy of origin and of lost irredeemable bliss. The emergence of Gaia out of Chaos, of course, reflects the infant's first object, the mother, who is the first structuring principle in the child's life. And with the perception of the object comes the initial experience of loss, frustration, and anxiety – as well as the first feelings of desire for the mother, security, and ultimately a return to the symbiotic state.

The experience of primal loss and the beginning of desire is reflected in the appearance of Tartaros and Eros. Tartaros punishes crimes and imprisons losers. The crimes of these losers are usually of a sexual nature. Either they have revealed the secrets of the gods, which is usually the secret of parental sexuality or the observance of a forbidden sexual sight, the primal scene – or they've stolen ambrosia, the food of the gods, which is another attempt to steal the parental prerogative. Of course, the parental possession that the son wants, but knows he will be punished for wanting, is the mother. So, we see that the myths symbolize the progression of the child from symbiosis to separation to the beginning of Oedipal desire, with its guilt and need for punishment. A great example of an Oedipal transgression is the theft of fire from Zeus by Prometheus. The theft of fire is a symbolic sexual crime. Zeus punished Prometheus by creating Pandora, the first human woman, who of course opened Pandora's box, unleashing all kinds of troubles on human beings. Thus, Pandora, or woman, is the root of all evils for mankind. And of course from the male point of view, the desired mother is the cause of all guilt.

Let's continue the story of creation according to the Greeks. The marriage of Gaia and Uranus is the joining of the earth and sky. Uranus rained down on Gaia to produce many offspring, including the Titans. Uranus feared the

Titans, because he was afraid that like himself, they would want to marry their mother and depose him. He tried to solve this dilemma by preventing his Titan children from being born. He did this by having perpetual intercourse with Gaia, preventing the children from leaving her body. Gaia got tired of this situation and gave her son Kronos, the youngest Titan, a sickle to solve the problem. Kronos cut off his father's penis inside Gaia's body, and this allowed him to be born. It also sets up the interesting situation of the youngest son being the first born, since Kronos preceded his older brothers in his exit from the body of Gaia. Kronos tossed Uranus' penis into the sea, and Aphrodite, the goddess of love, emerged out of the foam.

Now Kronos tried very hard to learn from the mistakes of his father. Seeing the danger of marrying your mother, he, like all the Titans, married a sister, but remembering the sickle, he was as reluctant as his father to bear children. An important theme in Greek myth is that each generation tries to get what it wants without repeating the mistakes of the previous one. The Titans, like Freud's primal horde, overthrew the jealous patriarch who denied his sons access to any of the sexual privileges he enjoyed. But, not wanting to share the father's fate, they denied themselves access to Gaia, setting up the prohibition against maternal incest.

So, Kronos had a problem. He avoided sexual intercourse with his mother, marrying instead Rhea, the sister who most resembled Gaia, but what to do about his sons? In order to keep his sons from overthrowing him, he must keep mother and sons separate. If the mother's body is too dangerous, he will use his own instead. And so, he swallows his children as soon as they are born. His children must not be allowed a separate existence, and most importantly, they must be kept away from their mother, a potential accomplice. Now eventually, Rhea gets annoyed at Kronos' seemingly unlimited appetite for her babies. When she is pregnant with her youngest son Zeus, she goes to Crete, delivers the baby in a cave, entrusts him to the care of nymphs, and returns with a stone wrapped in a baby blanket which she gives to Kronos to swallow. Kronos didn't find out about the deception until it was too late. Zeus ambushed Kronos and kicked him so hard that Kronos vomited forth his other five fully grown children: Hades, Hestia, Demeter, Hera, and Poseidon. Zeus was made leader by his grateful siblings, and each of the others took a portion of creation as their dominion. Zeus exiled Kronos to Tartaros, but later he allowed his broken and defeated father to enter paradise at the end of the world. Once deposed or castrated, the father can die and be allowed to go to heaven, a symbolic return to symbiotic bliss.

Now Zeus figures something out that ensures his position as king of the gods and ruler of the universe. He has learned from the fates of Uranus and Kronos that to put his children in either his wife's body or his own is no solution, and he also realizes that the real enemy is not his children, but his wife. After swallowing his first wife, Zeus marries six more times. His last wife, his sister Hera, is the most important. Hera proves extremely jealous, and subsequent myths have her torturing Zeus' other wives and children. Zeus himself, however, seems above such shenanigans. Although he has sexual relationships with two aunts, two sisters, and several maternal goddesses, Zeus observes at least a rudimentary distinction between permissible and non-permissible sexual objects. To compensate himself for this act of restraint, Zeus then proceeds to copulate with practically every woman in Greek myth. The secret of Zeus' success is a misogynist lesson he has learned from his predecessors – the female enemy in the succession myth is not the mother, but the wife, who regularly takes the side of her children against her husband. Rather than confining his children in the earth, he sets out on an ambitious program of reproductive activity. Like his father and grandfather, Zeus is a principle of male sexuality, a god of rain and lightning, but unlike them, he is not an enemy of generation. He is the Oedipal success story par excellence and the good father of unlimited power and knowledge. Zeus is a figure with which all sons (and that is all men) can identify.

In describing and explaining the origin of the world, the Greeks created a story that recalls and reanimates the deepest concerns of childhood. Sons overthrow their fathers, not because they are monsters but because mothers prefer their sons, and this is just the way things are. The way to prevent yourself from being killed and to become god-like is to be careful of both wives and mothers and spread your seed as far and wide as possible. The Greek myth of the origin of the world and the establishment of the gods is the story of gratifying childhood wishes and overcoming childhood anxiety. And if your goal is to populate the world with people and steal the power of the goddess, then Zeus is a great role model.

So far, we have brought human beings up to the Oedipal period and found one solution to resolving the Oedipal dilemma. Now I want to talk a little bit about heroes, because the story of the hero is the story of puberty, of giving up your infantile personality and becoming a responsible adult. This is a fundamental psychological transformation that everyone has to undergo, and the hero gives us a road map to make that perilous journey. Greek myth is full of heroes, some human, some gods. The story of the hero is the story of the spiritual quest, the search each human being must make for meaning. Greek heroes go about slaying monsters, which are symbols of both taming the world out of a dangerous and unshaped wilderness and grappling with our own primitive impulses of desire and fear. Greek heroes leave their old way of life and go up to the mountain or down to the depths of the sea, which is, of course, the unconscious. Here they wrestle with the power of the dark and emerge, at last, to a new way of life. Greek heroes who find something new on their journey, often come back to found a new city. Homer's *Odyssey* chronicles the story of the hero Odysseus. Odysseus left his home to fight in the Trojan War. He spent ten years away from his wife and children during the Trojan War, and another ten years roaming the Greek islands under the watchful eye of Athena, goddess of wisdom. He was sent to the underworld by Circe, where his true initiation began when he met Tiresias and realized the unity of male and female. This separation caused his family much suffering. In the story, Athena comes to the 20-year-old son of Odysseus, Telemachus, and says, "Young man, go find your father." This is the theme of all the hero stories. The boy must leave his mother and go to find the father, which is the search for a career, for the source of power and meaning in life. Odysseus was celebrated by Homer as a man of judgment and courage. He was able to enjoy fortunate living circumstances, a happy family life, and an easy old age when he came home.

In terms of heroes, strife is the creator of all great things. They teach us that it is not the destination that counts but the journey. The adventure of the hero is the adventure and rapture of being alive. Heroes do what Joseph Campbell says we all must do to live meaningful lives: follow our bliss wherever it takes us. But following that bliss, as we all know, can be a perilous journey, and the path is riddled with the monsters of psychopathology. Narcissus and Oedipus, who made big mistakes, can serve as a warning for anyone who aspires to good mental health.

Narcissus' mother was Liriope, a beautiful nymph who was raped and cast aside by a river god. Liriope took the infant Narcissus to a prophet to ask if the child would live a long life. "He will," the seer replied, "as long as he never knows himself." Narcissus grew into a handsome youth who rejected the advances of every young man or woman that he met. In some versions of the myth, Narcissus not only rejects lovers, he sends a sword to one suitor and invites him to commit suicide. Some early versions of the myth have Narcissus slain by a suitor, but the more durable versions of the myth have him dying from self-neglect. When Narcissus saw his own reflection in a pool of water, he could not tear himself away from the beautiful image. Finally, he died of self-neglect, and a beautiful flower appeared in his stead. Today the narcissus grows on the banks of rivers. It can reproduce sexually, but usually does so in an asexual fashion. It is extremely poisonous. Now let's look at this myth. What is usually emphasized is the high opinion that Narcissus had of himself. But the fact is that Narcissus died because he was so in love with his own reflection that he forgot to eat or take care of himself. This myth is as much concerned with destructive impulses as with libidinal ones. It's interesting to remember that Narcissus' father was a god of water, and that this god had found an object of desire in the water. Gazing into the water becomes a repetition compulsion for Narcissus. Part of the extreme fascination Narcissus felt at his own watery image stemmed from a longing for an absent father – and also an Oedipal striving, a yearning to repeat his father's pleasure with his mother. There is also another version of this myth that gives Narcissus a twin sister who died. Therefore, his adoring gaze at his own reflection could have been an incestuous wish to be reunited with his sister. Is this a myth of self-love or mourning for a lost object? Whichever interpretation we take, Narcissus was unable to withdraw his libidinal cathexis from the beloved image sufficiently to seek new objects and survive. Another interpretation of the myth is that Narcissus didn't realize that the image he saw was himself and thought he was in love with another beautiful young man. In this case, the myth becomes a study of homosexual yearnings. If all three possibilities are accepted then Narcissus was driven by a fusion of both sexes into primal scene fantasies. Analysis of the myth suggests that it is important to deal with a tendency to idealize beautiful but excessively frustrating objects and to wrap up in a cloak of self-love the destructive impulses provoked by such objects (Spotnitz, 1976).

I now want to discuss Oedipus, a man who unknowingly killed his father, married his mother, and had children with her. Apparently, the wrong kind of sexual love can be as dangerous as too much love for oneself. In the story, a sphinx – not an Egyptian sphinx, but a female form with the wings of a bird, the body of an animal, and the breast, neck, and face of a woman – has caused a plague in the land. To lift that plague, Oedipus has to solve her riddle: "What is it that walks on four legs, then two, and then on three?" The answer is "Man." The infant creeps about on four legs, the adult walks on two, and the aged man walks with a cane. The riddle of the sphinx is the image of life itself, and once you have faced and accepted the riddle, death has no further hold on you. The conquest of the fear of death is the recovery of life's joy. One can experience the rapture of being alive only when one has accepted death, not as contrary to life, but as part of it (Campbell, 1988).

Greek mythology is for the most part male oriented. It is also extremely dualistic in that all compassion and human kindness is reserved for your group or clan, while all aggression is projected outward onto the other, the monster who must be confronted and destroyed. This can be a helpful way to deal with aggression, but Campbell makes the point that it doesn't work as well for the world today as it did in ancient Greece. If the human race wants to survive, there can be no more out groups on this planet. What is needed now is a new myth, not Greek, Roman, Hebrew, Christian, Hindu or American Indian – but a world myth. A return to the goddess as metaphor could be helpful in the creation of a myth for our time. The goddess loves all her children equally; and if the earth is to survive, compassion must work for the whole of humanity. But the organization of the planet is going to be an enormous task, and the energy that it will require will be a masculine energy. A unity of masculine and feminine, a non-dualistic perspective, can be the next evolutionary step in the creation of myth. But then what happens to aggression, that completely natural and troubling instinct? This is the problem of our time. And, as we all know, modern analysis has something to say about that.

References

Campbell, J. (1988). *The power of myth*. New York: Anchor Books.
Graves, R. (1955). *The Greek myths*. London: Penguin Books.
Spotnitz, H. (1976). Psychotherapy of preoedipal conditions. New York: Jason Aronson, Inc.
Spotnitz, H. and Meadow, P. (1976). Treatment of the narcissistic neurosis. New York: Manhattan Center for Advanced Psychoanalytic Studies.

Chapter 14

Becoming an analyst
Learning to live with madness, aggression and the unknown

I met Phyllis Meadow in the fall of 1983. I had just been accepted as a student at the Center for Modern Psychoanalytic Studies (CMPS), and Dr Meadow was the instructor of my first course. The subject was drive theory and the preverbal personality.

I was ten years out of Texas and five years into my personal analysis. I was just beginning to realize that there was more to me than a honeyed Southern belle, that Winnicottian smoke screen I had draped around myself to live in the world. Initially exhilarated to find in psychoanalysis a place where I could drop the treacly charm and tell the truth to a person who seemed sincerely interested in understanding me, I was becoming anxious and sometimes downright frightened by the quantities of primitive aggression pouring out of me on the couch. Though I was beginning to accept that I was a very angry young woman. I still hoped that being a diligent, cooperative analysand would cure me of my rage. Fresh out of a degree in social work, immersed in the theories of Alfred Adler and Carl Rogers, I saw aggression as a pathological response to the denial, distortion, or frustration of my basic benevolent nature, and the wish to murder as a logical reaction to a toxic environment. If I could exorcise all those traumatic childhood memories in analysis, I would never have to be angry again.

I was, therefore, astonished to hear Dr Meadow say on the night of the first class that childhood memories are mostly fabrications, distortions created at a much later time to express unconscious wishes. We create these memories to express a wish in the here and now, and these wishes have to do with two basic human impulses: the drive toward pleasure and connection, and the drive toward inertia or tension reduction. Even more astonishing, the final aim of this latter drive toward inertia is to lead what is living into an inorganic state, and thus can be properly understood as a death instinct. As long as the instinct operates internally, as a death instinct, it remains silent; it only comes to our notice when it is diverted outward as an instinct of destruction (Freud, 1938).

How I struggled with this unsavory concept! Using the ideas I learned in my social work studies, I initially argued with Dr Meadow. Finally, I grudgingly accepted the dual drive theory but balked at the term "death instinct." I understood the pull toward the inorganic, the peace of not feeling, but "death" I associated with illness and violence. What was even more unsettling was that Dr Meadow seemed so intrinsically joyful and full of life when discussing Thanatos and the primitive aggressive impulses that are its expression. I wondered how she had managed to stay out of prison all those years with such a voracious appetite for murderous fantasy. I also felt a deep excitement. Here was someone who was obviously as aggressive as I, who was living a full, meaningful life and having a lot of fun doing it.

It was in that first class with Dr Meadow that I learned that the mind itself is born out of rage and conflict. It is not pleasure and love, but frustration that develops the ego. Dr Meadow didn't teach this by lecturing about it. Like all good drive theorists, she believed in working in the here and now, and so she created the concept of constructive aggression in the classroom. In our debates over the death instinct, she pointed out that I was very angry and that anger was the energy fueling my intellectual engagement with her. I saw in the here and now that learning is unpleasure, an anxiety-ridden confrontation with the new and unfamiliar, and that helped me to understand that the creation of the self occurs in an atmosphere of frustration and discomfort that is very irritating. Here was a constructive outlet for rage: its use as an engine for growth. In stimulating my mind in such an infuriating way, Dr Meadow was enabling the intrapsychic fusion of the life and death instincts, teaching me to draw my aggression away from destructive action turned against myself and others and focusing it on thinking and learning.

Dr Meadow saw aggression not as something we are to be cured of, but as an innate drive in every human being (and indeed as something intrinsic in every living creature). She believed that even the life drive seeks its own end. Any impulse, whether toward life or death, desires relief from its own tension, and aggression is the tool through which a desire can accomplish its discharge. Aggression, expressed in assertiveness, is necessary for life. Channeling aggression into constructive rather than destructive outlets is the major task of psychoanalysis. Modern analysts were among the first to separate aggression from destruction and conceive of any act that reduces tension as aggressive, but not necessarily destructive (Meadow, 2003).

The debate over the death instinct has been waged for almost 100 years, and some analytic students claim that the whole argument is overly intellectualized and largely irrelevant in clinical practice. I believe, on the contrary, that the analyst's attitude toward aggression drives every aspect of clinical work, from how we aim to be with patients in the here and now of the treatment room to how we define cure. Once the analyst can see aggression as a powerful and worthwhile force, not something requiring a cure, then treatment proceeds in a unique way. The focus moves away from giving support or gaining insight or retrieving traumatic memories. Our primary clinical goal becomes helping the people we work with discharge their primitive rage into words in the treatment so that their aggression can be released constructively toward the outside world and can serve as the indispensable engine and fuel for productive living (Spotnitz, 1976).

Looking into Dr Meadow's merry eyes while we argued over drive theory, I learned to accept, and even relish, my own aggression. That was the beginning of a period of tremendous growth for me. I was able to harness my rage into completing my training at CMPS and writing a doctoral thesis. Every time I sat down at a keyboard, I experienced how irritating it was to confront the demand of a blank sheet of paper (later a screen) and how determined I was that I would defeat it by filling it with thoughts. Every time I slogged through an impenetrable analytic paper on technique – knowing how angry I was at the obtuse author for making me feel stupid – it sharpened my perceptions and helped me understand what was being said.

It was that fear of being stupid, certainly too stupid to be an analyst, that became the focus of the second valuable lesson Dr Meadow taught me. Clearly, I was no match for her formidable intelligence in our debates over the death instinct. Those debates converted me to dual drive theory, but they also left me with the sinking feeling that, with no hope of being as brainy as my teacher, I should just go on back to Texas. I wrote in my log, "I will never be as smart as you, and the idea infuriates and depresses me because I am very competitive."

In our next meeting, Dr Meadow asked the class if you have to be smart to be an analyst. Everyone thought that indeed you do. Dr Meadow shook her head and said, "There's nothing worse than an analyst that's too smart – unless it's a patient that's too smart." She explained that extremely smart patients are hard to cure because they can explain everything, and extremely smart analysts are not very good at their work because they think they know everything. "Your job as an analyst is to try to *understand*," she said, "and you can't begin to understand until you are aware of how stupid you are."

Laquercia (1992) asserted that "I don't know" is the correct position to take when conducting an analysis. As analysts, we strive to be comfortable not knowing while still being available to feelings and ideas. The work of analysis is developing an understanding of someone else's private world. This is a lonely and chaotic realm, and here we are all lost, alone, and ignorant (Sherman, 1981). As an analyst, it becomes necessary to enter a pre-Oedipal world, to think in hallucination and in the language of the body, not in an intellectual or logical way (Winnicott, 1965). We must give up the world of thought itself for a state of meditation where there is very little thought. In this state, our grasp of the patient's reality is only partly thinkable, more akin to poetry or music than abstract thought (Bollas, 1992).

Winnicott (1989) made the startling observation that intelligence itself hides deprivation. If a mother fails to adapt to her baby's needs, the baby survives by means of the mind. As Winnicott (1989, p. 156) puts it, "The mother exploits the baby's power to think things out and to collate and to understand. If the baby has a good mental apparatus, this thinking becomes a substitute for maternal care and adaptation." Seen in this light, wanting to be too smart as an analyst precludes an emotional connection with our patients.

Smart analysts want to offer interpretations to their patients and, as Dr Meadow said, any explanation or interpretation – especially early in treatment – is made to quell the analyst's anxiety or to make her feel grandiose. Interpretation almost never helps the patient. In fact, when smart analysts try to educate their patients, it interferes with the development of the narcissistic transference relationship (Meadow, 1989).

Interpretation suggests that what is being interpreted is wrong and should be discarded. Declarative interpretations are perceived as, and indeed often are, attacks. The craving for interpretation – sadistic for the analyst, masochistic for the patient – can be a way of maintaining emotional distance in the treatment setting (Friedman, 1979). Unsolicited interpretation is essentially unhelpful in modifying narcissistic patterns in which the patient is still dominantly attuned to the more primitive communicative modes of tone, inflection, gesture, and body language (Nelson, 1981).

"If you *must* make an interpretation," Meadow told our class, "make sure it's an incorrect one. If your interpretation is correct, the patient has no work to do. Patients are cured by incorrect interpretations because the patient must correct them." Even incorrect interpretations are contraindicated for a patient who is too compliant. A patient must learn to say no before the analyst risks any interpretation, right or wrong. If an analyst can resonate with her patient's feelings, nothing else is required (Meadow, 1989). How freeing this was! It meant that I could sit in bewildered silence for at least the first few years of treatment with my patients, with nothing more to do than experience the feelings in the room and try to temper my stupidity with understanding.

"But what," I asked in my log, "do I do when a patient comes in with the same kinds of problems I have? It may be okay for the analyst to be stupid, but what if she is crazy?" Dr Meadow responded by asking the class if it's okay for the analyst to be crazy. Most of us answered that we certainly hoped so. Dr Meadow reassured us that being crazy ourselves gives us a unique understanding of and empathy for our patients. She told us, "When the analyst can be worse than the patient, the patient can get better." The important thing is to be able to contain all the primitive thoughts and impulses induced in the analytic hour. She advised us to feel all our crazy feelings, to ask three to five object-oriented questions in the 50-minute session, and otherwise to keep quiet and stay in our chair, no matter what we were feeling.

McDougall (1978) agrees with Dr Meadow that people who are "too well adapted to life" do not make good analysts. We are little apt to understand psychic ills in our patients if we cannot recognize symptoms and psychic suffering within ourselves. Being "normal" keeps the analyst out of contact with her imaginative life. Dr Meadow taught us that it isn't good to feel so crazy that we lose touch with the patient. If a person is just too difficult, too much like ourselves or our difficult mothers, it is okay to lose that patient. "It's a myth that the analyst has to keep all her patients. Sometimes we have to let them go. We can't treat everybody. Make a good referral and say goodbye."

I would go on to learn many more things from Dr Meadow in the 12 years I studied at CMPS. In fact, she was teaching me about the life and death instincts until the week before she died. But I will never forget that first class at CMPS where I learned two of the most important lessons of my life: how to enjoy and harness aggression, and how to loosen and laugh at my rather harsh superego, so intolerant of my imperfections. Being able to tolerate, savor, and use one's own rage, stupidity, and craziness can make the eye dance with glee.

References

Bollas, C. (1992). The psychoanalyst's use of free association. In *Being a character: Psychoanalysis and self experience*. New York: Hill and Wang, pp. 101–133.

Freud, S. (1938). An outline of psychoanalysis. *Standard Edition*. London: Hogarth Press, 23, 141–207.

Friedman, L. (1979). Marie Coleman Nelson's paradigmatic therapy: A variant reading. *Modern Psychoanalysis*, 4, 19–37.

Laquercia, T. (1992). The anaclitic environment: The emerging challenge for the analyst. *Modern Psychoanalysis*, 17, 35–42.

McDougall, J. (1978). *Plea for a measure of abnormality*. New York: Bruner/Mazel.

Meadow, P.W. (1989). How we aim to be with patients. *Modern Psychoanalysis*, 14, 145–162.

Meadow, P.W. (2003). Drives, aggression and destructivity. *Modern Psychoanalysis*, 28, 199–205.

Nelson, M.C. (1981). The paradigmatic approach: A parallel development. *Modern Psychoanalysis*, 6, 9–26.

Sherman, M. (1981). Siding with the resistance in paradigmatic psychotherapy. *Modern Psychoanalysis*, 6, 47–64.

Spotnitz, H. (1976). *Psychotherapy of preoedipal conditions*. New York: Jason Aronson.

Winnicott, D. (1989). New light on children's thinking. *Psychoanalytic Explorations*. Cambridge, MA: Harvard University Press, pp. 152–157.

Chapter 15

Wrestling with destiny

Do we believe in destiny? In the myths that are most meaningful to us – the fairy tales we cut our teeth on, in Shakespeare and the Greek myths, even in the novels of lesser and greater merit that entertain us on the beach in the summer, destiny is very real. In "Sleeping Beauty," a curse is put on a baby princess by a slighted and wicked fairy. She predicts that the baby will be pricked by the needle of a spinning wheel and fall down dead. Although this curse is softened by a kinder fairy who decrees a long sleep rather than death, nothing can prevent the princess's fate from being enacted. Indeed, the father's frantic efforts to change the story by banning all spinning wheels only helps bring about his daughter's destiny. The same is true of the myth of Oedipus. Oedipus's father maims him and casts him out to die to forestall the horrible fate, patricide and incest, predicted by the oracle, but his efforts only hasten the inevitable. Romeo and Juliet are "star-crossed," yet despite their goodness and beauty, they are doomed to meet a tragic end.

In all of these stories, there is a common denominator: *not knowing*. Sleeping Beauty didn't know what a spinning wheel was, and so when at last she had occasion to see one, she had to touch it. Oedipus was ignorant of the fact that his adoptive parents were not his biological ones, and so he didn't realize he was murdering his father and marrying his mother. Romeo didn't know that Juliet, like Sleeping Beauty, was not dead, but asleep, and so he killed himself. Can knowledge save us from malevolent destiny? If we can be courageous enough to confront what we don't know or, more importantly, what we don't want to know, can we win control over our own destiny?

This is the promise of psychoanalysis. Like the myth makers and the poets, psychoanalysts believe that destiny is real. Psychoanalysts, however, call it by the name of repetition compulsion. We believe that there is a dark power in every human being that if left unchecked could propel a person against his will to a tragic end. Though we design our own destinies with our repetitions, the true architect of our fate is the unconscious.

Destiny and the repetition compulsion

Freud (1924; 1928) understood destiny as related in the unconscious to the power of the parents, particularly the punishing father. The early father is projected onto the external world and called fate. When we were children, the father punished us when we were bad, and since we all go on being bad, we arrange to ensure that we will go on being punished. This is what makes us associate destiny with angry gods and tragic ends. In "Beyond the Pleasure Principle," Freud (1920) hypothesizes a compulsion to repeat that is more primitive, more elementary, and more instinctual than the pleasure principle which it overrides. Working in the service of the death instinct, this compulsion seeks to return the organism to an earlier state of affairs.

Laplanche and Pontalis (1973), p. 79) describe the repetition compulsion as "an ungovernable process originating in the unconscious. As a result of its actions the subject deliberately puts himself in distressing situations, thereby repeating an old experience, but he does not recall this prototype." As Freud (1920, p. 18) states, "what is not remembered will be repeated." The repetition compulsion, in the final analysis, expresses the most general character of the instincts, their conservatism. This is the concept of the inertia of living matter, the disinclination to abandon an old position in favor of a new one. Human beings like to maintain the existing state of things, even if this state is very painful indeed. So our fate becomes an automatic and impulsive repetition of unpleasurable situations.

Bibring (1943) felt that patterns of coping that we acquire at the very beginning of life are retained and reproduced over and over in a way that determines our destiny. A formative influence on an instinctual drive is brought about by a traumatic experience that influences the course and aim of the instinct. Repetitions occur when traumatic experiences have not been assimilated. If we have had to endure a lot of excessively traumatic stimuli in our early life, we use our adaptions and defenses to bind these stimuli by anticathexis. Instincts tend to cling to primary or intense experiences and to follow the way paved by these experiences, irrespective of pleasure or pain. As we continually repeat the traumatic situation, the toxins are discharged in fractional amounts in a way that makes them more bearable. In repeating dangerous situations, the unknown becomes familiar, with a decrease in emotional cathexis. Looked at from this perspective, the repetition compulsion has both a repetitive and a restitutive tendency. One of my female patients who has been divorced three times said, "I keep marrying my mother, hoping that I can change the story and finally get a happy ending with her." This repetitive tendency is a function of the id, while the restitutive hope for a happy ending is the work of the ego.

Freud (1924, p. 178) said famously that "anatomy is destiny," and he wrote extensively about how a penis, or the lack of one, can have profound effects on human beings. I (Holmes, 2000) have studied and written about how girls use the internalization of maternal and paternal objects in the same way that boys use the penis: to attain separation and mastery over powerful parental figures. All of these adaptions to being male and female occur very early in life on an unconscious level, and they get acted out over and over, for good or ill, as we go through the life cycle. Although women are making real gains in the working world, and men are becoming more comfortable taking responsibility for children and the home, our gender nonetheless guides us in ways conscious and unconscious toward our individual destinies.

Many human beings see fate as an expression of a divine will (Freud, 1930). They find the idea that destiny is just a monster created out of the garbage dump of a lifetime of mistakes totally repellent, and so they take solace in the idea that God has a plan for them on this earth. Even if that plan is to suffer and die, they find comfort in the knowledge that their pain is not their own responsibility, and if they can bear it with courage and grace, they will get their reward in heaven. How gratifying it is to feel that God exists and that we have no control! Like a child in the back seat of a car, we can enjoy the view and say, "I wonder where we're going." Reassuring as this concept is, it can also be dangerous. If you believe that God guides your hand, then you have no personal responsibility for all the unspeakable acts that are carried out in God's name. The murder, torture, barbarism, and destruction that human beings have inflicted on this long-suffering world in the name of God or gods have been with us throughout history, from the murder of the early Christians through the Holocaust to the recent acts of terrorism perpetrated by radical Islamists.

Bollas (1989) likes to differentiate between destiny and fate. He equates fate with neurosis. The person who comes to psychoanalysis with neurotic or psychotic ideas can be described as a fated person. Her symptom is the oracle predicting her doom. These unfortunate patients are interred in an internal world of self and object relations that endlessly repeats the same scenarios. They have no hope for the future; indeed, the idea of the future is simply the endless repetition of the past. A glimpse into the future is a vision from fate, echoing the voice of the mother, the father, or the toxic environment that oppresses the self. This sense of fate is a feeling of despair over one's inability to influence the course of one's life.

Destiny, according to Bollas, is another matter. Destiny is a positive drive, an urge to articulate our true selves. It is the creative potential in a person's life. One of the most important tasks of an analysis is to enable a patient to come into contact with his destiny, to articulate his true nature through the creative use of objects. Lacan's (1977) concept of *jouissance* (enjoyment) also embodies the idea that the individual can find pleasure in his choice and use of objects. The pursuit of *jouissance* is each person's true destiny, and if one is fortunate, determined, and aggressive enough, this enlightened state can be achieved. The work of analysis becomes a creative destruction of the past in order to see the potential of the future and to make a psychic investment in creating that future. When the future holds positive possibilities, destiny is no longer a matter of chance. It becomes a choice – not a thing to passively endure, but a thing to be achieved.

Gaining control over our destinies

Bollas' idea of a personal destiny is an optimistic and exciting one; all of us want to help our patients go from feeling fated to feeling that they can control and savor their own destinies. The question, therefore, becomes: how do we help people get there? When we see that a patient has gotten control over her repetitions, what has happened? How has she achieved it? How have we achieved it? What have we created together in the analysis which has enabled the patient to move forward toward a new and creative experience? I have thought about this question for many years. New patients often ask me, "How does psychoanalysis work? You don't say much, and I do all the talking." They find it hard to believe that just talking can help them. My patients and I have struggled over this question and come up with lots of different answers. Psychoanalysis provides a corrective emotional experience. There is something intrinsically therapeutic about spending time with a person who is completely focused on understanding you, a person not interested in inflicting his projections or fantasies or ideas on you, but trying to understand how you are trapped in your own inflexible fate. These ideas are among the answers or partial answers helping us to understand how we can help our patients. But I have always felt there was more to learn about how psychoanalysis helps a person shape his destiny.

Exciting new work in the field of neuroscience is providing physical and scientific corroboration of the psychoanalytic theories postulated by Freud and later theorists such as Hyman Spotnitz. For example, in 1969, Spotnitz was writing about the curative process in psychoanalysis as "the deactivation of certain neural pathways and the activation of others" (p. 99).

The neuroscientist Paul MacLean (Restak, 1979; Shepherd, 2005) describes the evolution of the human brain as expanding in a hierarchical pattern along the lines of three basic structures in the brain, each with "its own way of perceiving and responding to the world" (Shepherd, 2005, p. 48). These "three brains" have evolved methods of communicating with each other. Brain one, the first to evolve, is reptilian in nature and governs mechanical and unconscious behaviors. This is the seat of what we call instinct, and what Freud called the id. The mammalian brain, or the limbic system, was the next area to develop. Wrapped around the reptilian brain, the limbic system allowed sight, smell, and hearing to operate together and created a primitive memory system. It also made the nurturance of offspring possible. Emotions are generated in the limbic system but do not become conscious there. The third brain, which developed in the last several 100,000 years, is the cerebral cortex. This is the center of thinking and reasoning. The cerebral cortex evolved with the advent of language and is where consciousness resides. Freud called it the ego.

One of the most interesting things about these three brains is that the neuronal connections from brain one and brain two upward are a great deal stronger than those from the cerebral cortex downward. This explains the difficulty we experience in using logic and insight to change feelings. One goal of analysis is to strengthen the cerebral cortex to free the patient from the repetitive, obsessive behaviors that are characteristic of the lower two brains. I believe this is achieved by the constant conversion of primitive impulses and feelings into words. This is similar to the goal that Freud (1932, p. 80) stated for analysis when he said, "Where there was id, ego shall be."

Panksepp (1998) has studied the brains of cats and rats, and one of his most important findings is that feeling is older than thought. There were emotions in the brain millions of years before there was mind to interpret them. We are used to believing that feelings are caused by events or thoughts, but that is evidently not true. Feelings arise out of neurobiological circuits in the limbic system; they are the effect, not the cause, of arousal systems in the brain. Feelings are not actually felt until they are experienced by the cerebral cortex. These circuits are inherited by the species and by each individual organism. No specific thoughts or behaviors are directly inherited, but dispositions to feel, think, and act in various ways and in various situations are. Although these dispositions do not necessarily dictate our destinies, they powerfully promote certain possibilities and diminish others. While basic emotional circuits are among the tools provided by nature, Panksepp believes that their ability to control our destinies depends on the nurturance or lack of nurturance that the world provides. Emotional systems, like the body, can be strengthened by use and weakened by disuse.

This picture of the brain and of the origin of feelings has given me new ideas about how psychoanalysis can change one's destiny. In psychoanalysis, the contract is to "say everything." So we are constantly inviting the patient to convert into language the electrical impulses pulsing up from the reptilian brain and the feelings traveling along neurobiological circuits in the mammalian brain. In this process, we are granting the lower brains access to the cerebral cortex. And, I believe, we are strengthening the young and often overpowered upper brain against the instincts and primitive feelings that are all too often acted out in the world in a way that ensures a star-crossed destiny. When messages from the lower brains are put into words, instincts lose their primitive power, and feelings can be felt and verbalized, rather than acting as mandates to often destructive action. As analysis progresses, communication from the lower two brains gradually becomes data, not commands. The patient can evaluate this data and then decide how she wants to deal with it. At this point, the patient takes charge of her own destiny.

This is by no means an easy process. There are many pitfalls along the way. When patients decide to behave in ways that go against the familiar pathways of their repetitions, they may experience all sorts of terrible feelings as well as an enormous amount of anxiety. I remember a patient in a group of mine who for years had taken care of the men in the group. She had had a series of unsuccessful relationships outside the group, and inside it she compulsively mothered the men, while unconsciously feeling a lot of contempt for what she saw as their childishness and dependency, which she, in a way, had created. As this pattern became more conscious to her, she began to develop new longings. No longer so interested in taking care of the men, she developed a hunger to be loved by them. As she became able to put this new yearning into words, she induced new feelings in the men. They very cooperatively began to love her, and so we came to a point in the group where this woman took on a whole new role. No longer the caretaker, she began to be the object of a tremendous amount of masculine affection and attention. But it was interesting to me that instead of being delighted by this development, she began to feel primitive anxiety and got the idea that she had to leave the group. When the group explored this with her, all she could say was, "There's something not right about this. I don't deserve all this attention." I told her she didn't have to deserve it. "Nobody really deserves to get love," I said, "All you have to do is know you want it." Sometimes when a man in the group was talking to this woman with love and empathy, she would begin to cry, look at me in distress, and say, "Oh, my mother is going to kill me!" Anxiety about punishment and guilt always accompanies constructive change and must be worked through in the analysis.

A man I worked with described what it feels like to decide to go against your repetitions and change your destiny. He said, "When I behave in a way that is not self-destructive, I feel like I have a penny in my hand, and I release it. And instead of falling to the ground, it floats up into the sky. It's very disorienting and unpleasant."

Patients often report that their lives are not as exciting when they change self-destructive habits and find new, more satisfying objects. "I still think about Robert," a woman who had just made a new and happy marriage told me. "He was bad news with his drug use and his constant unemployment and his cheating on me, but God – he was so exciting. I think he was the love of my life." What is it that is so thrilling to many of us about these self-destructive repetitions? Why do we feel slightly bored when we find objects who so effortlessly make us happy? I think it is because the compulsion to repeat the old, sad story is fueled by the hope that this time, finally, the ending will be different. We will master the situation, triumph over it, make people who are incapable of love finally love us. What could be more exciting! It's the primitive thrill the *Tyrannosaurus rex* must have felt when he finally grabbed the *Pterodactyl* and ate him up. Reptilian pleasures probably are more exciting than day-to-day satisfaction. So, at some point, a conscious choice has to be made.

One of the most painful feelings involved in becoming the master of our own fate is a sense of mourning. Giving up old repetitions is often experienced as the death, or even the murder, of beloved early objects. Taking charge of our destiny means saying goodbye to those objects; being happy feels like a betrayal of the people who made us and taught us, for better or worse, how to be in this world. When I first came to New York, I was in an acting class in which the teacher could get any of the students to cry by having the student stand in front of the class and wave, "Bye-bye, bye-bye," like an infant. No matter how toxic or how painful the past has been, it hurts the heart to relinquish it.

Our repetitions haunt us like the spirits in ghost stories. They cannot be put to rest until psychoanalysis solves the mystery and breaks the spell. Most people come into analysis wanting to change their feelings. Making unpleasant feelings go away is, for them, the definition of cure. But this death of feeling is not really the goal of psychoanalysis. Feelings are like weather. When fated patients come to our offices, the weather is violent and dangerous, forcing the patient to take cover and defend himself with all sorts of pathological defenses and unconscious repetitions and re-enactments. As the talking cure progresses, the weather settles down a little, becomes less dangerous to the person, and finally, like the fluctuation of sun and rain, winter and summer, love and hate, or joy and grief, becomes a thing to be enjoyed.

A Buddhist yogi, Dharmaraksita composed a text titled "The Wheel Weapon Striking at the Vital Points of the Enemy." In this text, there is a reference to destiny and the very human obsession to repeat:

> Forsaking ethical discipline, the liberation path,
> I cling to my paternal home.
> Casting my happiness into the river, I chase after misery.
> Dance and trample on the head of this betrayer, false conception
> Mortally strike at the heart of this butcher and enemy, Ego!
>
> (Thupten Jinpa, 2005, p. 135)

In the dance we call psychoanalysis, patient and therapist endeavor to trample on the false conceptions of the repetition compulsion, that enemy which tends to butcher any hope for happiness or for control over our own fate. I have devoted my life to psychoanalysis because I believe it is an ethical discipline, a path to liberation.

References

Bibring, E. (1943). The conception of the repetition compulsion. *Psychoanalytic Quarterly*, *12*(4), 486–519.

Bollas, C. (1989). *Forces of destiny: Psychoanalysis and the human idiom*. Northvale, NJ: Jason Aronson.

Freud, S. (1920). Beyond the pleasure principle. *Standard Edition*. London: Hogarth Press, *23*, 3–64.

Freud, S. (1924). The economic problem of masochism. *Standard Edition*. London: Hogarth Press, *19*, 159–170.

Freud, S. (1928). Dostoevsky and parricide. *Standard Edition*. London: Hogarth Press, *21*, 175–196.

Freud, S. (1930). Civilization and its discontents. *Standard Edition*. London: Hogarth Press, *21*, 59–145.

Holmes, L. (2000). The internal triangle: New theories of female development. *Modern Psychoanalysis*, *25*, 207–226.

Jinpa, T., trans. & ed. (2005). *Mind training: The great collection*. Boston, MA: Wisdom Publications.

Lacan, J. (1977). *Écrits: A selection* (A. Sheridan, trans.). London: Tavistock Publications.

Laplanche, J., & Pontalis, J.B. (1973). *The language of psychoanalysis*. New York: W. W. Norton & Company.

Panksepp, J. (1998). *Affective neuroscience*. New York: Oxford University Press.

Restak, R. (1979). *The brain: The last frontier*. New York: Doubleday Publishing.

Shepherd, M. (2005). Toward a psychobiology of desire. *Modern Psychoanalysis*, 30, 43–59.

Spotnitz, H. (1969). Modern *p*sychoanalysis of the *s*chizophrenic *p*atient. New York: Grune and Stratton.

Chapter 16

Why talking cures

People often come to my office for a consultation, and at some point during the interview, they ask me how I can possibly help them. I usually tell them, "Talking helps." More often than not, this thought is met with profound mistrust. The potential patient will say something like, "I hope you're not one of those therapists who doesn't talk. I'm not paying you to listen to me talk. I could do that with a tape recorder." These skeptics want guidance, advice, the solution to their problems, or the secret to happiness, which they seem to fantasize I am willfully withholding from them. They doubt my competence and my ethics if all I am going to do is sit there and try to understand them. For years, when potential patients questioned the psychoanalytic process or refused to lie on the couch, I questioned myself. Their misgivings made me feel like a fraud.

I am a little more experienced now. After 25 years of working with psychoanalytic patients, I have conducted extensive research on my successes and my failures, and I can say with some conviction that Freud, Spotnitz, and Meadow were right all along. Saying everything is the key to a successful analysis. Perhaps it is because I find talking so easy that I tended to devalue it for all those years. Even after it became crystal clear to me that patients who adhere to the analytic contract of free association are the ones who get better, I was confused. How does talking help? What does it actually do for a patient? Lately, with the help of the exciting discoveries in the field of neuroscience, I have finally gotten some new ideas about how talking helps.

Clinical examples

Let me begin with a few of my talkative success stories. All of these patients had practically no resistance to speaking freely – but for very different reasons. A woman I'll call Sherri, who has been my patient for 25 years, is an ambulatory schizophrenic. She comes in for her session, immediately lies on the couch, and talks nonstop for the full 50 minutes. She doesn't like to be interrupted. Indeed, when I ask an object-oriented question, she stops talking and looks very distressed. For 25 years, I don't think I have said more than 100 words to her. For the first few years, Sherri's talk was mostly what we call "word salad," the incomprehensible meanderings of psychosis. She did make me understand that she was a single mother and had a young son named Jake. She came to treatment because she had poured a full can of paint over her infant son's head, very nearly killing him. Sherri and Jake were alone in the world. The boy's father was a very wealthy man with whom Sherri had spent one night. In the third year of treatment, still babbling nonsense on the couch, Sherri went to court and won a monthly settlement from this man for child support. He was furious, but DNA testing confirmed that he was indeed Jake's father, and he paid the child support. In the fourth year of treatment, when the boy was almost five years old, Sherri contacted Jake's paternal grandmother. Knowing that Jake's father was an only child and that Jake was his only child, Sherri wrote the grandmother a letter introducing her to Jake, her only grandchild, and enclosed pictures of the adorable little boy. She included drawings Jake had made in kindergarten. This began a ten-year relationship with the grandmother. The old woman encouraged her son to get to know Jake. She paid the boy's tuition for private school, and when she died, she left Sherri and Jake enough money to put the boy through an excellent college. After the grandmother's death, Sherri began to make more sense in the sessions. She had come to love this woman, and grief seemed to make her coherent. She mourned, and she worried about what her life was going to be like when Jake went off to college and she was alone. Though she was much less psychotic, she still made it very clear that she wanted no contact from me; I sat in silence while Sherri talked. Sherri went back to school and got a job as a temp in a neighborhood public school. She will be finishing her master's degree this year and hopes to get a permanent job as a full-time teacher in this school in September. I'm sure she'll do it – they love her there and think she is charmingly eccentric and rather gifted in relating to the kids.

I am quite proud of this case. I consider Sherri one of my great success stories though I didn't do anything except stay out of her way and try to understand her. I am convinced she has made such phenomenal progress because she is conflict-free about talking.

Another talker who has demonstrated dramatic growth in analysis is a patient I wrote about several years ago (Holmes, 2002; Chapter 9 of this book). This man had a fascination with death. He loved to dream about it, witness it, and act it out in various ways. For years, he tried to kill me off in the session by speaking in a deadly flat monotone. He droned on and on, and like Sherri, he wanted no contact with me. Indeed, the schizoid, unstoppable verbiage was a way to ensure that I could not talk or even be experienced as alive. I often slept during his session, and if I was able to stay awake, I had all kinds of uncomfortable somatic sensations: my head hurt, I felt nauseated, sweaty, and breathless. I have worked with this man for 17 years, and the change in him has been remarkable. He is now able to experience pleasure for the first time in his life. His affect is animated and labile. He has gone from a boring, low-paying job as a librarian's assistant to a position as the editor of a prominent food magazine. He has been with his partner for over ten years now. Lately, he seems to want me to talk a little more. I am reluctant to do it. I feel this man has saved his own life with his persistent defensive monotone. His talking has cured him.

Another patient, Sally, came into treatment so distressed and frantic about her husband's leaving her that words tumbled out of her in a waterfall of grief, rage, and despair. She refused to lie on the couch, but she had absolutely no problem with "saying everything." In the five years I have known Sally, she has divorced her husband, found a new relationship, and most importantly, gone from seeing herself as the perpetual victim to using her aggression creatively to get a better job, make new kinds of friends, and pursue her talent as a painter. She is very grateful to me and has referred quite a few patients to me. I haven't been able to help any of them as much as she claims I helped her. I think it is because most of these referrals have a resistance to talking. They question the process. They don't believe that talking can really help. They want guidance. They don't think they're getting their money's worth unless I say brilliant things to them. When I get worried that one of them is really going to leave, I try to accommodate the request and say something brilliant. Sometimes I am successful, and then the patient and I are very gratified, but it doesn't really change anything. No matter how brilliant I am, the patient stays stuck. What makes Sally different from all her friends is her understanding that she needed to talk. I consider all her friends to be pre-analytic in that my goal with them is to resolve their resistances to speaking freely. Until that happens, I will have to focus on these patients' lives when what I want to do is focus on their minds. They will expect insight, symptom relief, or behavioral changes, with no understanding that what we should be working on is the expansion of free association (Kris, 1992).

Bridging soma and psyche

Ever since Freud's patient Anna O. coined the phrase "the talking cure," psychoanalysts have been instructing their patients to just say everything. Freud (1910, p. 32) described free association as "the basic rule" of psychoanalysis. He insisted that the patient

> must say whatever comes into his head, even if he considers it incorrect or irrelevant or nonsensical, and above all, if he finds it disagreeable to let himself think about what has occurred to him. So long as this ordinance is carried out we are certain of obtaining the material which will put us on the track of the repressed complexes.

As early as 1895, Freud described language as energy discharge, and toward the end of his life (1938), he was still convinced that language binds the mobile energy of the drive to stabilize mental representations. Years later, Spotnitz (1985, p. 92) affirmed Freud's idea: "In saying everything, the patient engages in discharge and operates to produce the deactivation of certain nervous system patterns, and the activation and discharge of new patterns." Patients strive to understand themselves, but according to Spotnitz (1985, p. 169) this should not be the goal: "His mental energy should be wholly dedicated to saying whatever he thinks, feels and remembers at the moment." Meadow (1996a, p. 140) had the conviction that growth can occur only when a patient is allowed to say everything to an analyst who listens without judgment or evaluation. She urged the analyst to concern herself with creating an environment where a patient can give up his resistance to talking in the presence of the therapist (1996b, p. 236). From Meadow's point of view, the key to reversing pathology lies in discovering *why* the patient cannot say what she cannot say (1996c, p. 242).

Words bridge the gap between the body and the mind, between the neurological and the psychological (Kris, 1990). They are a derivative, an ideational representative, of instinctual forces (Rapaport, 1944). Talking has the potential power to evoke somatic states and bridge intrapsychic elements, thereby transforming the patient. It is both a hallmark of the secondary process and a bridge to the primary process. Indeed, in the word, primary and secondary processes are reconciled (Loewald, 1980a; 1980b). The patient's primary process thinking is being reactivated, but he is communicating the primitive impulses in language, thus imparting to the primary process important characteristics of secondary process thinking (Lowenstein, 1963). Free association combines an increased awareness of self with a liberating disregard for reality (Rosegrant, 2005). It breaks with the usual state of affairs within the psyche, where elements of both ego and id are repressed. Saying everything invites the patient to direct his perceptions toward these warded-off elements. This shifts the balance of forces between autonomous and defensive functions within the ego and between the ego and the id (Lowenstein, 1963). Language, like the ego, is both a structure and an evolving process. The operations of both take place mostly on a preconscious level. Speech creates ego. The ego is both a language-determined and a language-determining structure (Edelheit, 1969).

Many patients come into treatment with the goal of being "happy." They don't realize that happy is a feeling, and like all feelings, it comes and goes. Feelings, like the weather, are always changing. Maintaining a constant state of pleasure is an irrational definition of psychoanalytic cure. The ability to free-associate, to say everything, is in some sense a better definition of cure. It indicates that the talker has reached a point in her growth where primitive impulses of sex and aggression are able to be managed in a maturational way. They are no longer repressed, which causes them to be replaced with the pathological symptoms of mental illness, nor are they acted out in all the destructive ways that create so much misery in the world. A person who can truly say everything has control of her destiny; she is free to explore what it is she wants and how to get it in a way that will do no damage to herself or the objects in her life.

Spotnitz was foreshadowing recent advances in neuroscience when he talked about the changes in nervous system patterns that talking facilitates. Neuroscientists, using new technologies, are now able to study the human brain in great detail and more importantly to watch it in action. They have found that the human brain should be thought of as three different brains. Brain one was the first to evolve; it is reptilian in nature, essentially no different from the brain of a *Tyrannosaurus rex*. It governs mechanical and unconscious behavior and is the seat of instinct, what Freud called the id. Millions of years ago the second brain, the limbic system, evolved. This brain is mammalian in nature. It allowed for the nurturance of offspring, and it also enabled the senses to work together to create thought and a primitive memory. The limbic system generates feelings, but they are not experienced or connected with ideas there. For that, we need the third brain, the cerebral cortex. This is a relatively small part of the brain, and it evolved only in the last several hundred thousand years (Restak, 1979). Language probably hastened its development. Although it is quite small in comparison to the other two brains, the cerebral cortex is certainly the center of what Freud called the ego.

It is important to remember that this center of thinking and reasoning is often overwhelmed by the lower two brains. The neural connections from brain one and brain two upward are a great deal stronger than those from the cerebral cortex downward. Electrical impulses are constantly pulsing up into the cerebral cortex from the reptiles and the mammals below, but the more evolved cerebral cortex has practically no influence at all on the lower brains. That's why it is so hard to use logic or insight to control our impulses and feelings. It also explains why human beings so often act like animals.

Consider though what happens neurologically when we ask the patient to say everything. We are inviting the patient to convert into language powerful electrical impulses pulsing up from the unconscious. This process gives the cerebral cortex, where language resides, some control over the tyranny of the lower brains. When these electrical impulses conveying primitive instincts are verbalized, the drives lose their primitive power, and feelings can be felt and verbalized rather than acted out in all sorts of destructive behaviors. Freud educated us about how the ego represses the instincts and creates symptoms. Free association invites the repressed impulses to the surface and creates words. In talking, the patient gets the repressing ego out of the way and encourages other ego functions, such as self-observation and communication. Telling replaces repeating pathological patterns; speech takes the place of the symptom. Patients get better.

I have heard psychoanalysis described as a sort of religion for intellectuals. This analogy can certainly be interpreted in a number of ways, some complimentary, others derogatory. And yet after 25 years as an analyst, I do consider the practice of free association as a sort of sacrament of the most ethical kind.

The word can convert an impulse to kill, rape, commit suicide, or start a war into a thought or a feeling. It enables the most primitive instincts of sex and aggression to be utilized in poetry, painting, or social action. Within the psychic system of the speaker, each word is an act of love toward her own mind, a containment, a motherly protection and care for the primitive animal that resides neurologically within each of us.

Neurologist and Nobel laureate Eric Kandel, who has studied psychoanalysis and the biology of the mind extensively, was asked by Charlie Rose (2006) at the end of a round table called "From Freud to the Mysteries of the Human Brain," what he wants to study next. Kandel replied:

> I have the sense that psychotherapy is a learning experience. And, therefore, there should be anatomical changes to the brain that occur as a result of psychotherapy, and we should be able to detect it. So, I would like to see imaging done on people before, during, and after a psychotherapeutic experience in order to see whether one can detect changes in the brain as a result of therapy.

Rose asked if anyone is doing that. And Kandel said they're beginning to. Freud would have been very pleased.

References

Edelheit, H. (1969). Speech and psychic structure—The vocal-auditory organization of the ego. *Journal of the American Psychoanalytic Association*, 17(2), 381–412.

Freud, S. (1895). Project for a scientific psychology. *Standard Edition*. London: Hogarth Press, 1, 283–397.

Freud, S. (1910). Five lectures on psycho-analysis. *Standard Edition*. London: Hogarth Press, 11, 9–55.

Freud, S. (1938). An outline of psycho-analysis. *Standard Edition*. London: Hogarth Press, 23, 141–207.

Holmes, L. (2002). A single case study of a fascination with death. *Modern Psychoanalysis*, 27, 113–131.

Kris, A.O. (1990). The analyst's stance and the method of free association. *Psychoanalytics Study of the Child*, 45, 25–44.

Kris, A.O. (1992). Interpretation and the method of free association. *Psychoanalytic Inquiry*, 12(2), 208–224.

Loewald, H. (1980a). On the therapeutic action of psychoanalysis. *Papers on psychoanalysis*. New Haven: Yale University Press.

Loewald, H. (1980b). Primary process, secondary process and language. *Papers on psychoanalysis*. New Haven: Yale University Press.

Lowenstein, R.M. (1963). Some considerations on free association. *Journal of the American Psychoanalytic Association*, 11(3), 451–473.

Meadow, P. (1996a). How we aim to be with patients. *Modern Psychoanalysis*, 21, 137–154.

Meadow, P. (1996b). Treatment beginnings. *Modern Psychoanalysis*, 21, 233–240.

Meadow, P. (1996c). The myth of the impersonal analyst. *Modern Psychoanalysis*, 22, 241–259.
Rapaport, D. (1944). The scientific methodology of psychoanalysis. In M.M. Gill (Ed.), *The collected papers of David Rapaport* (p. 1967). New York: Basic Books.
Restak, R. (1979). *The brain: The last frontier*. New York: Doubleday Publishing.
Rose, C. (2006). Part one of the Charlie Rose Science Series: From Freud to the mysteries of the human brain. October 31. Available from www.charlierose.com/view/interview/154.
Rosegrant, J. (2005). The therapeutic effects of the free associative state of consciousness. *Psychoanalytic Quarterly*, 74(3), 737–766.
Spotnitz, H. (1985). *Modern psychoanalysis of the schizophrenic patient* (2nd ed.). New York: Human Sciences Press.

Chapter 17

Beyond cure

Although patients come to psychoanalysis hoping to be cured, there are a multitude of theories about what that actually means. Given that a cure – as an idea and a goal – must be derived through the dynamics of transference–countertransference, conscious and unconscious fantasy, and unresolved childhood conflicts, it is not surprising that a precise definition of cure is elusive. Each patient, and indeed each analyst, probably has a unique understanding of it.

Sigmund Freud grappled with the concept of cure throughout his professional life. In "Studies on Hysteria" (Breuer and Freud, 1895), he focused on his patients' pathological symptoms and saw the goal of treatment as clearing up those symptoms one after another. When the symptoms were gone, the patient was said to be cured. Later, he framed the work of analysis as the process of making the unconscious conscious through the lifting of repressions. Freud (1916–1917, p. 435) said, "The neurotic who is cured has really become another man; though at bottom, of course, he has remained the same, that is to say, he has become what he might have become at best under the most favorable conditions." Later still, in the closing sentences of Lecture XXXI of "New Introductory Lectures" (1933), Freud wrote that the intention of psychoanalysis is to strengthen the ego, to widen its perception and enlarge its organization. It was here that he made his famous statement, "Where id was, there ego shall be" (p. 80). Still, Freud was never very optimistic about the potential of psychoanalysis to effect miraculous cures. The most he thought he could promise was that psychoanalysis could "convert hysterical misery into common unhappiness" (Freud, 1893–1895, p. 305).

Freud's disciples expanded on his ideas about cure. Ferenczi (1955) thought that if the transference neurosis were completely resolved, then the patient would be able to pursue realistic methods of gratification, and at that point, the analysis would die a natural death. Fenichel (1938) theorized that when all resistances were removed, the patient was cured. Continuing this line of thought, Nacht (1965) wrote that the disappearance of a symptom is not an indication of cure. He saw the aim of therapy as the removal of internal obstacles that would free the patient to live in harmony with himself and others.

This harmony, along with a checking of inappropriate reactions to frustration, would allow a person to live in peace. In this sense, a cured patient would be freed from the burden of fear – fear of himself and others and fear of outer and inner reality.

Nevertheless, the concept of cure as freedom is variously defined. Loewald (1978) described this freedom by reversing Freud's famous idea about ego and id. He said that at the end of a successful analysis, "where ego is, there id shall come into being again to renew the life of the ego" (1978, p. 16). Loewald felt the id had been given a bad name by analytic theory and that too much rationality can only be irrational. Instincts and affects, along with an ability to enjoy primitive feelings, must be integrated into the psyche under the control of the managing ego. Only a balanced combination of affect and cognition constitutes the means and ends of analytic cure. Phillips (1998) asserted that helping the patient regain his infantile curiosity about the world is a more significant outcome than the development of insight.

Karl Menninger (1966, cited in Novick (1982), p. 357 described various models that diversified how we might think about goals in analysis and the question of the termination of treatment. There is the medical model where treatment is ended when the analysis becomes more of a burden to the patient than his illness has been. Under a parent–child model, cure is similar to emancipation at adolescence. An educational model would see the goal of therapy as helping the patient to learn for himself without the guidance of the analyst. Menninger describes a "visiting-an-art-gallery model" in which the analysis is a pleasurable and enriching experience, but not absolutely necessary. When one goes to an art exhibit again and again, a point is reached where the law of diminishing returns sets in, and the analysis is terminated. This is in direct contrast to a "life and death model," where the stakes are very high; the analysis is perceived as literally saving the patient's life, and in this case the treatment, both more primitive and more desperate in character, is crucial.

Still, many patients and some analysts have an unrealistic idea about cure. As early as 1938, Schmideberg (p. 126) wrote about the unconscious fantasies many patients have about what it means to be fully analyzed. These fantasies are replicas of little children's ideas about what it will be like to be grown up. The patient's notion that a perfectly analyzed person lives in complete and uninterrupted bliss expresses not only a childish fantasy about being an adult, but also "a longing for past happiness; an idealized memory of his babyhood is projected into the future." Schaffer (2006) and Werbart (2007) described utopic ideas among patients and their analysts that involve a decisive and total cure, a psychological rebirth to a better existence. These utopic ideas have an almost religious fervor. When psychoanalysis becomes a new religion, the patient will never be satisfied with a mere alleviation of some or all his symptoms or an improvement in functioning. The patient expects that after being analyzed, he will never again have to experience difficulty or disappointment. Guilt and anxiety will be banished from his life, and he will develop the intellectual and aesthetic powers of a genius. He will be blissfully happy, perfectly balanced, superhumanly unbiased, and free of all neuroses and bad habits. He will never make a Freudian slip. Most extraordinary of all, he will never be burdened with aggression or the unruliness of the sexual instinct (Schaffer, 2006). This wish and theory of a utopian cure can also be present in mental techniques like meditation. Meditation and religious ideas of purge and salvation express a longing to become another person and transcend existential limitations. This wish is also alive in addictions, psychosis, artistic creativity, and ecstatic sexual experience.

Modern analysts have developed new ideas about the concept of cure. Spotnitz and Meadow (1976) wrote that the *sine qua non* of cure is the ability of both analyst and patient to feel all their feelings, understand them and talk about them. Spotnitz (1976, p. 297) described the cured person as "emotionally mature and emotionally versatile." In 1985, Spotnitz (pp. 287–288) wrote at length about what constitutes recovery in psychoanalysis:

> It involves an ability to experience the full range of human emotions. The cured patient demonstrates the rich orchestration of the mature personality. He commands an abundance of behavior patterns, and since he can express feelings appropriately, he does not have to lose contact with others, however great the provocation, to prevent himself from acting destructively. He acknowledges that emotional problems are universal and knows that difficulties and problems will be encountered in the future, but he can face that future with a new resiliency. The cured person can accept the analyst's shortcomings and can constructively criticize the treatment process. He understands other people and can function effectively among them without isolating himself behind "the stone wall of narcissism." He has an abundance of psychic energy and experiences the pleasure of operating at his full potential. He conveys the attitude that he has completed a "successful voyage of self-discovery."

Meadow (2000, p.10) put it more succinctly: a patient is cured when he can "think and say everything." That involves getting in touch with, understanding, and resolving preverbal conflicts. Bernstein (1995, p. 52) suggests that "One does not cure a person in the same sense that a physician cures an illness – by eradicating it – but rather in the sense that a tobacco farmer cures tobacco – by exposing it to conditions that allow it to mature." To cure in modern psychoanalysis means to introduce a person to experiences that encourage growth and maturation, diminish suffering, and increase the capacity for happiness (Bernstein, 2001).

The modern group analyst Louis Ormont (1992, p. 214) put it succinctly when he described a cured person:

Such a person can identify with others, can process experience before acting. He can tolerate high frustration, even in the area of his presenting problem. He can identify, understand and take responsibility for his own feelings. He has empathy and an appreciation of what other people feel.

Historically, psychoanalysts have used the medical model in conducting treatment. Often the goal has been to get the patient cured in an efficient and timely manner and out of analysis as soon as symptoms disappear. Indeed if psychoanalysis became interminable, it was seen as an indication that the analyst was incompetent or the patient was intractable or comically self-involved. Modern psychoanalysis accepts the idea that truly long-term treatment is *beneficial*. These analysts argue that extended treatment can promote deep character change, expand consciousness, and facilitate therapeutic personal development in a constantly expanding and unfolding manner. Bernstein (1995, p. 50) contends that:

> Long-term treatment adds a dimension to the treatment process that allows it to develop into a mutative relationship that promotes changes in attitudes psychotherapy does not even address. For, like much of the practice of medicine, brief psychotherapy is really crisis intervention. Wanting to spare patients unnecessary pain, time and money is a laudable aspiration, when it can be accomplished. But a short story is not the same as a novel, and brief psychotherapy is not the same as long-term treatment.

Bernstein (1995, p. 50) further points out that psychotherapists and their clients take it for granted that their relationship must end:

> A prolonged therapeutic relationship is more likely to be a source of embarrassment to them than a cause for rejoicing. Quite the contrary is the case when other human relationships come to an end. When marriages, families, friendships, and loveships break up, it is generally conceded that something went wrong. But it is important to keep in mind that psychosocial systems are not held together by biological bonds but by psychological bonds; and that all of the basic human drives and their characterological derivatives, as well as the transferences and resistances, that we observe during the course of the treatment are at work shaping behavior and feelings in all other psychosocial contexts as well.

Bernstein believed that there is a correlation between the length of treatment and the depth of cure. During long-term therapy, patients can begin to realize that there is more that psychoanalysis has to offer than relief from pain and suffering. Patients no longer continue treatment because they have to, but because they want to pursue the goal of ever-expanding awareness.

Ormont (1992, p. 213) also addressed the advantages of an extended analysis:

> As for the creative people who keep using group profitably, we revel in their expansiveness, in their romanticizing their own lives, which they see as glorious odysseys. We watch them continually use what they learn from others. To them, every personal limitation is a challenge. Such people are, as a rule, flexible and adaptable. It is not a failure for them to work with us years, or even decades, so long as their inner lives keep enlarging.

Kohut (1984) argued that a permanent reliance on the analyst as a selfobject, as a caretaker who can meet emotional needs, is not an indication of maladaptation.

Many people come to analysis because they are in a crisis and need help to resolve it or because they have specific symptoms that impair their functioning. When the crisis is over or the symptom disappears, they consider themselves cured and leave. Sometimes this is painful for the analyst. A supervisee told me about a female patient who had come to treatment to process a heartbreaking divorce. The patient's husband had left her abruptly for another woman, and the patient was suicidal. After two years of treatment, the patient was feeling considerably better. She told my supervisee that she had moved on and was ready to start dating again. She thanked the analyst and left. Despite the fact that, at least according to the patient, the analysis had been a great success, my supervisee felt bereft. She said, "When I think of all the hours I sat with this woman trying not to fall asleep listening to her depressed monotone! And now that she is beginning to be interesting and fun to listen to, she leaves!" I joined my supervisee, telling her the patient was an ungrateful wretch and psychoanalysis an impossible profession. She laughed, acknowledging that the patient was totally justified in declaring herself cured and terminating. She had articulated her goal at the beginning of treatment and when it was accomplished, she left, a satisfied customer. If she had stayed in analysis, could she have enjoyed more growth and gain? Undoubtedly. But her definition of goal and gain was both coherent and legitimate, and her perception of cure must be respected.

I had a patient who came to analysis for what he called "anger management." The patient had a terrible temper, which was always getting him in trouble with his boss, his family, and his friends. He yelled at his wife and children, insulted his colleagues at work, and was even threatened with arrest when a woman he met at a bar charged him with sexual harassment. In treatment, this man was intelligent, lively, and articulate. He understood instinctively that talking could cure him. Working with him was a pleasure. Early in treatment, I joined his rageful thoughts, telling him that most people are extremely annoying and that he had the right feelings. I told him that his feelings were not the problem. The problem was that he acted on his feelings. He immediately grasped this important difference between feeling and action. Instead of torturing himself about his aggression, he began to enjoy it. He would relate dreams of smothering his son and publicly humiliating his boss with great glee. He reported with pleasure his sexual feelings for all the beautiful women in the world. As his superego softened, he noticed that he was able to have his feelings without acting them out. Gradually he gained control of his rage. He told me his wife, his father, and even his boss had noticed that he was a "changed man." One day soon after, he came in for his session and told me the analysis was complete. I noticed that I was extremely disappointed, and I realized I had plans for this man. He was working as a high school English teacher, and he didn't enjoy his job. Without being entirely conscious of the idea, I had assumed my patient and I would work together for many years, and eventually he would become an analyst like me. I silently scolded myself for putting my need for narcissistic gratification ahead of what he wanted, but that didn't stop me from trying to keep him. I asked him if he had achieved all his goals. He thought and said, "Well, no. I hope I have goals till the day I die. But I didn't come into analysis to achieve all my goals. I came to learn to manage my anger. And I've done that." I asked him if he thought anything positive would come out of his continuing. He said, "Absolutely. If I was an investment banker instead of a teacher, I would want to stay in analysis. I like coming here and talking to you. But money is a big issue for me and my wife. She and I agree that I'm cured of my anger problem, and it's time to stop." Reluctantly, I told him he had used the process very effectively, that I wished him well, and that he should know the door was always open should he feel the need to return.

Was this man cured? He was certainly cured, at least at the time of his termination, of his initial problem. The treatment he received was reflective of the medical model. He came to the doctor with an illness – his tendency to act on his angry feelings. I administered the medicine – educating him about the idea that all feelings are to be enjoyed and understood, but that going into action on some feelings is self-destructive. He took what I prescribed, and it worked. He gained control of his aggressive impulses and became a changed man. He was very satisfied with the treatment and the outcome, and my reluctance to let him go was ultimately irrelevant, even impertinent, given his view of therapy.

And yet there is an important idea to be considered in my wish that the patient stay in treatment and continue to grow. It is a conceptualization about the use and value of the psychoanalytic process that while not denigrating my patient's concept of a concrete cure, goes beyond it. It is the principle that having a place to engage in the evolved articulation of psychoanalysis on a regular and ongoing basis is a practice that promotes good mental health, just as exercise or flossing one's teeth on a regular and ongoing basis are practices to ensure good physical health.

Talking is important to the development of the brain (Holmes, 2008). The human brain is made up of three distinct areas, having evolved over hundreds of thousands of years. The more primitive parts of the brain, the reptilian and mammalian brains, are much larger than the cerebral cortex, which is the seat of language and logic and was the last part of the brain to develop. Our sexual and aggressive instincts and our intense feelings are generated in the reptilian and mammalian brains, and they constantly send up powerful electrical impulses for the cerebral cortex to process. This is a daunting task for an area of the brain that is newer and smaller than the bullies below. That is why people so often act like primitive animals ruled by their basest impulses. The basic rule of modern psychoanalysis – to just say everything – is an exercise that constantly converts instincts and feelings into words. I believe the very act of talking strengthens the cerebral cortex and helps it gain control. It is an enlightened practice that constantly examines and reflects on the rigors of life.

I have a patient who enters the treatment room, and if I ask, "How are you?" she replies, "I don't know. I'll find out when I lie down and start talking." It seems she is telling me that the analytic hour is a time in her busy life to reconnect with herself and her inner experience, to be reflective. Mental health professionals with an interest in neuroscience have written that analysis helps people convert implicit memory into explicit memory (Badenoch and Cox, 2010). Implicit memory is formed very early in life, even in utero, when our experience of the womb and of the pre-Oedipal mother establishes neural pathways in the brain. Because the cerebral cortex is still developing in these early days of life, implicit memory is not cognitive. We are not conscious that we know what we know. Rather it's experienced as visceral and sometimes somatic. Though we don't remember implicit memory, we experience it as reality, as the way the world works. For example, a person who had a very anxious mother when he was a baby may experience the world as a dangerous place. He may feel constantly anxious, but the anxiety may not be connected to any thoughts. A person who had a mother who tried to abort her may feel that she is worthless and unloved, no matter what the reality of her situation as an adult may be. Explicit memory begins in the second year of life when the developing cerebral cortex begins to be aware of a timeline between past and present, when we begin to feel ourselves in our personal history in time and space and when we first begin to develop words to say things like, "I remember when we went to the circus last summer."

Even after many years in analysis, patients can regress to preverbal levels, activating implicit memory. This regression may be triggered by the fresh hells that reality constantly bombards us with, or it may happen because of the structure of the analytic situation, the dream-like state of the couch, the silence of the analyst. Pain, fear, and rage, which heretofore have had no words, may emerge. This is a good thing. Unconscious structures that make themselves known by primitive feeling and bodily sensation can be verbalized, and when that happens, the patient gets more control over the neural pathways laid down before there was cognition. The implicit memories that may have silently dominated our lives come under the influence of the cerebral cortex and words. This is not a process that has a beginning, middle, and end. It is ongoing and remarkably fresh in each session of long-term analysis.

It is precisely because there is no such thing as a utopic cure that a regular place to talk is so important. No matter how well analyzed and symptom-free we are, we still have to contend with rage, unruly sexual feelings, anxiety, grief, loss, trauma, aging – all of the turbulence of being alive. If we are fortunate, we have spouses, friends, and family we can talk to, but those kinds of conversations are not the kind of talking that is done in analysis. Ultimately, it is not a good idea to "say everything" to the people we love. Relationships work best when we have and understand all our feelings, while being disciplined enough to voice only those thoughts and feelings that are in the best interest of our personal relationships. In psychoanalysis we are uniquely free to verbalize the primitive, the murderous, the perverse; the discharge of all these primal impulses into language ensures that we don't repress thoughts to create symptoms or act them out in the world to hurt ourselves and others. An ongoing analysis provides a constant psychic housecleaning, freeing the mind to pursue satisfaction and pleasure in a way that doesn't harm others.

Interminable psychoanalysis is a particularly good idea for those who decide to make their living as analysts. It is a profession that can be meaningful and satisfying, but it is also true that analysts are constantly assaulted with toxins in the form of painful transference and countertransference feelings. Analysts need a place to discharge all those toxins, or they risk their own physical and mental health. New graduates of psychoanalytic institutes sometimes decide to terminate their analysis and supervision because of financial concerns. Becoming an analyst, with its demand for a personal psychoanalysis and hours and hours of supervision, is an expensive proposition, and when training is complete, new analysts are faced with the challenge of building a private practice. Terminating all that expensive, and now no longer required, analysis and supervision may seem like a good idea. Supervision groups can be a good solution to this problem. Young analysts can get together to form peer groups or share the expense of a supervisor to lead the group. These sorts of groups can be amazingly effective. Unlike therapy groups, supervision group members have all been analyzed for many years, and the talking that goes on in these environments is often bracingly honest, laced with humor, and remarkably intelligent.

This appreciation for language as a tool that gives us the potential to be constantly moving toward the light is a concept that goes beyond cure. Psychoanalysis can relieve us of symptoms, but abandoning the practice when the symptoms cease deprives us of the opportunity to explore the enormous potential of putting our lives into words on an ongoing basis. I once asked my analyst of 30 years how much longer I should stay in analysis. He smiled at me and replied, "How much can you grow?"

References

Badenoch, B., & Cox, P. (2010). Integrating interpersonal neurobiology with group psychotherapy. *International Journal of Group Psychotherapy*, 60(4), 463–481.

Bernstein, A. (1995). Some clinical observations upon the emergence of the "wonder child." *Modern Psychoanalysis*, 20, 43–54.

Bernstein, A. (2001). Beyond countertransference: The love that cures. *Modern Psychoanalysis*, 26, 249–255.

Breuer, J., & Freud, S. (1895). Studies on hysteria. *Standard edition*. London: Hogarth Press, 2, 1–323.

Fenichel, O. (1938). Problems of psychoanalytic technique. *Psychoanalytic Quarterly*, 7(4), 421–442.

Ferenczi, S. (1955). *Final contributions to the problems and methods of psychoanalysis*. New York: Basic Books.

Freud, S. (1893–1895). The psychotherapy of hysteria. *Standard edition*. London: Hogarth Press, 2, 253–306.

Freud, S. (1916–1917). Introductory lectures on psychoanalysis. *Standard edition*. London: Hogarth Press, 16, 243–463.

Freud, S. (1933). New introductory lectures on psychoanalysis. *Standard edition*. London: Hogarth Press, 22, 3–184.

Holmes, L. (2008). Why talking cures. *Modern Psychoanalysis*, 33, 71–77.

Kohut, H. (1984). *How does analysis cure?* Chicago, IL: University of Chicago Press.

Loewald, H.W. (1978). *Psychoanalysis and the history of the individual*. New Haven, CT: Yale University Press.

Meadow, P.W. (2000). Creating psychic change in analysis. *Modern Psychoanalysis*, 25, 3–22.

Nacht, S. (1965). Criteria and technique for the termination of analysis. *International Journal of Psycho-Analysis*, 46, 107–116.

Novick, J. (1982) Termination: themes and issues. *Psychoanalytic Inquiry*, 2(3): 329–365.

Ormont, L. (1992). *The group therapy experience: From theory to practice*. New York: St. Martin's Press.

Phillips, A. (1998). *The beast in the nursery*. New York: Vintage.

Schaffer, A. (2006). The analyst's curative fantasies: Implications for supervision. *Contemporary Psychoanalysis*, 42(3), 349–366.

Schmideberg, M. (1938). After the analysis. *International Journal of Psycho-Analysis*, 21, 122–142.

Spotnitz, H. (1976). *Psychotherapy of Preoedipal conditions: Schizophrenia and severe character disorders*. Northvale, NJ: Jason Aronson.

Spotnitz, H. (1985). *Modern psychoanalysis of the schizophrenic patient: Theory of the technique* (2nd ed.). New York: Human Sciences Press, Inc.

Spotnitz, H., & Meadow, P.W. (1976). *Treatment of the narcissistic neuroses*. New York: The Manahattan Center for Advanced Psychoanalytic Studies.

Werbart, A. (2007). Utopic ideas of cure and joint exploration in psychoanalytic supervision. *International Journal of Psycho-Analysis*, 88(6), 1391–1408.

Chapter 18

Reaching the repetition compulsion

> Don't believe everything you think.
> *Graffiti on an overpass in Austin, Texas, 2013*

André Green (2008, p. 1037) called the repetition compulsion "the murder of time," and anyone who has worked as a mental health practitioner has experienced the dispiriting drudgery of witnessing patients attempt to kill themselves and the analyst with their toxic obsession with treating the present like the past. We can sit with a patient for years while he demonstrates in his talking that time spent in analysis has had no effect whatsoever on his compulsion to find the same bad objects, use the same self-destructive defenses, and create the same gloomy prisons for himself over and over again.

A 50-year-old patient of mine doesn't sleep well. She wakes in the night and has obsessive feelings of self-attack, dread, and hopelessness. She reports that these are very familiar feelings. "I've had them all my life," she says, "but I think menopause has made them worse." This patient is interested in Buddhism and has taken up meditation to see if she can quiet her thoughts. She tells me that when she goes into a deep meditative state she experiences her own mind as a visual image. She says, "My mind is a loop, a loop that goes round and round endlessly, pushing up against something painful and then looping away from it, and then back around to confront it again." This is a picture of the repetition compulsion. This repetitive tendency seems to be immune to insight, reason, and even the affection or rage of the analyst.

Slavoj Žižek (2000) advises that human beings should enjoy their symptoms. Since the symptom is our unique system for the discharge of pleasure and pain, we might as well claim and embrace it. There is a sort of cynical wisdom in this, because I believe the repetition compulsion is a life sentence. The neural pathways that were laid down in our infant brains before we could talk are going to be buzzing electrical impulses from our reptilian brains to the more evolved cerebral parts of the mind until we breathe our last. So, can anything be done? What can we as analysts do to help our patients free themselves from the malevolent destiny that the repetition compulsion dictates?

The first thing we can do is understand what is going on in the brains of our patients when we talk about a compulsion to repeat. The repetition compulsion is so hard to influence because it is created in a part of the brain that is almost inaccessible through language or cognition. It is organized very early in the life cycle. Long before a baby can speak, he is learning about the way the world works. Neuroscientists talk about two kinds of memory: implicit and explicit (Badenoch and Cox, 2010). Implicit memory is laid down in the brain before a human being develops language and before the most highly evolved part of the brain, the cerebral cortex, is completely developed. The human infant can't talk yet, but he is very busy. His infantile brain is perceiving and learning about his environment. Upon the *tabula rasa* of his brand-new brain, he is creating the neural pathways that are his unique response to his experience. He isn't able yet to think cognitively about what is happening to him, but the structures of implicit memory that he is creating will inform his awareness for the rest of his life.

Bollas (1987, p. 4) called implicit memory the "unthought known," which I think is an apt description. We don't "think" these impressions, but they are deeply, almost viscerally, perceived. Implicit memories are the working tools of the repetition compulsion. We are not conscious that we know what we know; it's just that we experience these unconscious memories as reality, as the way the world works. Unconsciously, we choose objects and situations that may be highly unpleasant but give us the reassuring sense that our implicit memories are absolutely correct, that we are of sound mind, that the brains we depend on for survival can be trusted. Those infantile neural pathways also dictate that, again and again, we will respond to the pathological people and situations we choose because they are so familiar, with the defenses that we were able to muster in the first year of life. Never mind that those defenses are ineffective, even nonsensical in the present.

The clinical example I like to give is of a female patient I work with who over and over finds herself involved with men who abuse and hurt her. As her analysis progressed, she began to put into words an idea she had never really examined, but which she was convinced was true: all men are dangerous. This implicit memory has been running her life. Again and again, she chooses sadistic objects to give her the sense that she understands and can cope with the way the world works and that her implicit memory is correct. It was quite correct when she was born into a family with an alcoholic, angry father, a violent older brother, and a passive, neglectful mother. The problem is the murder of time; my patient treats the present as if it were 1959. In the group, I watch this woman infuriate and frustrate some perfectly good men to the point that they want to hurt her. She reports to me in her individual sessions that the men in the group who treat women empathically are "kind of boring." She unconsciously creates her own hell when she brilliantly turns current objects into toxic figures from the past.

My patient is fated by an idea that was powerful but unspoken for most of her life. Her intense idealization of angry men is the repetition of a strategy learned very early in childhood, when as a vulnerable baby she found herself unloved and unprotected by her parents. She defended herself by taking on the idea that she was bad, and her parents were good. She thought that if she could find a way to be less bad, her parents would stop hurting her. Most small children would rather be bad themselves than face the terrifying fact that their survival depends on bad objects. Criticism of the bad objects is kept at bay and replaced by a misplaced and highly charged idealization. This is an aspect of what modern analysts call the narcissistic defense.

My patient's infantile brain created a neural pathway that is generally impervious to later learning and experience. She is doomed to select withholders, deprivers, and abusers, who personify the original frightening but also exciting and highly desired object. Struggling to relate to a dangerous object has become her template for intimacy. These toxic relationships are eroticized and addictive. Relinquishing the repetition or even contemplating its nature can be experienced as annihilating. Who am I if not the person who tries to be good enough to get this scary man to finally love me? A patient of mine said to me, "You're going to cure me of my symptoms and then what will I have?" It is important that we as analysts appreciate the power of the repetition compulsion. In expecting our patients to give it up, we are really asking them to lose their minds. Their minds may be faultily wired, but they have enabled them to survive in a dangerous world. How would you feel if someone asked you to give up your lumpy, imperfect life raft in the middle of a stormy sea?

One of the most discouraging things about the repetition compulsion is that insight has practically no effect on it. My patient has lots of insight. She knows that she chooses her alcoholic father again and again. After ten years in analysis, she told me, "I can walk into a wedding reception where there are 200 people in the room and spot the sadist because he is the one I will be attracted to." A lot of good this insight has done her. Her new boyfriend, whom she describes as "so sexy, so exciting," got mad at her and killed her cat, leaving its body on her welcome mat. When she told me this, she brought her hands to her face and said despairingly, "Oh, God! I've found Daddy again, haven't I?"

The problem with this symptom is that the repetition compulsion resides deep in the primitive brain, where it is almost completely inaccessible to the most classic intervention of psychoanalysis, interpretation. Giving a patient an intelligent, reasonable, and well thought-out idea about why he does what he does speaks to the cerebral cortex, the most highly evolved but also the smallest part of the brain, where reason, logic, and ethics, not to mention language, reside. But talking to the cerebral cortex is like trying to prevent a lion from killing a child by explaining to the lion tamer that his animal is misbehaving – it doesn't begin to confront the problem where it lies. The repetition compulsion is created out of instinct and emotion, which are generated in the reptilian and mammalian regions of the brain: the brain stem, the cerebellum, and the limbic system. Talking to the more rational cerebral cortex just doesn't work because the cerebral cortex is too small to control the lions, tigers, and bears in the more primitive parts of the brain.

I have written and spoken extensively about why I think talking in psychoanalysis cures. The free association, the mandate to "just say everything" that we give to our patients, is an invitation to exercise and strengthen the most evolved part of our brain, the cerebral cortex, where language resides. When we talk in analysis, we create the potential to convert implicit memory into explicit memory. Psychoanalysts call this process "working through." Freud (1916–1917) described "making the unconscious conscious the goal of psychoanalysis." Freud (1932, p. 80) also famously said, "Where id was, there ego shall be." Neurologically speaking, he is describing the strengthening of the cerebral cortex, so that it can gain control over the more primitive reptilian and mammalian parts of the brain. Talking is the constant conversion into words of the electrical impulses pulsing up from the cerebellum and brain stem, which are the reptilian parts of the brain, and the feelings traveling along neurobiological circuits in the mammalian limbic system. Primitive instincts and feelings can then be pondered, thought about, and considered. But it is important to remember that they are not obliterated. The best we can hope for is that they can be contemplated, understood, and controlled. Psychoanalysis does not get rid of painful feelings. Lots of people come into psychoanalysis wanting to be happy, but this is an unrealistic goal. Happy is a feeling, and feelings, like the weather, are transitory and change all the time. It is not feelings that a successful analysis changes. People who believe that psychoanalysis has cured them do not have fewer feelings than they did before they began treatment. They probably have more. It is also a myth that healthy people never have crazy or regressed feelings. They do. Life is hard, and when we are sick, bereaved, overworked, or mistreated, we are going to have weird and primitive feelings no matter how well analyzed we are. What changes with a good analysis is a sense of awareness and control. Those primitive, crazy feelings no longer steer the ship. They are no longer imperatives to take action and run toward a painful destiny. Rather they become information, data to consider that helps us understand what is going on and what we want to do about it. Between the impulse and the action, psychoanalysis inserts the word. We can call ourselves successful as analysts when our patients get as addicted to talking as they have been to their repetitions. They will still have obsessive urges to do things that are self-destructive, but they learn to talk about them rather than act them out. Do the feelings ever change? Maybe not. My personal experience is that years of talking can mute them. Like the witches and ghosts who scared us in childhood, we come to view our primitive feelings with nostalgia, something that once terrified and controlled us but now have no ability to hurt us.

A patient of mine used to experience panic attacks in the middle of the night. She would leave long, wordless, sobbing messages on my voice mail at four in the morning. When she came in for her session, she would report having felt during her panic attack that her life was a misery, that there was nothing she could do about it, that she deserved to have a miserable life, and that no one cared anyway. She has been in treatment for eight years. A few weeks ago, she came in and said, "I didn't sleep well last night." I asked her why, and she chuckled and said, "I had a little visitor from Yonkers." She told me she had wakened with the familiar, old feelings of worthlessness and despair. "But," she said, "I just thought, 'Oh boy, here we go again. Mother, leave me alone. I need to sleep.' And eventually I did go back to sleep." Is this woman cured? She still has the feelings. What she has gained is an observing ego and an ability to soothe and guide herself into better functioning. She has developed the capacity to contemplate her own mind, which has created a layer of processing with increased integration between the cerebral cortex and the lower brains (Badenoch, 2008). I believe that the lower brains eventually grow more peaceful through this integration. Or perhaps it is better described as a reduction in volume – the primitive instincts and impulses go from screams to fitful murmurs. Reactivity, both internal and behavioral, decreases, and a calm, holding capacity increases (Badenoch, 2008). One part of the mind is observing and caring for another part of the mind.

My patient, whose "mind is a loop," is developing that capacity. She has recently been associating that image of a loop with the fact that she was in an incubator for the first three weeks of her life. When she told me this, I commented that all her terrifying infantile feelings and impulses had nowhere to go. They couldn't be discharged onto and into her mother, so they had to loop back into her own mind. Last week, she reported that since I made that remark, she has been trying to be her own mother in the night when she can't sleep, and it has helped. "My mind loops, and I just try to hold it in awareness and empathy."

In my book *Wrestling with Destiny* (2013), I enthusiastically endorsed talking as the best method to achieve an integration between the primitive and more evolved parts of the brain. Modern analysts observe the contact function. That is, they speak only when spoken to. They trust that if they don't arouse the patient's defenses and resistances by making him feel attacked or stupid with their brilliant interpretations, the patient can pretty much cure himself with words. Over time, talking changes the structure and functioning of the brain. Spotnitz (1969, pp. 58–59), who had medical degrees in neurology and psychiatry, hypothesized that everything deactivates certain neural pathways and activates new neural pathways. The more highly evolved portions of the brain gain control over the more primitive brains that have bullied them.

But lately, I have been thinking that there is more to be said about this than simply "talking cures." (Holmes, 2008) One of my students recently made an interesting comment in class. He said, "I am beginning to realize that if I want to have a satisfying life, I am going to have to change my behavior. And I don't want to." This was a deceptively simple and fascinating remark. He is right. We can gain tremendous insight by talking in psychoanalysis and even considerable ability to resist our impulses, but ultimately, we have to make a conscious decision not to act on our pathological and gratifying repetitions. What makes us finally reconcile ourselves not just to the fact that we create our own misery, but also that if we don't want to be miserable, we have to make active choices?

One answer to this question is that we just get sick of ourselves. Talking helps us accept and understand our self-destructiveness. As we repeatedly confront the same resistances and repressions, as we get new insights and then forget them and return to old modes of thinking, and as we repeatedly work though the same dreary dynamics, we just run out of steam and begin to bore ourselves. This process is greatly enhanced if the analyst is a good enough analyst to know that she should pretty much keep quiet as the analytic process unfolds. Intervening to try to show the patient the error of his ways only makes the patient defensive and resistant, and so slows the therapeutic process. But if the analyst observes the contact function and the patient says everything, a gradual, unconscious erosion of reactivity and impulsivity occurs in the mind of the patient. Everything has been said, everything has been understood; the patient arrives at the simple but profound truth, "I have to change my behavior." This simple truth is not so simple. He probably is finally able to confront it because all those years of talking have strengthened his ego to the point that he is capable of deciding to change.

When my student said what he said, I began to think about myself and my own analysis. I consider myself cured of some of my most controlling and toxic repetitions. I still can be attracted to the wrong kind of people, and I still have impulses to behave in ways that are hurtful to me but, most of the time, I don't act on these impulses. How was I able to stop it?

Thinking about this made me remember a pivotal moment in my analysis. I had been in analysis for 17 years. During that time, I had managed to get myself out of a very unhappy marriage and developed tremendous insight about why I had chosen an object who had made me so miserable. I started dating again. I met a man I was very attracted to. He was handsome, intelligent, and intense. But as the relationship developed, I realized he was mistreating me in much the same way that my ex-husband had treated me. I went in and told my analyst all about it. And then something very curative happened. My analyst, who was a good modern analyst and had let me talk for 17 years, now intervened. She said, "Listen, Dr Holmes, I'm not going through this with you again! This is not my treatment plan for you! If you don't get rid of this guy and find yourself a kind, loving man who thinks everything you do is wonderful, I'm going to have to discharge you!" I was dumbstruck, but in that moment I could almost feel my brain rewiring. I didn't say much at the time, but I left the session and followed my analyst's orders. I got rid of the guy I was dating, and I found a man who was kind and loving and who thought everything I did was wonderful. I went in and told my analyst about this new man. I said, "He's so nice to me. It's kind of boring." You see, I was not so different from my patient! My analyst said, "Now we're getting somewhere!" I was so happy that I had pleased her that I married the man. That was probably the first truly self-enhancing act I had ever pulled off, and it is evidence enough for me that I am cured.

So what happened? Though I didn't understand it then, my analyst gave me a powerful emotional communication that reached a deeper part of the brain, probably the limbic system where feelings are generated. What she communicated to me was, "It is not okay with me for you to hurt yourself. It is not okay, and I will not permit it. Now you had better damn well change your behavior or there will be hell to pay." This rewired my brain. I had never in my life experienced someone I loved and who was vital to me tell me I was not allowed to be self-destructive. It changed the whole circuitry. It also changed my life. Can I still be attracted to difficult, frustrating men? You bet. But I have integrated my analyst's love for me. I would like to eat that second bowl of ice cream, get involved with sadistic people, sacrifice my own needs to the victims in the world, but I am not allowed to anymore because my brain has a new neural pathway. I am not allowed to hurt myself. The emotional communication from my analyst, which expressed a remarkably evolved fusion of love and hate, created a neural pathway that made it possible for me to change my behavior. For years, she just let me talk, and her silent presence helped me feel safe enough to give voice to the implicit memories that had been running my life. Those 17 years of preparation strengthened my ego and gave me insight and empathy about my own story. But ultimately, it was a powerful emotional communication that threw the switch in my brain and allowed me to decide to change my behavior.

When I tell this story, I am invariably asked, "Did she have to wait so long? Why couldn't she have said this to you in the first or second year of analysis?" If she had, I would have left treatment. My ego was too fragile and my resistances too rigid to tolerate anyone questioning my repetitions. The long, long period of free association in an environment of acceptance and low stimulation had strengthened me to the point that I could use the powerful emotions she communicated to me to change my mind.

The clinical techniques that Hyman Spotnitz developed over 50 years ago were brilliantly intuitive in predicting what we now know about brain structure and function. The Spotnitzian techniques of object-oriented questions, the contact function, joining and mirroring, soothe the reptilian and mammalian brains, and this means that the repetition compulsion, which was created and resides in these brains, loses much of its primitive power. The emotional rather than intellectual interventions that modern analysts use reach more primitive levels of the brain than the didactic interpretation favored by classical analysts and are, therefore, more effective in changing the mind at a very deep level. Language, the capacity to love, and to use our aggression creatively in the service of that love are things that distinguish human beings from animals. These are also two of the most effective tools in our work to control the animals within our own minds and defeat the repetition compulsion.

References

Badenoch, B. (2008). *Being a brain-wise therapist: A practical guide to interpersonal neurobiology*. New York: Norton.

Badenoch, B., & Cox, P. (2010). Integrating interpersonal neurobiology with group psychotherapy. *International Journal of Group Psychotherapy*, 60(4), 463–481.

Bollas, C. (1987). *The shadow of the object: Psychoanalysis and the unthought known*. New York: Columbia University Press.

Freud, S. (1963). Introductory lectures on psychoanalysis. In J. Strachey (Ed. & Trans.), *The standard edition of the complete psychological works of Sigmund Freud* (vol. 16, pp. 243–463). London: Hogarth Press. (Original work published 1916–1917)

Freud, S. (1964). New introductory lectures on psychoanalysis. In J. Strachey (Ed. & Trans.), *The standard edition of the complete psychological works of Sigmund Freud* (vol. 22, pp. 3–184). London: Hogarth Press. (Original work published 1932)

Green, A. (2008). Freud's concept of temporality; differences with current ideas. *International Journal of Psycho-Analysis*, 89(5), 1029–1039.

Holmes, L. (2008). Why talking cures. *Modern Psychoanalysis*, 33(2), 71–77.

Holmes, L. (2013). *Wrestling with destiny: The promise of psychoanalysis*. London: Routledge.

Spotnitz, H. (1969). *Modern psychoanalysis of the schizophrenic patient: Theory of the technique*. New York: Grune and Stratton.

Žižek, S. (2000). *Enjoy your symptom! Jacques Lacan in Hollywood and out* (2nd ed.). New York: Routledge.

Chapter 19

The analyst in winter

The late writer Phillip Roth once told an interviewer, "Old age is not a battle. Old age is a massacre." When I first read this interview several years ago, I thought Roth was betraying his narcissism and his talent for drama with these remarks. But having recently joined the ranks of official old age myself, I can now agree with empathy and enthusiasm that growing old is one of life's greatest challenges, a battle we are all going to lose, since it inevitably ends in annihilation. Freud gave us some advice about this bloody, ultimately doomed war. Recalling the old adage, "If you want peace, get ready for war," Freud (1915, p. 300) suggested changing it to "If you want to endure life, prepare yourself for death." In their haunting song "Old Friends," the very young and precociously wise Simon and Garfunkel sang, "How terribly strange to be seventy." And aging does begin with a shock of strangeness as the body starts to betray you (Bromberg, 2003). Grotjahn (1955) described growing old as a narcissistic wound which shatters the unconscious illusion of everlasting youth. A 65-year-old patient of mine said:

> When I wake in the morning, I forget that I'm old. I open my eyes, and I could be 16 or 20 or 35. I feel like I always have. I feel like myself. But then I put my feet on the floor, and my arthritis makes me wince in pain, and I stagger a little on the way to the bathroom, and I realize that I could easily fall and break a hip. And I think, "Who is this old lady? It can't be me."

This woman is in a rage about getting old. She has a profound indignation about it and has laughed when she has admitted to me that she feels like she is the first and only person this has ever happened to. I understand her to mean that like our birth, our death is something that all of us must go through alone.

Old age is similar to adolescence. In both stages we struggle with what De Masi (2004, p.88) calls "inner chaos." There is the same shock at the passing of time and the same resistance to taking the next step. Changes in the body, always overstimulating and usually unwelcome, assault human beings in their teens and again at the end of life. Adolescents have to mourn their childhood and gather strength to face adulthood. The elderly mourn their youth and try to find methods to cope with the anxiety of knowing that death is near. Identity and identity confusion are adolescent problems that are reawakened in old age (Erikson et al., 1994). Adolescents must give up their toys and their play, long-cherished activities which have helped them establish a sense of self, to face the reality of coping in the world. Older people struggle to maintain a sense of competence as they are forced to relinquish physical health, athletic talents, professional successes, the authority and control of being a parent to young children, and the power, rarely appreciated until it is gone, of being sexually attractive. In both adolescence and old age, you hear patients say, "I've never been here before. I don't know how to go forward. I don't know how to be."

Modern culture is particularly challenging for the elderly. In primitive cultures, traditions and history could not be passed on by the media and the internet. The old were honored as the keepers and teachers of tradition. Experience was a valuable tool, and those who had it were revered for their wisdom. In today's world, experience has a short life, and what is respected, whether a film star or the latest technology, is the new (Penziak, 1982). An 80-year-old member of a group I lead shrugged and said, "I don't know the world anymore. It's moving too fast for me. I can hardly get my phone to work or turn on the television. I'm in a fog."

Aging is often associated with hypochondria, frequently linked with depressive episodes and feelings of neglect and persecution. Often this is because growing old involves new and frightening aches, pains, and symptoms, and those who have never been old before can develop anxieties and obsessions about life-threatening illnesses when in reality they are only experiencing the physical challenges of aging. Old people are very vulnerable to depression, but elderly depression often has different underlying dynamics than the depressions of people earlier in life. Rather than the classic description of depression, the turning inward of unconscious hostile impulses, the depression of the aging is associated with the loss of self-esteem caused by the recognition of a new weakness and inability to obtain necessary narcissistic supplies and to defend oneself against threats to basic security. The onset of depression is often linked to a specific stimulus, such as increased physical suffering, lower financial, professional, or social status, or any increase in stress. Elderly depression does not appear to be an attempt to force an object to give necessary love, nor does it appear to be aimed at placating the super ego (Busse et al., 1958).

I became depressed when I first began to deal with the challenges of aging. I experienced my decline as a narcissistic wound, and the inexorability of the aging process left me feeling impotent and stuck. I gave up all creative pursuits. I stopped playing the piano and singing, pastimes that had always given me tremendous satisfaction, because my arthritic hands and my suddenly weak and trembling voice were painful reminders of what I had lost. I stopped writing, because it was humiliating to realize that my facility with language had deserted me, and now I had to struggle to get the words on the page. When I had a bad fall on the street, a sympathetic colleague, who is a little older than me, said softly, "Lucy, you're not young anymore. You must treat yourself gently and slow down a little." I wanted to strangle her. But of course, she was right. I have had to realize hating myself for growing old is gratifying on some sadistic level, giving me the fantasy that I can whip my aging body into submission; but ultimately self-flagellation is a waste of time and discouraging to the creative energy I still possess. I have had to face the fact that, no matter how old and wise I like to think I am, I have, like all human beings, a terrified infant within me. I have had to try to become a good parent to the strange old lady and the terrified infant I have become. Developing a capacity for self-comfort and nurturance and managing depressive or anxious feelings becomes an important discipline in old age. I now mindfully structure my life to continuously give myself something to look forward to. Like a good mother counting the days until Christmas with her small child, I plan pleasures like Caribbean vacations or special dinners with my children to cheer myself with the anticipation of a future full of good things. I have had to learn to adapt to my limitations. I gave up the arias I used to sing and moved to the smokier, husky songs favored by aging saloon singers. I became an alto rather than a soprano. When my fingers stumbled on the keyboard, I reminded myself what excellent exercise I am giving my arthritic hands. I learned to enjoy the struggle to find words, realizing it was similar to the pleasurable challenge of finding an answer in the crossword puzzle in the Sunday *New York Times*. This allowed me to write again, and I was delighted to see that the return of my creative process was a very helpful tonic for my depression.

Psychoanalysts are more fortunate than most people entering old age. Our profession is unique in its respect for the elderly. Maybe because it takes so long to become an analyst, our professional community is much older than is the case in the worlds of business, law, academia, or civil service. Though Freud (1905, p. 264) thought that no one over the age of 40 or 50 should embark on an analysis, he had no compunction in continuing his analytic practice almost until his death. His last 17 years were burdened by his battle with a painful cancer, but he worked almost to the very end of his life. Many analysts in their sixties and seventies are completely comfortable today about beginning an analysis with a new patient. We psychoanalysts sustain a "fantasy of immortality" (Junkers, 2013, p. 4) within ourselves reinforced by the unconscious conviction that our own analysis has made us immune to illness and aging. When I was working on my research paper at the Center for Modern Psychoanalytic Studies (CMPS), I was studying a patient who had a fascination with death. I had many negative feelings working with this patient, and at one point, Dr Phyllis Meadow, the director of CMPS, advised me that if I wanted to cure my patient, I had to learn to enjoy the idea of death. I told her that a resistance I struggled with was my horror at the thought of my own death. Her eyes twinkled, and she said, "Don't you know that when you're well analyzed you never have to die?" This fantasy of existential immunity did help me write my paper. Dr Meadow, who was then 75, would lose her battle with cancer five years later, but she had taught me the advantages of that usually denigrated defense, denial, in helping elderly people live creatively and fully until the end.

Eissler (1975) talked about the increase in narcissism that comes with old age. He explained that increase as a reduction in super ego function in the aging analyst that produces a feeling of omnipotence and entitlement to special privileges. When it comes to death, psychoanalysts have a tendency to use theory defensively. For example, Freud theorized that since the unconscious is timeless, it cannot conceive of death. He concluded that fear of death is really fear of castration, something that can be worked through in the course of a good analysis (Freud, 1923, pp. 57–59). By pathologizing the fear of death, psychoanalysis can be used to rationalize and deny the catastrophic impact that the fear of death has on all human beings, including psychoanalysts. Analysts might employ every available means to show their patients how their fears are symptomatic, while unconsciously, they themselves are in the grip of the same anxiety (De Masi, 2004). When the uncomfortable topic of the analyst's illness or death is broached by a patient, the analyst can circumvent it by interpreting the patient's concern and calling it "separation anxiety."

Of course, sometimes the distraction of focusing on the possible senility of the analyst provides the patient defensive opportunities or masks the patient's own insecurities regarding intelligence and mental functioning. I recently had a patient who was constantly screaming at me that I was "losing it." She would insist that she had cancelled appointments that I had in my book. She would ask me if she had told me something, and when I said no, scream that yes indeed, she had. She recommended that I retire, stop writing, and "buy a rocking chair." She told me that I had always been "stupid," but now I was "senile." Because of my advanced age, I was particularly vulnerable to these charges, and so I began to defensively keep both a written and electronic calendar, and I took detailed notes after all of our sessions. I soon began to realize that the patient was clearly wrong when she asserted that she had cancelled an appointment or told me something. It wasn't until later in the analysis, when the patient was able to verbalize her envy of my professional success, my writing, and her fear that she wasn't "smart enough" to be an analyst that I realized the defensive nature of her attacks on me.

This focus on the aging analyst's deficiencies can sometimes be a manifestation of a negative transference or a psychic protective maneuver to avoid the possible shock of the analyst's sudden death (Chessick, 2013). I have reached an age where I frequently have to deal with people in my groups who want to obsess about my death. Usually these ideas are presented tearfully. The group member weeps that she will be devastated by my death, which she implies is imminent. Despite the tears, I often experience these soliloquies as an attack. I usually tell the person that I have no plans to die yet. After researching for this article, however, I realize that my curt answer may be cutting off an opportunity to have a discussion about how the group should handle the reality of my advancing years and inevitable death.

Sometimes the patient's obsession with her analyst's cognitive decline can be a realistic perception of the aging of the analyst. We have all heard stories from colleagues who are dealing with their elderly analysts with whom they have had long term relationships. They have now reached a point in the treatment when the beloved analyst is beginning to show signs of mental decline. Whenever these colleagues try to bring up the subject of the analyst's advancing age or attempt to begin to discuss termination, many of these analysts deny any mental challenges and interpret the patient's anxieties as "transference." Trapped by love, gratitude and guilt, patients in this situation feel the need to support and protect their analyst from his or her own diminished sense of self-worth, fear of death, and increased dependency. These analysands are not only prevented from leaving, but also from expressing any aggressive feelings at all, for the fear they will hasten the analyst's death (Kaplan, 1993).

Long term patients handle terminations with their analysts in various ways, some more gracefully than others. Some stay until the analyst's death, sacrificing their own needs for many months or even years in a loving and masochistic compulsion to accompany the beloved analyst to the grave. Others suffer until their gratitude and masochism turn to rage at the analyst, whose cognitive fog finally makes them feel mistreated and abandoned. These terminations are almost always abrupt and carried out without the consent of the elderly analyst and without any attempt to make the termination process as therapeutic as possible. I have one colleague who had this problem for several years. When her analyst was clearly lost in dementia, my colleague told her gently that she was terminating treatment and asked permission from the analyst's caretaker to come once a week to have a cup of tea with her analyst. The first week she came for tea, she brought a final check and told her analyst that they were "beginning a new chapter" in their relationship. She came weekly until her analyst died, and she told me that at these weekly tea parties, just as she had in the analysis, she did most of the talking, sharing memories of the long analysis and gratitude for the role the analyst had played in her life, while the elderly analyst nodded or slept. My colleague said, "My analyst didn't respond to my chatter much at all, but I think she was glad I was there, and for me, it provided a constructive way to say good-bye."

My own 90-year-old analyst is as sharp mentally as he has always been, but the death of a beloved mutual colleague three years ago prompted a discussion of how we want to handle the end of the analysis we have created together. My colleague and friend, who had lost her battle with cancer, had decided when she got the terrible diagnosis that she wanted to keep it a secret from her patients and from the institute where we both taught. She forbade me to even talk about her cancer with my analyst. The reason she gave was economic. If the truth were known, she would lose patients and be excluded from teaching and participating in the business of the institute. I held this secret until the final few months of her battle, but when she made it clear that she could no longer see me or even talk to me on the telephone, I felt such distress that I talked to my own analyst about her choice to sever all but familial relationships in anticipation of death. I got my analyst to agree that, if he gets sick, he will not keep it a "secret" from me. I told him I want to be informed of what he is facing and have a chance to participate in decisions about when and how to terminate treatment. He agreed to this plan. Of course, neither of us can be sure which of us will die first. We can't know if he dies first, how long he will be capable of participating in our plan. But the discussion allayed my intense anxiety about the finality of death and provided me with some therapeutic, if delusional, sense of control.

I have yet to face a terminal illness, and so have no idea how I will feel and what choices I will make when I do. I have watched more than a few friends and colleagues die and thus have several models of how a psychoanalyst dies well. Keeping illness a secret can protect our patients and maintain the analytic neutrality until the bitter end. It can also make the people you love feel excluded and abandoned. Being honest, as Dr Meadow did when she told her many patients, "I have a terminal cancer and probably have only a few months to live. What are your thoughts and feelings about it?" certainly includes the patient in the process, giving them a chance to "say everything." But some analysands feel assaulted and overstimulated by this brutal candor.

Traesdale (2013, p. 86) suggested that it is vitally important that psychoanalysts are able to face the fact of their own mortality with honesty and acceptance, "so that we can handle the topic in an undefended way when working with our patients." The aging of the analyst threatens the transference, which, like the unconscious, is timeless. Aging and physical and mental maladies in the analyst get harder and harder to hide and create primitive anxieties in both analyst and patient (Issroff, 1994). The concept of co-creating with each patient an emotional environment to deal with the fact that *I am getting old, and I am going to die* can provide a "transformational process" (McKamy, 2015, p. 733) where patient and analyst can acknowledge their attachment to each other, grieve its ending, and let go in a healthy manner. This can involve working through together previous traumatic losses and building resilience to future disappointments. A colleague of mine reported that he had begun this important work with his analyst of over 40 years when she said at the beginning of a recent session, "I am 89 years old. What shall we do about it?" This opens the door to inviting the patient to be a consultant about what lies ahead, and it is a process that can be therapeutic to both analyst and patient.

A "good enough" termination of a long-term analytic relationship develops the capacity of the patient to keep the analyst alive in his internal world, offering some comfort for the loss of the real object. When a patient has had an important and therapeutic relationship with the analyst and an opportunity to work through the termination of the analysis, he or she does not lose the ability to remember it after they have parted and to use the internalized object of the analyst to comfort and guide going forward (De Masi, 2004). This internalization of an important object is also crucial to the analyst. Junkers (2013, p. 14) says "When I finish an analysis, my couch is empty in connection with external reality, but it is occupied in regard to my internal world."

Eissler (1975) suggests that, at the right moment, it may be necessary to tell patients whom to turn to for advice and treatment should the analyst die, but finding that right moment is up to the analyst's tact and intuition, since the subject may precipitate severe resistances and stir up a host of unfavorable reactions. Dr Benjamin Margolis, a supervisor of mine, chose just the right moment to make this intervention with his patients and supervisees. It was only a few weeks after I had begun to notice Dr Margolis' decline that he started a session with me by saying, "I am in my nineties now, and I have had time to consider who you should work with as a supervisor after I am gone." He made a recommendation of another faculty member he thought I would work well with. I protested saying, "You're going to live forever, Dr Margolis!" He smiled wanly and said, "I hope so, and I plan to, but when I die, I want you to call the person I recommended." What was touching about this was that after Margolis' death, I found out that he had had this conversation with all the people he worked with, and what was remarkable was that he made a different recommendation to each person. He really had given each of us a lot of thought, and the fact that my recommendation had been tailor-made just for me made me feel surrounded in a care and concern which I still feel many years after his death. And by the way, my work with the supervisor he recommended has been very successful.

Weiner (1990) has asserted that psychoanalytic institutes should intervene in the challenges of the aging analyst by setting up guidelines for retirement. Many institutes are mute about the competence of their esteemed elders, probably because all human beings utilize strong and rigid defenses against the idea of human transience, and analysts are no exception. Too often, the cognitive decline and illness of aging analysts are met by the community with silence and denial or whispers about the shameful secret that an aging analyst has "lost it." But this is not always the case. Today, some institutes restrict analysts over the age of 65 or 70 from accepting analytic candidates for long-term analysis. Elderly analysts are not restricted from accepting psychotherapy patients in their private practice or taking on limited time supervision with students, but they are not allowed to be training analysts for the institute after they reach a certain milestone. Other institutes require analysts over a certain age to present themselves before a committee every two or three years for an evaluation of their mental clarity. Certainly, these policies protect students and patients, but I question their rigidity and their overriding of the importance of the relationship between analyst and patient. Not all, not even most 70-year-old human beings have lost their mental acuity, and requiring elders to submit to a form of IQ test every so often completely discounts the importance of the relationship between the analyst and his long term patients.

Rather than restricting and evaluating, institutes should put their energy into assisting patients and supervisees who find themselves in a no longer therapeutic relationship with a faltering analyst. Many students are afraid to talk to anyone at their institutes about a declining analyst for fear that criticizing a luminary or terminating their supervision or analysis with him may damage their own reputation at the institute, or even prevent them from getting credit for the work they have done with the aging analyst. Frank discussions about the challenges of our mortality should be part of classroom discussions, faculty meetings, conferences, and workshops, and protocols should be established whereby patients dealing with an analyst with dementia, Alzheimer's or a debilitating illness have places to talk about how to proceed. Institutes can play a role in helping each analyst plan what Junkers (2013, p. 13) called a "personalized retirement" that allows an analyst not to withdraw from all his different psychoanalytic activities at the same time. Students who are dealing with the death of a long-term analyst need the support of their institutes. Traesdale (2013, p. 89) talks about the experience of "a type of insanity," characterized by a loss of voice, speech, and language, that analysands who have lost their analyst experience. The analyst's death forecloses for the patient the possibility of fully retrieving his mind, a mind that has not been his exclusive possession for the duration of his analysis with the deceased analyst.

The field of psychoanalysis is populated with many more old people than most professions, and since the appearance of psychotropic medications and short term therapies, it has gotten a reputation for being old fashioned and outdated. Institutes have a responsibility to ensure that young people are attracted to the idea of pursuing analytic careers, and that institute training is not so prolonged that even the young become old before they can practice and survive economically. Institutes can foster a creative atmosphere where a body of theory associated with that institute is identified, promoted, and honored, and where an ongoing development of new theoretical ideas is encouraged. Psychoanalytic theory is both timeless and constantly reinventing itself in a way that makes it feel immortal. The history of an institute and the collection of shared myths about the community build a social group identity that can honor the past and project into the future in a way that allows the fear of death to achieve a certain equilibrium (De Masi, 2004, p. 122). Though each individual in the institute won't find an easy solution to the fear of death, the institute can provide a place where psychoanalysis can be immortal, because it is transmitted to others. As Paul Denis (2013, p. 33) says, "My immortal psychoanalytic soul will be carried onwards by my former patients who have become psychoanalysts." If the institute is able to protect the vitality, the human and social relevance of psychoanalysis, it facilitates an ability in each of its members to witness with pleasure young colleagues who are moving the profession forward, and assist them in a shared mission of protecting the legacy of psychoanalysis.

So, is there anything good to say about getting old? In my experience, the challenges far outweigh the advantages, but there are some advantages. And there are habits of mind and experiences that can help focus on the gains that have been attained in reaching an advanced age and find ways to cope with all the losses that old age involves.

Aging often brings an enhanced appreciation for the beauty of the world. Knowing that death is near helps us to cherish the here and now and open our hearts to all the loveliness around us. Junkers (2013, p. 12) describes this when she says:

> When I take leave of a patient, I expect to see him next week. But I am not as sure of that as I used to be. Far from weakening me, these thoughts give me stability and strength because the present is experienced with great intensity and becomes a sense of wonder, constantly renewed.

I was complaining to a physician who was about to retire about some of the annoying symptoms my aging body had, and he nodded with empathy. Then he smiled and said:

> One thing I notice though that I like. Everything seems so beautiful to me as I get older. I walk through the park, and the babies and the dogs and the birds and the young girls – they all look so beautiful. The spring flowers, the autumn leaves. I never took them in so deeply as I do now. I guess I was too busy. But I just seem to have an intense appreciation of the world around me lately.

Enjoyment of the images, smells, and sounds the environment presents to us on a moment to moment basis ripens in old age, and this awareness of the shimmering radiance of the world has the power to lift us up and away from the burden of our carnality and mortality and bring us back to the ephemeral moment (Holmes, 2013, p. 166). The elderly who are able to confront their aging honestly and actively will be able to acknowledge with regret, but not desperation, that there are limits to putting things off for the future, to the idea of, "I'll do that later." It becomes less and less rational to reassure ourselves of our continuing existence by projecting goals into the future. When all energy is focused on what is possible right now, life can be lived with a new immediacy. This approach to the end of life can be a new beginning that we can shape actively and consciously and which could be thought of as "wisdom" (Junkers, 2013, pp. 23–24).

Being old is often associated with being wise. Cozolino (2008) argued that the elderly are indeed respectable, valuable custodians of wisdom because experience has given them a capacity for compassion, thoughtfulness, and the ability to see the big picture. He also describes a maturity of emotion that comes with age. As long as we have a history of secure enough attachments and/or have gone through a successful analysis, the aging brain will have developed a capacity to regulate and not be overwhelmed by intense affect. A study of the brains of 60–80-year-olds found that the elderly develop a bias against what activates fear and anxiety. This means that old people tend to be less fearful and more empathetic than the young. Neurobiological research has shown that the capacity for love is characterized by an absence of an activated fear circuit in the brain. The general downgrading of fear later in life may open us up to a deeper understanding and compassion for others and more passion for humanity in general (Cozolino, 2008, p. 154).

One of the important developmental tasks of old age is integrating the emotionally important moments of our lives into an organized and intelligible story. To leave life in peace, we must focus on imbuing our life story with an overall coherence. Stephen Sondheim, a Broadway composer and lyricist now in his nineties, wrote about his tendency to reminisce and remember. He wrote, "When asked my place of residence on a customs form, I always want to write, 'The Past'" (Sondheim, 2011). Rather than judging this as a narcissistic, isolating habit, we need to understand the therapeutic value of this activity.

Erikson (1950), writing about the developmental stages of human beings, described the final stage as a conflict between ego integrity and despair. Despair is a state of mind characterized by a non-acceptance of the life one has led and a desperate feeling that time has run out, and there will be no opportunity to get things right. In this state, death is a thing to be dreaded and feared. Integrity, on the other hand is creating and honoring the meaning of one's life, forgiving ourselves for our repetitions, forgiving the parents who helped us create those repetitions by realizing they too had a story and were caught in their own destinies. Erikson (1950, p. 268) called this multigenerational awareness the "patrimony of the soul," and he asserted that, "in such consolidation, death loses its sting."

I have a 70-year-old patient who is struggling with a difficult husband. This alcoholic man is very depressed and has made three suicide attempts in the last five years, all under the influence of alcohol. My patient came in one day, elated and excited. She told me her husband had found a new psychiatrist:

> She started by asking Dan if he wanted to live or die. Dan said, without much enthusiasm, that he wanted to live. She said, "Okay then. I want you to do three things. First, you are never to touch alcohol again. Second, I want you to take an hour-long walk every day. And I don't mean on the treadmill. I want you to walk in nature – in the woods if you're in the country and in the park if you're in the city. And the third thing I want

> you to do is write the story of your life." Dan said, "But I'm not a writer." And she said, "I didn't ask you if you were a writer. I don't expect you to publish what you write. I just want you to focus on making your life a meaningful story."

My patient told me that these three instructions had changed her husband's life.

> Dan was in Vietnam as a young man, and he has never wanted to talk about it, but now he is writing about it every day. He shares the most gruesome, brutal stories with me. The funny thing is, he tells me these awful things with a pleasure I haven't seen in him in a long time. He's stopped drinking, and we walk together in the park, and yesterday, we were walking in the rain, and he kissed me under the umbrella and said, "Maybe I do want to live."

After the publication of my last book, *Wrestling with Destiny*, in 2013, I decided I wanted to write a novel I had been thinking about for 30 years. I had an idea about an analyst whose patient is found dead in the bathtub with her throat cut. The death is ruled a suicide, but the analyst is convinced that the patient was murdered. The analyst solves the murder by understanding the transference in the case and drawing parallels between her life and the life of her murdered patient. I worked happily on this project for four years, but the interesting thing about the book was that, as I wrote, I kept losing my focus on my murder mystery plot to veer off into the analyst's childhood in Texas, particularly her relationship with her sister, and her difficulties after she moved to New York City. Of course, this was my story. When I finished the novel, I sent it out to a long list of agents. No one was interested. More importantly, I gave the book to my daughter to read. She said, "Mom, you can't publish this. Your sister will kill you!"

I felt strangely relieved when she responded in this way, and I began to realize I didn't want to publish it. I had written it for another reason. I was trying to make sense of my life. I had been depressed about getting old, and I was attempting to treat myself. By reappraising my past, I was trying to achieve a balance between despair and acceptance. Writing my story helped me come to a new equilibrium without grudge or too many regrets. I was able to accept responsibility for my life, developing a capacity to mourn what is lost and becoming aware that what has been done can no longer be changed (Spagnoli, 1995).

This attention to life stories has another role in the challenge of growing old. They connect us to younger people, particularly grandchildren. Grandchildren are one of the great pleasures of old age. They are experienced as ongoing extensions of the self beyond the boundaries of our individual lives (Erikson et al., 1994). They are one's genetic immortality, the only part of the self that is youthful and survives our own death. Grandchildren draw grandparents to the beginning of life, a time of reality for the child and memory for the grandparent, where the future seems endless, full of adventure and potential (Holmes, 2013, p. 167). Young children, like the old, are more interested in just being than having. Rather than making long term plans or worrying about tomorrow, the very young and the very old focus on the moment. Grandchildren demand that we "be here now" in a delightful distraction from our fears about death.

My grandchildren have an endless appetite for stories about my life, particularly the ones that involve aggression, emergencies, and disasters. Some of their favorites include the time a waiter dropped a tray filled with two dozen glasses of ice water on my sister's head, the Halloween when my brother put on a bear suit and chased me with a cap gun, and the summer my father ran after a raccoon with a slingshot because the raccoon had climbed up my father's peach tree and taken one bite of every piece of fruit on the tree. Bettelheim (1977) wrote about the usefulness of fairy tales in helping children deal with violence, death, and all the negative emotions, and I found that my grandchildren loved dark stories and games best. My oldest granddaughter wanted to play endless games with me after her little sister was born. I was cast as the "jealous big sister" in these games while my granddaughter took the role of loving mother with a new baby. Holding her doll to her flat little chest to feed, she would also feed me my lines, which always focused on sending the baby back where she came from. When her sister got old enough to ride in a car seat, my granddaughter asked me to hold her doll in the pretend back seat while she drove. I was then instructed to throw the baby out the window. My daughter was not thrilled with these games, and she asked me to cease and desist. So, the next time I was invited to take a drive and throw the baby out, I said to my granddaughter, "No Mommy. I've learned that it's okay to want to throw the baby out the window, but I don't have to act on the feeling." My granddaughter looked at me in horror, and then exclaimed, "LuLu! This is my house and my game! Now throw that baby out the window or go home!" The first thing my granddaughters say to me when I arrive for a visit is, "LuLu, tell us a horrible story!"

Grandchildren serve defensive purposes. Intense investment in and idealization of grandchildren buffer the traumas of old age and the imminence of death and help us forgive imperfections in ourselves, since grandchildren are almost always perceived as perfect in every way (Colarusso, 2000). Grandchildren help us deny the passage of time and the reality of old age. We can observe, if not participate in their animal exuberance that denies mortality with a childish innocence and ignorance that cannot even be described as denial. Even the sobs of childhood are full of life. Old people are usually too wise and too tired to cry much. Grandchildren provide a chance for the magical repair of one's own life through observing the advantages that grandchildren have that we didn't. Of course, healthy grandparents realize the falseness of their idealization of their grandchildren, but that doesn't prevent them from enjoying the continuity that multigenerational object ties bring.

The recognition that death is final enhances the appreciation of the limited ways in which the self lives on through one's creations and one's offspring (Nemiroff and Colarusso, 1980).

When I became a grandmother, it took me a while to settle into my new role. After all, I had never been a grandparent before. I had the grandiose delusion that I was my granddaughter's mother. I tried to carry her around with the ease that her mother did and get down on the floor to diaper her. A herniated disc provided a painful lesson that I was too old to be a mother. Even more distressing, my infant granddaughter had no delusions about who her mother was. I realized quickly that my importance in her life was a disappointing fourth place, behind her mother, her father, and the nanny. I had to learn to assume what Issroff (1994) called the "third position." This is a type of relationship where one is an observer of a situation rather than a participant. It is the attainment of this position that enables a grandparent to accept her child's partner and the birth of their baby and to learn to enjoy being the audience of a show in which her daughter and her daughter's husband are the stars. The type of anxiety aroused by attaining this third position depends, according to Issroff, on the extent to which the grandmother has been able to resolve her Oedipal anxieties, the first encounter with learning to accept being a "third wheel" in a drama that involves two people who are not focused on you. This is a significant life event which is a new pathway out of narcissism and a fresh introduction to the pleasure of object relations.

But even if one doesn't have grandchildren, there are young friends and relatives, students, analysands, and mentees to feed what Colarusso (2000, p. 1470) called "the intense desire to fuse with objects" that comes with the acceptance of one's death. In old age, a kind of "grand-generativity" (Erikson et al., 1994) may occur in which one performs the roles of aging parent, grandparent, old friend, advisor, and mentor. This can result in an integration of outward looking care for others with inward looking care for one's self. A focus on procreativity rather than productivity expresses a new generativity (Erikson et al. 1994, p. 81). De Masi (2004, p. 112) calls this internalizing the maternal function and describes how it can be used consciously and unconsciously to protect an aging person from anxiety. We can project the "inexhaustible potential of our being" (De Masi 2004, p. 124) into children, friends, pupils and institutions who can accept and constructively use those projections.

At the beginning of life, we could not survive without an object. Dr Meadow used to say that when they are born, babies want to die. They are terrified by the light and noise and painful sensation of the world, and they long to return to the dark peace of the womb. It is the love and care of the maternal object and later other objects which makes the infant begin to want to live. This vital need for the object returns in old age. A rush towards objects in a desire, which almost feels sexual, compels people at the end of their lives to put parts of themselves in younger people. When the elderly are forced to relinquish professional success and a wish for power, they compensate with a new drive toward interpersonal effectiveness. In the face of death, reparation consists in the arduous journey of many individual selves who leave themselves in other selves that will follow. Reparation can only be achieved through the past, through the projection of our past into the future, into the future of others (De Masi, 2004, p. 125).

If envy is not too strong, old people can not only project into but also identify with and introject the young. The establishment and presence of good and reliable internal objects enables the aging individual to face the losses and unknowns at the end of life with psychic integrity (Kavka, 2013, p. 132). Cozolino (2008) asserted that stimulating interpersonal relationships are crucial for the health of the aging brain. The challenges of aging threaten to bind us in a narcissistic self-preoccupation that can be experienced as a living death. But with the healthy use of objects, the elderly can feel the satisfaction of a sense of generativity and vicarious identification with the young which reinforces the life drive, making one feel needed and still able to give.

In our modern world, everything in life happens later. Education continues for a longer time. Women become mothers later. Our active parental and professional lives are extended well into old age. People are retiring later and living longer (Junkers, 2013, p. 7). If the final chapter of life is to be lived with meaning and satisfaction, the elderly must face the challenge of working through the pain caused by the awareness of human transience. Of course, dealing with our mortality is a lifelong process, but that challenge becomes a crisis in old age. Just as in all developmental challenges of the life cycle, the pathway to mental health in old age involves a journey out of narcissism and into object relatedness.

Dr Arnold Bernstein described dying as "like being very, very tired and wanting to go to sleep" (personal conversation). This is a comforting notion. Certainly, we all have memories of being an exhausted, cranky child who longs for his bed or his mother's arms. The depletion of energy in old age brings a return to the appeal of a fusion with the mother that both infantile sleep and death represent. As we age and face our physical decline, death is not as terrifying as it was when we were possessed of a youthful exuberant energy.

A patient of mine, a candidate at the Center for Modern Psychoanalytic Studies, was talking on the couch about her struggles with Freud's theory of the death instinct. She said:

> So, if I understand it correctly, the death instinct is connected to aggression. It's aggression turned inward. So my job as a modern analyst becomes to help my patients turn their aggression outward into the world and use it creatively, right?

I agreed that that was the idea. She went on:

> But the death instinct is also a wish for peace, a return to the peace of the womb, an impulse to return to primordial nothingness. Looking at it that way, death can be seen as a fusion with the mother, a state of symbiotic bliss.

She had no idea how helpful she was to me.

References

Bettelheim, Bruno (1977). *The uses of enchantment*. New York: Vintage Books.
Bromberg, P.M. (2003). One need not be a house to be haunted: On enactment, dissociation, and the dread of "not me" – A case study. *Psychoanalytic Dialogues*, *13*(5), 689–709.
Busse, E.W., Barnes, R.H., Silverman, A.J., Thaler, M., Frost, L.L. (1958). Strength and weakness of psychic functioning in the aged. *Psychoanalytic Quarterly*, 27, 143, 896–901.
Chessick, R.D. (2013). Special problems for the elderly psychoanalyst in the psychoanalytic process. *Journal of the American Psychoanalytic Association*, *61*(1), 67–93.
Colarusso, C.A. (2000). Separation-individuation phenomena in adulthood: General concepts and fifth individuation. *Journal of the American Psychoanalytic Association*, *48*(4), 1467–1489.
Cozolino, Louis (2008). *The healthy aging brain: Sustaining attachment*. New York: Norton.
DeMasi, F. (2004). *Making death thinkable*. London: Free Association Books.
Denis, P. (2013). Psychoanalyst: A profession for an immortal. In G. Junkers (ed.), *The empty couch* (pp. 32–40). London: Routledge.
Eissler, K. (1975). On possible effects of aging on the practice of psychoanalysis: An essay. *Journal of the Philadelphia Association for Psychoanalysis*, 11, 316–332.
Erikson, E., Kivnick, Helen Q., Erikson, J. (1994). *Vital involvement in old age*. New York: Norton.
Erikson, E.H. (1950). *Childhood and society*. New York: Norton.
Freud, S. (1905). On psychotherapy. *Standard edition, volume 7* (pp. 257–270). London: Hogarth Press.
Freud, S. (1915). Thoughts for the times on war and death. *Standard edition, volume 14* (pp. 273–301). London: Hogarth Press.
Freud, S. (1923). The ego and the id. *Standard edition, volume 19* (pp. 3–66). London: Hogarth Press.
Grotjahn, M. (1955). Analytic psychotherapy with the elderly. *Psychoanalytic Review*, *42*(4), 419–427.
Holmes, L. (2013). *Wrestling with destiny: The promise of psychoanalysis*. London: Routledge.
Issroff, R. (1994). Becoming a grandmother: The third position. *British Journal of Psychotherapy*, *11*(2), 260–266.
Junkers, G. (ed.). (2013). *The empty couch*. London: Routledge.
Kaplan, A. (1993). The aging and dying psychotherapist: Death and illness in the life of the aging psychotherapist. In J.H. Gold and J.C. Nemiah (eds.), *Beyond transference: When the therapist's real life intrudes* (pp. 51–70). Washington, DC: American Psychiatric Press.
Kavka, A. (2013). Psychoanalyst assistance committees: Philosophy and practicalities. In G. Junkers (ed.), *The empty couch* (pp. 130–149). London: Routledge.
McKamy, E.H. (2015). Closed for business: Reflections on a psychoanalytic psychotherapist's voluntary retirement. *Contemporary Psychoanalysis*, *51*(4), 727–746.

Nemiroff, R.A., and Colarusso, C.A. (1980). Authenticity and narcissism in the adult development of the self. *Annals of Psychoanalysis*, 8, 111–129.

Penziak, Z. (1982). The experience of time and hope in the elderly. *Contemporary Psychoanalysis*, 18(4), 635–645.

Sondheim, S. (2011). *Look I Made A hat*. New York: Alfred A. Knopf.

Spagnoli, A. (1995). *"e divento sempre più vecchio" Jung, Freud, la psicologia del profondo a l'invecchiamento*. Torino: Bollati Boringhieri.

Traesdale, T. (2013). Analysis lost and regained. In G. Junkers (ed.), *The empty couch* (pp. 82–90). London: Routledge.

Weiner, M. (1990). Older psychiatrists and their psychotherapy practice. *American Journal of Psychotherapy*, 44(1), 44–49.

Index

9/11, trauma 143–148

activity 46
adolescence 58–60
adolescents 204; September 11 healing processing 143–148
Adventures in Teaching and Counseling (ATC) 143
aggression 48–49, 130, 166; boys 52; constructive aggression 167; death instinct 216–217; girls 53–54; groups 68; primitive aggression 50; projected aggression 103; against representations of baby 19; toward men, pregnancy 11, 13
aging 203–205; advantages of 211–212; cognitive decline 207–210; death 206–208; grandchildren 213–215; life stories 213; narcissism 206; objects 215–216
all-girls schools 72–73
American culture, childbirth 40
analysts, becoming 166–170
anesthesia, childbirth 36–37
anger *see* aggression
anger management 190–191
Arms, S. 36

baby, as self 18–19; *see also* infants
bad objects 197
Benjamin, J. 13–15, 52, 60
Bernstein, A. 189, 216
Bettelheim, B. 214
Bibring, E. 172
Bibring, G.L. 8
birth centers 37
bisexuality 56; prepubertal period in girls 57
bleeding, menses 59
Blos, P. 57–58, 111
Bollas, C. 68, 88, 129, 173, 196

Bonaparte, M. 47–48, 57
boundary confusion 63
boys: aggression 52; mothers 51; mothers and 53; Oedipal conflict 86; Oedipus complex 107; pre-Oedipal 62–63, 86
brains 174, 183–184, 192
breasts 49
bridging 146

Campbell, J. 158, 163
castration, menses 59
castration fantasies 15
Center for Group Studies (New York City) 154
cerebral cortex 174–175, 183, 192, 197–198
Chamberlen, P. 33
Chaos 159–160
Chasseguet-Smirgel, J. 52
childbirth 4–5; birth centers 37; control 40–41; C-sections 37; culture 32–40; death 16, 40; drugs 35–36; eroticism 38–39; fear 36; female development milestones 87–89; intervention 35; Naomi 21–30; natural childbirth 36; oppression 31–32, 42–43; pain 34–38; pain relief 43; phallus 14–15; pre-Oedipal 10; sexual intercourse 33; sexuality 39–40; support 43
childhood memories 166
children: genitals 86; play 150; sexual theory of 45–46
chloroform, childbirth 35
Chodorow, N. 15, 20, 51
clitoris 46–47, 49
cloaca 48
co-creating 208
cognitive decline 207–210
coitus, childbirth 33
Colarusso, C.A. 215

Index

competitive triangles, pregnancy 12
confessions 129–130
consciousness 175
constructive aggression 167
control, childbirth 40–41
countertransference 129
Cozolino, L. 212, 216
Crowell, M. 10, 51
C-sections, childbirth 37
culture, childbirth 32–40
cures 186–194

dance of mutual recognition 14
dark continent 45
de Beauvoir, S. 14
De Masi, F. 203, 215
death 127–129, 205–206, 216; aging 207–209; childbirth 16, 40; masochism 130; Mr B 127–141; repetition compulsion 132
death instinct 167, 216–217
deficient men 95
DeLee, J. 35
Denis, P. 210
depression, elderly 204
destiny 171; control over 174–177; repetition compulsion 172–174
Deutsch, H. 8, 57, 58, 90; childbirth 33; feminine core 46; menstruation 59
developmental phase 8
Dharmaraksita 177
Dick-Read, G. 36
Dinnerstein, D. 56
domination of women 62
dreams, play 151–152
drives 49
drugs, childbirth 35–36
Duncan, I. 39

early theories of female development 45–49
educational model, cures 187
Ego 48, 175
Eissler, K. 206, 209
elderly, depression 204
emotions 174
empathy 98
ENACT, *Finding the Words* 143
epidurals, childbirth 36–37
episiotomies, childbirth 35
Erikson, E. 212
Eros 48, 160
eroticism 57; childbirth 38–39
erotics 156

erotogenicity 49
experience 204
explicit memory 192
externalization, introjected objects 19

families, groups 111
fantasies 50, 187; infants 128; projected fantasies 88
fate 173
father imago 57
fathers 52, 111–112; daughters and 51–52; identification with 89–90
fear: childbirth 36, 40–42; cure 187; of death 206–207
female development: early theories of 45–49; internal triangle 62–64; modern psychoanalytic theory on women 49–53; new theories 53–60
female development milestones; childbirth 87–89; groups 68–69
female masochism 47, 90
female narcissism 90
female Oedipal complex 51, 55–56
female passivity 46, 90
female superego 56
feminine 46, 86–96; childbirth 19–20
feminine adolescence 58
feminine core 46
feminine masochism 46–47
feminine women, in groups 64–68
femininity 45, 47, 48, 56
feminism, childbirth 31–32
Fenichel, O. 186
fetus 88; shifting object representations 17–21; *see also* childbirth; pregnancy
Finding the Words 143
forceps, childbirth 33, 35
free association 181–183, 198
Freud, A. 150
Freud, S. 3–4, 20, 86, 122, 175, 198; aging 203, 205; cure 186; dark continent 45; death 206; destiny 172; early theories of female development 45–49; feminine 34; free association 181; humor 152; Oedipal conflict 86; penis deficiency 87; pregnancy 9; primal hordes 112, 155–156; superego 91

Gaia 159–161
gender 5–6
gender dynamics, group therapy 107–116
gender identity 6
genital differences 47

genitals, children 86
getting even 75–85
Gilligan, C. 57, 72, 91
girls: adolescence 58; aggression 53–54; mother-in-me 50; mothers and 53; Oedipus complex 51, 100, 107–108; pre-Oedipal 46, 63; prepubertal period 57; sexual impulses 59
God 154–155
gods 158
grandchildren, old age 213–215
grand-generativity 215
Graves, R. 158
Greek myth 157–164
Green, A. 195
Groddeck, G. 39
Grotjahn, M. 203
group leaders, gender dynamics 110–113
group therapy 98–99; gender dynamics 107–116
groups 62, 64; aggression 68; feminine women 64–68; menopausal groups 70–72; mixed-gender groups 72–73; organized around female developmental milestones 68–69; pregnancy groups 69–70
guilt, homosexuality 130

happy 176–177, 182, 198
Hera 162
heroes, Greek myth 162–163
Hesiod 159
heterosexuality 6
Homer 159, 162
homosexuality 130
Horney, K. 20, 47–49
humor 150–153

"I am I" 58
identification 60, 64, 89, 183; internal triangle 56–57; partial identification 97–105, 109
identifying with objects, revenge 80–84
implicit memory 192–193, 196
incest, Greek myth 160–161
infants 111; fantasies 128; mothers and 53; *see also* baby
infertility 9–10
inner chaos 203
institutes 155; analysts with cognitive decline 210–211
integration 95

intelligence 168–169
internal objects 88
internal triangle 55–56, 60, 88, 90; clinical examples 91–94; female development 62–64
internalization 89; introjected objects 19
interpretation 169
intersubjectivity 15, 60
intervention, childbirth 35
introject, defined 68
introjected objects 19, 60, 73, 105
intuition 98
Issroff, R. 215

Jacobson, E. 57
Jones, E. 47, 50
Joseph, B. 130
jouissance 173
Junkers, G. 210–211

Kandel, E. 184
Kauff, P. 145
killing, pregnancy dreams 11–12
Klein, M. 49–53, 89, 128
Kohut, H. 190
Kronos 161

Lacan, J. 111, 173
Langer, M. 13
language 182
Laplanche, J. 172
Laquercia, T. 168
latency 57
laughter 153
leadership 154–156
libidinal longings 138
libido 18, 20, 47–48, 53–54, 141
life and death model 187
life stories, old age 213–214
limbic system 174–175, 183, 198, 201
Liriope 163
Loewald, H.W. 187
long-term treatment 189–190
loops 199
love and hate 50, 104

Maccoby, M. 154, 156
MacLean, P. 174
Margolis, B. 209
masculine 46, 86–96; childbirth 19–20
masculine morality 91
masculine superego 56

masculinity 47, 87
masculinity complex 47
masculinization of childbirth 33–34
masochism 46, 48, 130
maternal function, internalizing 215
maternal identification 9
maternal imago 10, 15, 19, 27, 53, 56–59, 63, 67
maternal instinct 20
maternal introject 10
McDougall, J. 130, 169
Mead, M. 41
Meadow, P. 123–124, 130, 166–170, 182, 188, 205–206, 215
medical model, termination of treatment 187, 189
memories, childhood memories 166
memory: explicit memory 192; implicit memory 192–193, 196
memory romances 58
men: penis 14; pregnancy, paternal image 11–12; *see also* penis
Menninger, K. 187
menopausal groups 70–72
menses 59
menstruation 59
Mitchell, J. 15
mixed-gender groups 72–73, 105
modern psychoanalytic theory on women 49–53
morality 91
mother-child dyad 20
mother-in-me 50, 53, 63, 89
mothers 5, 52, 111; becoming my mother 9–10; identification with 89; phallic mother 11
motherself 17
mourning 177
multigenerational awareness 212
myths 157–164

Nacht, S. 186
Naomi, pregnancy/childbirth 21–30
narcissism 15, 46–47, 90, 97–99; old age 206; productive narcissists 154
narcissists 156
Narcissus 163–164
natural childbirth 36
neglect 129
neuroscience 174, 183
new theories of female development 53–60
not knowing 171
numbness, trauma 147

object relations theory 141
objects, old age 215–216
obsessives 156
obstetricians 34
Odyssey (Homer) 162–163
Oedipal conflict 89; boys 86
Oedipus 164, 171
Oedipus complex 46, 58; boys 107; female Oedipal complex 51, 55–56; girls 100, 107–108; pregnancy 10
old age 203–205; advantages of 211–212; cognitive decline 207–210; death 206–208; grandchildren 213–215; life stories 213; narcissism 206; objects 215–216
oppression, childbirth 31–32, 42–43
oral period 49, 55–56
Ormont, L. R. 66, 68, 98, 104, 108–109, 145, 188–190

pain, childbirth 34–38
pain relief, childbirth 35, 43
Panksepp, J. 175
parent-child model cure 187
partial identification 97–105, 109
passivity 48, 90
paternal image, pregnancy 11–17
paternal signifier 111–112
patricide 155
patrimony of the soul 212
penis 14, 86, 172–173
penis envy 46–47, 50–53, 59, 86, 100
personalized retirement 210
phallic mother 11
phallus 43, 49–50, 52, 54, 111; pregnancy/childbirth 14–15
Phillips, A. 187
Piontelli, A. 18
play 150–151
Pontalis, J.B. 172
pregnancy 8–9; maternal identification 9; Naomi 21–30; paternal image 11–17; phallus 14–15; pre-Oedipal 9–11; projected fantasies 88; shifting object representations 17–21
pregnancy dreams, killing 11–12
pregnancy groups 69–70
prejudice 145
pre-Oedipal 62–63; boys 86; girls 46, 51; pregnancy 9–11
prepubertal period in girls, bisexuality 57
primal hordes 112, 155–156
primary identification 80
primitive aggression 50, 166–168

primitive competitive triangles, pregnancy 12
primitive love and hate 50
productive narcissists 154
projected aggression 103
projected fantasies, pregnancy 88
psychoanalytic theory 31
psychosomatic fusion 129
puberty; *see also* adolescence

Rabuzzi, K.A. 17, 38
recovery 188; *see also* cure
relationships 193; termination of treatment 189
religion, childbirth 33
repetition compulsion 125, 195–202; death 132; destiny 172–174
repetitions 177
resistance 144–147
revenge 75–85, 129
Rich, A. 17
Rose, C. 184
Rosenthal, L. 144
Roth, B. 144
Roth, P. 203

Schaffer, A. 187–188
Schmideberg, M. 187
scopolamine 35
second sex 62
seduction, revenge 78–80
self: baby/self 18–19; internal triangle 56
self-destructive actions 129–130
self-punishment 129–130
separating from objects 89
September 11 healing processing, adolescents 143–148
sexual impulses, girls 59
sexual intercourse, childbirth 33
sexual theory of children 45–46
sexuality, childbirth 39–40
Shepherd, M. 124
shifting object representations, pregnancy 17–21
significance of childbirth 42–43
Simpson, J. Y. 35
Socarides, C.W. 130
social childbirth 34
Sondheim, S. 212
sovereign equal 13
Spotnitz, H. 58, 124, 130, 146, 174, 182, 188, 199, 201
story of the world, Greek myth 159–160

subordination 48
suffering 104; revenge 76–77
suicide 77, 81–83
superego 56
supervision groups 193
support, during childbirth 43
symbiosis, pregnancy 10
symbolic space 111

talking 179–184, 198–200
Tartaros 160
termination of treatment 187; analysts with cognitive decline 207–209
third position 215
Titans 160–161
Traesdale, T. 208, 210
transient identification 98–100, 109
trauma: menses 59; September 11 143–148
treatments, termination of 187, 207–209
triadic perspective 108
twilight sleep, childbirth 35

unborn babies 88
unconscious collusion, childbirth 41
unconscious identification 80
unconscious structures 192
unthought known 129, 196
Uranus 160

vagina 48–49, 59
visiting-an-art-gallery model 187

weak superego 56
Weiner, M. 209
Weltanschauung (view of the world) 57
Werbart, A. 187
Winnicott, D 168
wisdom, old age 212
Wolfenstein, M. 130
woman envy 49
women's groups 64; female development milestones 68–69; feminine women 64–68; menopausal groups 70–72; pregnancy groups 69–70
word salad 180
working through 198

Yalom, I. D. 111
Zeus 161–162
Zilboorg, G. 49

Žižek, S. 195

Taylor & Francis eBooks

www.taylorfrancis.com

A single destination for eBooks from Taylor & Francis with increased functionality and an improved user experience to meet the needs of our customers.

90,000+ eBooks of award-winning academic content in Humanities, Social Science, Science, Technology, Engineering, and Medical written by a global network of editors and authors.

TAYLOR & FRANCIS EBOOKS OFFERS:

- A streamlined experience for our library customers
- A single point of discovery for all of our eBook content
- Improved search and discovery of content at both book and chapter level

REQUEST A FREE TRIAL
support@taylorfrancis.com

Printed in the United States
By Bookmasters